"There is not one among us in whom a devil does not dwell; at some time, on some point, that devil masters each of us; he who has never failed has not been tempted; but the man who does in the end conquer, who does painfully retrace the steps of his slipping,...shows that he has been tried in the fire and not found wanting. It is not having been in the Dark House, but having left it, that counts...."

—Theodore Roosevelt

OTHER BOOKS BY THE AUTHOR

*New Left Diplomatic Histories*
*and Historians* (1973, 2d ed., 1993)

*The American Diplomatic Revolution:*
*A Documentary History of the Cold War,*
*1941-1947* (1976)

*Australian-American Relations Since 1945:*
*A Documentary History* (1976)
with Glen Barclay

*The Impact of the Cold War* (1977)

*The Testing of America, 1914-1945* (1979)
with Daniel M. Smith

*A History of United States Foreign Policy*
(4th ed., 1980)
with Julius W. Pratt and Vincent De Santis

*The Changing of America, 1945 to the Present*
(1986)

*Safe for Democracy: A History of America,*
*1914-1945* (1993)

*America's Australia: Australia's America* (1997)
with Yeong-Han Cheong

# INTO THE
# DARK HOUSE

## AMERICAN DIPLOMACY &
## THE IDEOLOGICAL ORIGINS
## OF THE COLD WAR

JOSEPH M. SIRACUSA

READER IN AMERICAN DIPLOMACY
THE UNIVERSITY OF QUEENSLAND

Regina Books
Claremont, California

**Library of Congress Cataloging-in-Publication Data**

Siracusa, Joseph M.
    Into the dark house : American diplomacy & the ideological origins of the Cold War / by Joseph M. Siracusa.
            p.      cm.
    Includes bibliographical references and index.
    ISBN 0-941690-81-4. -- ISBN 0-941690-80-6 (pbk.)
    1. United States--Foreign relations--1945-1989. 2. Cold War.
I. Title.
E744.S56367    1998
327.73--dc21                                        97-47380
                                                         CIP

𝕽𝖊𝖌𝖎𝖓𝖆 𝕭𝖔𝖔𝖐𝖘

Post Office Box 280
Claremont, California 91711
Tel: (909) 624-8466 / Fax: (909) 626-1345

Manufactured in the United States of America

For my students at
The University of Queensland, 1973-1998
—they gave as much as they got.

# CONTENTS

# PREFACE

The purpose of this book, which presupposes that the nature of the Cold War[1] was basically ideological and political—a point of view generally held by the principals themselves—is twofold. First, recognizing in the words of Norman A. Graebner, "the significant relationship between the intellectual milieu in which a foreign policy is conducted and the foreign policy itself",[2] it seeks to delineate the constellation of ideas, beliefs and assumptions (both spoken and unspoken) that informed American diplomacy[3] in the period from the last stages of the Grand Alliance to the Korean War, i.e., from Franklin D. Roosevelt's shift in Soviet policy in the autumn of 1944,[4] in the wake of the Warsaw uprising, to the resumption of the Korean armistice talks in late 1951. Second, it seeks to provide students of the early Cold War period with an opportunity to confront for themselves some of the major historical documents that have been the bases of historical interpretations during the past fifty years. Such documents have constituted the foundation of pivotal interpretations among traditional historians of the Cold War, moderate revisionists, the New Left—whose origins and significance I have dealt with elsewhere[5]—and the post-revisionists. These early Cold War documents, not unlike the pamphlets examined by Harvard historian Bernard Bailyn in *The Ideological Origins of The American Revolution* thirty years ago, reveal an exceptional *"explanatory"* quality, "not merely positions taken but the reasons why positions were taken", the very motives, intentions and values that informed America's world view. These documents, as the following chapters attest, indicate—in the words of Bailyn about an earlier time of troubles—"that there were real fears, real anxieties, a sense of real danger behind these phrases and not merely a desire to influence by rhetoric and propaganda the inert minds of an otherwise passive populace".[6]

The "revolution" that occurred in American diplomacy in the late 1940s was, in fact, a revolution that had occurred first in the hearts and minds of Americans—to steal some thunder from John Adams of an earlier Revolution. By this, I mean it is impossible to comprehend, in Arthur M. Schlesinger Jr.'s felicitous expression, "the brave and essential response of free men to Communist aggression",[7] without understanding the intellectual world of the Americans who articulated this view. These were the same politicians, policymakers and diplomats who had experienced the disillusionment of the Versailles system and the folly of isolationism; struggled through the Great Depression which had reduced half of America's population to penury; witnessed the rise of communism (with its forced collectivization and purges), fascism and nazism; recoiled from the West's abandonment of Czechoslovakia to Hitler in 1938 under the aegis of appeasement; and were dragged into a second world war in their own lifetime, the death toll this time probably reaching 60 million, a figure which included the 6 million murdered because they were Jewish.[8] They also perceived a shrinking world in which war and peace were judged indivisible—the hard lesson of Munich, learned on both sides of the Iron Curtain and the analogy that shaped a generation of diplomacy. Moreover, modern warfare, with its awful weapons of death and destruction and the equally awful contemplation that they could be delivered anywhere with impunity, caused the majority of Americans to rethink past policies and their role in the world. Pushed by the guilt of the past for abdicating their part in the League of Nations prescribed by the Versailles Peace Settlement and pulled along by their felt responsibility for the future, especially the future of their children, usually cautious Americans placed their faith in collective security of the fledgling United Nations. The fact that the UN would not or could not play this promised role became the moment of truth: whether or not the US would play the keeper of the balance of power. That the answer would be in the affirmative is what W.W. Rostow once described as the "American Diplomatic Revolution" to an Oxford audience long ago.[9]

The second part of the problem was to make sense out of the USSR. Americans were as perplexed about the motives and intentions of the Soviet Union in late 1944 as they were in November 1917.[10] How does a nation deal with a regime that regards it as the root and branch of all evil? In the end, American attitudes towards the Bolsheviks revolved around a single question: Whether Soviet Russia was a messianic ideology in the service of a traditional Great Power or was a traditional Great Power in the service of a messianic ideology? Uncertain initially, fearful perhaps, and with the taste of the Nazi experience still in its mouth, America, with the prompting of the British, chose to believe the worst.[11] Post-Cold War revelations from Soviet archives proved Washington (and London) right: Stalin could be a monster, with the soul of a killer.[12] As a Cold War opponent, he was an opportunist and a realist: he would take what he could, but he understood the limits of power. What "we now know", to borrow a line from a recent review of John L. Gaddis's latest work, has turned out to bear an uncanny resemblance to what Western diplomats thought they knew then.[13] Scholars who contend that it could have been otherwise, miss, I submit, this historical revulsion to totalitarianism in general and Bolshevism in particular and fail to place proper emphasis on it. Both threatened the American ideals of individualism—politically, culturally, and economically. For if it is assumed that policymakers in the West were so moved by such images, and I think we can, then it would have been well-nigh impossible to expect them to have behaved differently. Pragmatic realists to the core, they drew the line in the sand and chose to fight even if it meant asking Americans for continued sacrifice. Is it any wonder, then, that members of the early Cold War generation believed their critics had no ground to stand on?[14]

The author's intellectual debts, not unlike any other scholar of the early Cold War period, are numerous and should be evident both in my footnotes and in the bibliographic essay that follows. More immediately, however, the author should like to acknowledge the assistance he has received over the years from archivists from the Presidential Libraries of the National Archives and Records Administration, particularly the Franklin D. Roosevelt Library and the Harry S. Truman Library, as well as from the Library of Congress and Harvard University's Houghton Library. For other parts of the story, the author is also indebted to the Public Record Office (London) and the Australian Archives (Canberra). Lastly, I should like to thank Suzanne Lewis for her cheerful and generous cooperation in the preparation of this manuscript.

Joseph M. Siracusa
St Lucia

## NOTES

1. By Cold War, I mean "the protracted conflict between the Soviet and Western worlds that while falling short of 'hot' war nonetheless involved a

comprehensive military, political, and ideologically rivalry", lasting from late 1944 to 1991. Fred Halliday, "Cold War," in *The Oxford Companion to Politics of the World* (New York, 1993), pp. 151-53. Also see Joseph M. Siracusa, "Will the Real Author of the Cold War Please Stand Up?" The Society for Historians of American Foreign Relations, *Newsletter* 13 (Sept. 1982); William Safire, "On Language," *New York Times Magazine*, 26 Sept. 1982; and Coral Bell, *The Cold War in Retrospect: Diplomacy, Strategy and Regional Impact* (Canberra, 1996)

2. Norman A. Graebner, *Ideas and Diplomacy: Readings in the Intellectual Tradition of American Foreign Policy* (New York, 1964), p. vii.

3. By diplomacy, I mean the conduct of relations, formal and informal, between one group of human beings and another group alien to themselves. Harold Nicolson, *Diplomacy* (New York, 1939); and *The Evolution of Diplomatic Method* (London, 1954).

4. See the September cables of Ambassador W. Averell Harriman to Harry Hopkins and Secretary of State Cordell Hull, respectively, in Joseph M. Siracusa, ed., *The American Diplomatic Revolution: A Documentary History of the Cold War, 1941-1947* (Sydney, 1976), pp. 55-61.

5. Joseph M. Siracusa, *New Left Diplomatic Histories and Historians: The American Revisionists*, (2nd ed., Claremont, CA, 1993). For the state of the profession on the literature of the Cold War, see Michael J. Hogan, ed., *America in the World: The Historiography of American Foreign Relations since 1941* (New York, 1995); and John Lewis Gaddis, "The Tragedy of Cold War History," *Diplomatic History* 17 (Winter 1993): 1-16.

6. Bernard Bailyn, *The Ideological Origins of the American Revolution* (Cambridge, MA, 1967), pp. vi, ix.

7. Arthur M. Schlesinger, Jr., "Origins of the Cold War," *Foreign Affairs* 46 (Oct. 1967): 22-52.

8. See Gerhard L. Weinberg, *A World At Arms: A Global History of World War II* (Cambridge, 1994).

9. W.W. Rostow, *The American Diplomatic Revolution* (Oxford, 1946).

10. For example, see Daniel M. Smith, *Aftermath of War: Bainbridge Colby and Wilsonian Diplomacy, 1920-1921* (Philadelphia, 1970), pp. 64-65.

11. Daniel Yergin, *Shattered Peace: The Origins of the Cold War and the National Security State* (Boston, 1977), pp. 366-410; and Melvyn P. Leffler, *A Preponderance of Power: National Security, the Truman Administration, and the Cold War* (Stanford, 1992), pp. 15, 513-18.

12. According to minutes from the 5 March 1940 session of the Politburo, presumably chaired by Stalin, the NKVD, the Soviet Secret police and the forerunner of the KGB, was instructed to carry out "the supreme punishment" (execution by firing squad) of more than 25,000 Poles, including thousands of Polish Army officers whose bodies were dumped in a mass grave in the forests of Katyn. The documents surfaced in 1992 two years after former Soviet leader Mikhail S. Gorbachev first admitted Soviet guilt in the Katyn massacre. *International Herald-Tribune*, 15 Oct. 1992. Also see Alan Bullock, *Hitler and Stalin: Parallel Lives* (London, 1991); Robert W. Tucker, *Stalin in Power: The Revolution from Above, 1928-1941*; and Robert Conquest, *The Great Terror: A Reassessment* (New York, 1990).

13. David C. Hendrickson, review of *We Now Know: Rethinking Cold War History*, by John L. Gaddis, in *Foreign Affairs* 76 (Jul./ Aug. 1997): 153.

14. "I am not going to argue with the revisionists. They have no ground to stand on." Letter from W. Averell Harriman to the author, 30 Oct. 1978.

# INTRODUCTION

The following chapters constitute a thematic history of American diplomacy and the ideological origins of the Cold War. Taken together, they illustrate the extent to which United States Cold War policies developed in fits and starts, as the idealism of liberal internationalism gave way to the "realism" of containment. Chapter 1 demonstrates how difficult it was for American leadership to give up its illusions about international behaviour—the "liberal" view of international affairs. The clash between Churchill and Stalin, on the one hand, and FDR and the State Department, on the other hand, over spheres of influence, self-determination and the role of national interest provides the essential background for understanding the dilemma of the Roosevelt Administration, after repudiating "the balance of power concept as one of the techniques of an evil and war-ridden past".[1]

Chapter 2 highlights the origins of an unvarnished "realistic" view of world of politics which aimed at limiting the expansion of the Soviet Union, the basic intellectual concept of containment, together with the role the British played. The particular focus emphasizes George F. Kennan's relationship with his opposite number in the British Embassy, Frank Roberts, and the authorship of the "Long Telegram" sent from Moscow in February 1946. Chapter 3 reveals problems inherent in developing working policies to translate the concept of containment into an actual program. While developing "realistic" policies to enforce containment, the danger of over-estimating the Soviet threat was already evident in the differences between George Kennan and Paul Nitze. The former understood what George C. Marshall meant, when as Secretary of State, he once cautioned that if political problems were dealt with in military terms, they were likely to become military problems. Chapter 4 deals with the transformation of FDR's Indochinese policy of international trusteeship to Harry S. Truman's commitment to French restoration. It relates the difficult decisions that were made to gain France's support for containment and how vulnerable Washington was to demands, often unpleasant, by its allies. Chapter 5 shows again that to maintain allies, one had to bend to some of their demands. The ANZUS treaty, while not initially desired by the United States, did, in the end, anchor the southwest Pacific part of containment.

Moreover, it became evident in the study of these diplomatic episodes that the onset of the Korean War, coupled with the "loss" of China, played a major role in drawing all of the components of containment together, some for the better while some for the worst. Until then, America and its allies had successfully confronted the forces of international Communism in northern Iran, Greece, Turkey and Berlin. Then there was Korea. Or as Randall B. Woods put it, "Had it not been for the fall of China and the Korean War, the Cold War as a fifty-year phenomenon involving the expenditure of billions of dollars and the destruction of millions of lives in Vietnam, Cambodia, and other parts of the developing world, might never have happened".[2] The North Korean attack against South Korea on 25 June 1950 provided the Truman Administration with all the proof it needed that Stalin and his ilk were on the move; the introduction of Mao's Communist People's Volunteers in late November silenced critics of NSC-68 and ushered in a new, more dangerous world.

## NOTES

1. Julius W. Pratt, Vincent De Santis and Joseph M. Siracusa, *A History of United States Foreign Policy* (4th ed., Englewood Cliffs, NJ, 1980), p. 380.

2. Randall B. Woods, "Substitute War", review of *The Korean War: An International History*, by William Stueck, in *Diplomatic History* 21 (Fall 1977): 642.

# CHAPTER 1

# FRANKLIN D. ROOSEVELT & THE NIGHT STALIN AND CHURCHILL DIVIDED EUROPE

Of the many fascinating episodes that punctuate the diplomatic history of World War II, few have intrigued scholars more than the secret Balkan spheres-of-action agreement worked out by Prime Minister Winston Churchill and Marshal Josef Stalin at the Anglo-Soviet conference (British code-named TOLSTOY) held in Moscow in the autumn of 1944. It was late in the evening of 9 October. In his first encounter with Stalin since the meeting of the Big Three at Teheran in 1943, Churchill, believing "the moment...apt for business", appealed to the Soviet dictator to "Let us settle about our affairs in the Balkans". Specifically, he went on, "We have interests, missions, and agents there. Don't let us get at cross-purposes in small ways. So far as Britain and Russia are concerned, how would it do for you to have ninety per cent dominance in Rumania, for us to have ninety per cent of the say in Greece, and go fifty-fifty about Yugoslavia?" In the time this was being translated, the British leader recalled in his memoirs:

I wrote on a half-sheet of paper—

| | | |
|---|---|---|
| Rumania | | |
| | Russia | 90% |
| | The others | 10% |
| Greece | | |
| | Great Britain | |
| | (in accord with USA) | 90% |
| | Russia | 10% |
| Yugoslavia | | 50-50% |
| Hungary | | 50-50% |
| Bulgaria | | |
| | Russia | 75% |
| | The others | 25% |

In the presence of the small gathering that had come together that night in the Kremlin, Stalin looked on, listening for the translation. Having finally understood, he paused slightly and "took his blue pencil and made a large tick upon it, and passed it back to us". Thus, concluded Churchill, "It was all settled in no more time than it takes to set down".[1] With only minor variations—80-20 per cent predominance in favour of the Soviets in Hungary and Bulgaria, reached by Foreign Secretary Anthony Eden and Minister for Foreign Affairs Vyacheslav Molotov in two additional meetings amidst resolution of the tangled Bulgarian armistice dispute—the original agreement remained intact or so it was thought.[2]

Upon his return to London, the Prime Minister reported confidently to the House of Commons that so far as the Balkans were concerned, he and Stalin had been able to reach complete agreement. Moreover, he added, "I do not feel there is any immediate danger of our combined war effort being weakened by divergence of policy or of doctrine in Greece, Rumania, Bulgaria, Yugoslavia and, beyond the Balkans, Hungary. We have reached a very good working arrangement about all these countries, singly and in combination, with the object of concentrating all their efforts, and concerting them with ours against the common foe, and providing, as far as possible, for a peaceful settlement".[3] Though it is commonly agreed that the subject of Balkan percentages was not again officially raised at Yalta—or at any other time during the remainder of World War II—historians continue to debate the significance of that "very good working arrangement" concluded at TOLSTOY.[4] Needless to say, there are almost as many explanations as there are historians to enunciate them.

In one of the earliest accounts of the rise and fall of the Grand Alliance, *America, Britain and Russia,* published in 1953, William Hardy McNeill argued that an "agreement" had indeed been reached by Churchill and Stalin, one that "reflected the new military balance in the Balkans". What McNeill found odd about the arrangement was what he regarded as the curious effort made to reduce the matter to percentages", which he speculated, "might [have] serve[d] as a guide to the numerical division between pro-British and pro-Russian cabinet members in the Governments to be formed in the various Balkan states".[5] Though there was much room for speculation as to the meaning of the percentages themselves, few Western scholars have since doubted that a Balkan deal of one kind or another had been reached in Moscow. What has been debated extensively was the meaning of the nature of the agreement and to what extent it represented a short-term or long-term commitment, whether it was a formal or an informal agreement or merely a wartime understanding. Here American scholarship has been found wanting. From the otherwise substantial achievements of Herbert Feis, John Lewis Gaddis, and Lynn Etheridge Davis one learns little, save the standard reference to the Churchill-Stalin talks and President Roosevelt's apparently ambiguous response to them.[6]

Similarly from the efforts of Daniel Yergin, Albert Resis and Bruce R. Kuniholm one learns little more. In *Shattered Peace*, a full-length study of the ideological origins of the Cold War, not without merit, Yergin informs us that "The actual minutes of the [Churchill-Stalin] conversation [of October 9] demonstrate that Churchill knew exactly what her was doing, that he was seeking a permanent understanding [in the Balkans]", and that Stalin, characteristically preferring "such practical arithmetic to the algebra of declarations", understood perfectly.[7] In point of fact, however, a close reading of the minutes in question reveals no such certitude. Elsewhere, Resis concluded that with the exception of Bulgaria, Churchill and Stalin had fashioned "a comprehensive informal understanding on the Balkans", which, "in effect, extended into perpetuity the Anglo-Soviet agreement of May 1944 [sic], which allowed Britain the predominant voice in Greek affairs and the Soviet Union the predominant voice in Rumanian affairs".[8] Echoing the arguments of Churchill and Eden, Kuniholm, in *The Origins of the Cold War in the Near East*, reverted to the view that percentages reached at Moscow amounted to little more than "a rough guide to Allied influence in the Balkans", albeit with "long-range political implications", another chapter in the extension of Britain's and Russia's "historical struggle for power along the Northern Tier".[9] That the Anglo-Soviet agreement was never in fact consummated (about which more will be said) does not much deter Resis, who like Yergin had access to important declassified materials from the Public Record Office.

Equally disturbing, from the standpoint of coming to grips with Washington's view of the proposed Anglo-Soviet division of responsibilities in the Balkans, is Resis's misreading of Roosevelt's message of 4 October 1944 to Stalin in which the Soviet leader was reminded "that in this global war there is literally no question, political or military, in which the United States is not interested". Brushing aside the involved character of this cable, which if anything suggests a very different Presidential attitude toward the Balkans, Resis attributes to Roosevelt the responsibility for the first round in the Cold War: "If then we wanted to fix an exact date for the beginning of the Cold War in southeastern Europe, that date would be October 4, 1944. For on that day Roosevelt informed Stalin that the President reserved for the United States the right to do nothing less than have a voice at least equal to that of each of the other Big Three powers in arriving at and executing decisions on all international problems—including those in southeastern Europe—while denying the Soviet Union the same right in the Western spheres—in Italy, for example".[10] That this particular cable, which was in fact drafted by presidential advisers, was meant as much to rein in the Prime Minister as to put the Marshal on notice that Washington would not be extending a blank check to the allies in Eastern Europe in advance of the Presidential election in November is nowhere taken into consideration.

American historians have also attempted to resolve the question regarding the role of spheres of influence in United States's political thinking during the closing stages of World War II, most agreeing that the US government officially opposed spheres of influence. Yet controversy arose from attempts to implement this policy. Eduard Mark has suggested that in fact Washington's opposition to spheres of influence was "conditional rather than categorical".[11] Mark continues that while policymakers still opposed what they considered 'exclusive' spheres, by early 1944 a certain tolerance was being exhibited towards 'open' sphere arrangements which would allow smaller nations of the region to manage their domestic affairs while the Soviet Union controlled their foreign and domestic policy. Yet Gier Lundestad had earlier argued that while a two-spheres approach may be useful, it does not recognise that acceptance of Soviet control in international affairs would lead to control in domestic matters.[12] Elsewhere Warren Kimball has suggested that Churchill's pursuit of a spheres of influence agreement in Europe was a proposal opposed by the State Department but approved by Franklin Roosevelt.[13] Kimball uses as his evidence some open-ended remarks made by Roosevelt such as this comment to Ambassador Harriman: "My active interest at the present time in the Balkan area is that such steps as are practicable should be taken to insure against the Balkans getting us into future international war".[14] Had the US been uncompromising in its policy regarding spheres of influence, Eduard Mark adds, the Cold War would have been an "irrepressible conflict", especially considering the reluctance of the Soviet Union to forego unilateral guarantees of its interests. "American efforts in Europe, consequently, represented neither a utopian scheme to rid the continent of spheres of influence nor a Faustian bid to dominate it, but a search for stable spheres of a kind consonant with the interests of the principal victors of World War II".[15]

Recent post-Cold War American literature sheds little new light on these issues. Introducing a post-revisionist perspective, Lloyd Gardner in his substantial work *Spheres of Influence*, suggests, as Walter Lippman had earlier predicted, that spheres of influence were the only solution in the Balkan situation. In retrospect Gardner suggests that not only was it inevitable that eastern and central European nations fell to the Soviet Union, "a power politics truth that Wilson had tried to deny at Versailles", but that these hostile Soviet spheres encouraged the co-operation of Western European nations. In turn, Gardner continues, a real war was prevented. "The partition of Europe had been largely accomplished before the Cold War began. Had it not happened that way, there might not have been a Cold War, or, as seems more likely, it could have been worse, certainly for Europe".[16] Gardner presents "a Roosevelt torn between Woodrow Wilson's idealism and Churchill's European pragmatism".[17] In contrast, another recent account of this issue, Remi Nadeau's *Stalin, Churchill and Roosevelt Divide Europe*, implies a definite degree of naivete about FDR's leadership.[18] According to Nadeau, Churchill was the only leader aware of the dangers of Soviet control over Eastern Europe, and Roosevelt, "competing with centuries of political intrigue" served only to strengthen the Soviet cause by failing to support Britain fully. "It is not a story of American wrongdoing", he writes, "but of American innocence. The very idealism that made Roosevelt a surpassing global leader in winning the war also kept him, at least in Europe, from winning the peace". Nadeau's essential argument is reduced to the suggestion that Europe was divided because the United States had enough power but did not know how to use it, the British knew how to use power but did not have enough and the Soviets had enough and knew how to use it.

In turning to major British secondary sources, one finds little dispute that a percentage agreement had indeed been struck at Moscow and that the proceedings fairly much square with Churchill's own account, especially his insistence that the arrangement was to be viewed only as an "interim guide". With the exception of further elaboration of details of the two subsequent meetings between Eden and Molotov concerning Bulgaria, Sir Llewellyn Woodward's treatment of the subject in *British Foreign Policy in the Second World War* is probably the premier example in this category.[19] Others such as Sir John Wheeler-Bennett and Anthony Nicholls went on to characterize the arrangement merely as a temporary "rule-of-thumb agreement with Stalin about the amount of influence to be exercised by Russia and her Western allies in the Danube Basin".[20] Stressing the hopelessly unequal military position of the Western Allies in southeastern Europe in the fall of 1944, Elisabeth Barker underscored the essential reality of the situation. "The agreement", Barker observed after noting the Red Army was in effective control of the Balkans save Greece, "merely formalized an already existing situation, except that the original percentages, in so far as they had a meaning, understated actual Soviet predominance".[21]

Interestingly, but again perhaps not surprisingly, retrospective appraisals of various contemporaries of the significance of the percentage agreement evidence a similar diversity of judgment. Though not quite certain what it was, a number of American policy-makers, below the level of the President, believed the percentage agreement to be in the world tradition of power politics and spheres of influence and for that reason branded the arrangement as "cynical" and "notorious". What most bothered diplomats such as Charles Bohlen, chief of the Eastern European desk in State, and Averell Harriman, United States ambassador to Moscow, was what Churchill supposedly hoped to accomplish. "I don't understand now, and I do not believe that I understood at the time", Harriman repeated in his memoirs, "just what Churchill thought he was accomplishing by these percentages".[22] Bohlen thought the Prime Minister "unrealistic" in the sense that one could never count on the Kremlin to keep its word anyway. Assuming the percentages were designed as a sort of formula for the division of ministries, Bohlen went on to make his point: "Even though Communists would be limited in the number of ministries they controlled in a coalition government, they would continually attempt to extend their influence. A non-Communist Premier with Communist Ministers would be like a woman trying to stay half-pregnant".[23] At the time, President Roosevelt had little more to say than that he was pleased that Churchill and Stalin had reached a meeting of the minds. Similarly, little new is found in Eden's memoirs.[24] Sir Alexander Cadogan, permanent under secretary of the Foreign Office expressed the view that "We...seem to be reaching some understanding...to Balkans generally".[25] What kind was not certain. Still, others such as F.W.D. Deakin, who had served as first British liaison officer at Tito's headquarters in 1943, wrote off the agreement as a ploy on Churchill's part "to provoke Stalin into giving him some idea [of] where the Russian Army was going to end up.... He [Churchill] was not trying to divide up the Balkans. Maybe he gave the wrong impression...".[26] And perhaps he did.

Within the context of these introductory observations and with particular emphasis on the American perspective, this chapter will address itself to the following questions: What factors prompted Churchill to travel to Moscow in search of a Balkan agreement? What precisely did he hope to achieve by it? What did Stalin hope to achieve by affixing his mark to that half-sheet of paper? To what extent, if any, were the Anglo-Soviet leaders conditioned, constrained or otherwise influenced by the United States Government's declared hostility to spheres of influence generally and in the Balkans especially? Did America's official attitude necessarily reflect the private attitude of Franklin Roosevelt? And, finally, and in light of the relatively rapid disintegration of the Grand Alliance, might we not ask if a legitimate opportunity to avert at least one aspect of the Cold War had not been missed?

As to the question—"What factors prompted Churchill to travel to Moscow in 1944 in search of a Balkan agreement?"—few scholars have had any reason to doubt the Prime Minister's own account of his decision to embark on this journey. Against the background of the aftermath of the Soviet offensive of the summer of 1944, which witnessed the occupation of Bucharest and a declaration of war against Bulgaria, to be followed shortly by an armistice, Churchill "felt the need of another personal meeting with Stalin, whom I had not seen since Teheran, and with whom, in spite of the Warsaw tragedy, I felt new links since the successful opening of 'Overlord'".[27] The Prime Minister observed furthermore that while, "the arrangements which I had made with the President in the summer to divide our [Anglo-Soviet] responsibilities for looking after particular countries [Greece and Rumania, respectively] affected by the movements of the armies had tided us over the three months for which our arrangement ran", the time had come to rethink the agreement anew. The first Balkan agreement, so-called, originated with the British leader's concern in early May that something had to be done to put the Russians in their place. "I am not very clear on it myself" the Prime Minister minuted Eden on 4 May, "but evidently we are approaching a showdown with the Russians about their Communist intrigue in Italy, Yugoslavia and Greece...I must say their attitude becomes more difficult every day". Initially, Churchill requested that the foreign minister draft a paper "for the Cabinet and possibly for the Imperial Conference setting forth shortly,...the brute issues between us and the Soviet Government which are developing in Italy, in Rumania, in Bulgaria, in Yugoslavia and above all in Greece".

For Churchill, the issue was unequivocal: "Are we going to acquiesce in the Communization of the Balkans and perhaps of Italy"?[28] The paper, which was placed before the War Cabinet on 7 June, suggested that an effort ought to be made "to focus our [British] influence in the Balkans by consolidating our position in Greece and Turkey...and, while avoiding any direct challenge to Russian influence in Yugoslavia, Albania, Rumania and Bulgaria, to avail ourselves of every opportunity in order to spread British influence in those countries".[29] Even while the paper was being drafted Eden himself sought out the Soviet Ambassador in London in order to establish Balkan ground rules.

On 5 May, only a day after Churchill had minuted his concern, Eden called on Soviet Ambassador Gousev and raised "the possibility of our agreeing between ourselves as a practical matter that Rumanian affairs would be in the main the concern of the Soviet Government, while Greek affairs would be in the main our concern, each Government giving the other help in the respective countries". Less than two weeks later the Soviets replied to the suggestion positively with the proviso, to quote Eden's cable to his ambassador in Moscow, that "before giving any final assurance in the matter, they would like to know whether we had consulted the United States Government and whether the latter also agreed to this arrangement. If so, the Soviet Government would be ready to give us a final affirmative answer". The Foreign Secretary's final remarks are instructive:

> I [Eden] said that I did not think we had consulted the United States Government in the matter but would certainly be ready to do so. *I could not imagine that they would dissent.* After all the matter was really related to the military operations of our respective forces. Rumania fell within the sphere of the Russian armies and Greece within the Allied Command under General Wilson in the Mediterranean. Therefore it seemed natural that Soviet Russia should take the lead in Rumania and we in Greece, and that each should support the other.[30]

Inasmuch as it was common knowledge that Secretary of State Cordell Hull "was, in fact, flatly opposed to any division of Europe or section of Europe into spheres of influence" or, to paraphrase his comments to Congress upon his return from the foreign ministers' conference at Moscow in late 1943, "any other of the special arrangements through which, in the unhappy past, the nations strove to safeguard their security or to promote their interests", it is in itself hard to imagine how Eden expected to carry the Americans along.[31] It is also tempting to think that the Kremlin had deliberately nudged the Foreign Secretary into a trap.[32]

In any case, the British Ambassador Lord Halifax called on Hull on 30 May to broach the subject. Concealing the fact that Eden had already spoken to the Russians and representing the suggestions as the fruit of the Foreign Secretary's "own independent reflection",[33] Halifax inquired how the United States "would feel about an arrangement between the British and the Russians to the effect that Russia might have a controlling influence in Rumania and Great Britain a controlling influence in Greece". Though promising to give the matter serious attention Hull voiced deep reservations about the wisdom of abandoning "the fixed rules and policies which are in accord with our broad basic declarations of policy, principles and practice".[34] Before receiving Halifax's report of his meeting with Hull, and still anticipating no difficulty in State, Eden requested the Prime Minister to send a personal message to Roosevelt in order to "reinforce" the Foreign Office's representations to Hull.[35] It was at this juncture, however, that Churchill and Eden crossed signals raising serious doubts, at least in some American minds, as to the true aims of British policy in the Balkans.

After observing that there had "recently been disquieting signs between ourselves and the Russians in regard to the Balkan countries and in particular Greece", Churchill let the proverbial cat out of the bag when he told FDR that, "[W]e therefore suggested to the Soviet Ambassador here that we should agree between ourselves as a practical matter that the Soviet Government would take the lead in Rumanian affairs, while we would take the lead in Greek affairs, each Government giving the other help in the respective countries". In asking Roosevelt to give this proposal his "blessing", the Prime Minister took pains to point out to the election-bound President that "We do not of course wish to carve up the Balkans into spheres of influence and in agreeing to the arrangement we should make it clear that it applied only to war conditions and did not affect the rights and responsibilities which each of the three Great Powers will have to exercise at the peace settlement and afterwards in regard to the whole of Europe", the thrust of which was repeated to Halifax a week later.[36] In the meantime, Halifax conveyed to Eden his only reason for concealing Whitehall's initiative in approaching the Soviets first. "I purposely did not disclose the fact that you had already taken the matter up with the Russians", he cabled Eden on 5 June, "because I thought we were more likely to get the Americans along with us in that way". Furthermore, he went on to remonstrate, "Subject to what you and the Prime Minister may feel and to obvious necessities of urgency that may arise, it would seem wise, when you have instructed me to take up something with Mr. Hull, to defer action through the higher channel of the President until I have been able to report progress with Mr Hull, and further action that you may wish to take can be taken with the knowledge of what has passed at lower level. Otherwise we risk confusion and embarrassment".[37] Halifax got both for his trouble.

After some debate in State between the European and Near Eastern Desks, Acting Secretary of State Edward Stettinius handed the file over to Assistant Secretary of State Breckenridge Long for a recommendation. During the next several days Long prepared an answer in the negative,[38] which in turn was approved without change by the President on 10 June. Roosevelt advised Churchill in no uncertain language that his government was "unwilling to approve the proposed arrangement". Washington's position was as follows:

> Briefly, we acknowledge that the militarily responsible Government in any given territory will inevitably make decisions required by military developments but are convinced that the natural tendency for such decisions to

extend to other than military field would be strengthened by an agreement of the type suggested. On our opinion, this would certainly result in the persistence of differences between you and the Soviets and, in the division of the Balkans into spheres of influence despite the declared intention to limit the arrangements to military matters.

What to offer in its place? "We believe", the President gently lectured the Prime Minister, "efforts should preferably be made to establish consultative machinery to dispel misunderstandings and restrain the tendency toward the development of exclusive spheres".[39] Though, to be sure, without any risk of disturbing his special relationship with Roosevelt, Churchill replied with a forcefulness of his own.

"Action is paralyzed", he cabled the same day, "if everybody is to consult everybody else about everything before it is taken. The events will always outstrip the changing situation in these Balkan regions". Besides which, "Somebody must have the power to plan and act"; consultative machinery "would be a mere obstruction, always overridden in any case of emergency by direct interchange between you and me, or either you and Stalin". Explaining the realities of the prospect of Soviet troops on Romanian soil—"they will probably do what they like anyhow"—and the British investment both of blood and treasure, in Greece, Churchill appealed to the President's vanity with several questions: "Why is all this effective direction to be broken up into a committee of mediocre officials such as we are littering about the world? Why can you and I not keep this in our hands considering how we see eye to eye about so much of it"? In conclusion, the Prime Minister proposed that the President agree to a trial period of three months, although clearly, it seem, Churchill would have settled for two months as preferable to nothing.[40] Roosevelt was apparently impressed with the Prime Minister's logic. For, without notifying State for over two weeks that he had reversed course, the President acquiesced in Churchill's proposal, with the provision, "[W]e must be careful to make it clear that we are not establishing any postwar spheres of influence".[41] Needless to say, Churchill, who doubtless must have congratulated himself both on his power of persuasion and his ability to override the State Department, was grateful. All that remained was to pass on the information to the Soviets.

"The United States Government have now been consulted", Eden wrote to the Soviet Ambassador in London on 19 June, "and they agree with the arrangement proposed". More to the point, the Secretary noted, "They feel some anxiety, however, lest it should extend beyond the immediate circumstances for which it has been devised and should lead to the partition of the Balkan countries into spheres of influence", a prospect at variance with London's intentions "that the arrangement should apply only to war conditions and should not affect the rights and responsibilities which each of our three Governments will have to exercise at the peace settlement and afterwards in regard to the whole of Europe". In any case, he finished in a manner intimating only a hint of disagreement, "In order to guard against any danger of the arrangement extending beyond the purpose for which it has been devised we have suggested to the United States Government, and they have agreed, that it should be given a trial of three months after which it would be reviewed by our three Governments. I hope, therefore, that the Soviet Government will agree to the arrangement coming into force on this basis".[42] The Soviet Government had other plans, however. Ambassador Gousev replied on 8 July that in light of changed circumstances, particularly certain apprehensions expressed by the United States, the Kremlin would consider it necessary to give the question further consideration. Moreover, he added, "the Soviet Government deem it advisable to make a direct approach to the United States Government in order to obtain more detailed information as to their attitude to this question".[43] This was done on 1 July. Moscow had called Eden's bluff.

The State Department, with Hull back in the picture and the President in the midst of an election campaign, replied to the Soviet request two weeks later on 15 July, observing that "It is correct that the Government of the United States assented to the [Balkan] arrangement, for a trial period of three months, this assent being given in consideration of present war strategy". This particular "overriding consideration" aside, State continued, the United States "would wish to make known its apprehension lest the proposed agreement might, by the natural tendency of such arrangements, lead to the division, in fact, of [the] Balkan region into spheres of influence", [which] would be an unfortunate development, "in view of decisions of Moscow Conference...". As a consequence of those decisions, State had hoped that no projected measure would "be allowed to prejudice efforts towards direction of policies of the Allied governments along lines of collaboration rather than independent action, since any arrangement suggestive of spheres of influence cannot but militate against establishment and effective functioning of a broader system of general security in which all countries will have their part". Still—no doubt with due respect to the President's previous determination to do otherwise—the Secretary of State let it be known that he would have no particular objection to a three months' trial period so long as Anglo-Soviet actions in no way affected "the rights and responsibilities which each of the three principal allies will have to exercise during the period of re-establishment of peace and afterwards in regard to the whole of Europe". And, finally, in case anyone missed the point, State went on notice in assuming aloud "that the arrangement would have neither direct or indirect validity as affecting interests of this Government or of other Governments associated with the three principal allies".[44] In addition to the arguments against spheres of influence contained in this memorandum there were other perhaps less lofty considerations to be taken into account.

In a top-secret letter written to Hull in May 1944, Admiral William D. Leahy, Roosevelt's chief of staff, advanced a number of military arguments in opposition to spheres of influence along the lines of the proposed Anglo-Soviet agreement. According to Leahy, whose diary records that he did "not intend to sacrifice American soldiers and sailors in order to impose any government on any people, or to adjust political differences in Europe or Asia, except to act against an aggressor with the purpose of preventing an international war", the nation's best interests in postwar would be served in maintaining "the solidarity of [the] three great powers",[45] until such time "arrangements will be perfected for the prevention of world conflicts".[46] Furthermore, and as any world conflict in the foreseeable future would most likely find Britain and Soviet Russia in opposite camps with Moscow in an overwhelmingly dominant military position on the continent, about which the United States could presently do little, it would be prudent for America to "exert its utmost efforts and utilize all its influence to prevent such a situation arising and to promote a spirit of mutual cooperation between Britain, Russia and ourselves". Put another way, Leahy was saying that in the case of war between London and Moscow, probably occasioned by a territorial dispute on the continent, "we might be able to successfully defend Britain [proper], but we could not, under existing conditions, defeat Russia...we would find ourselves [therefore] engaged in a war which we could not win even though the United States would be in no danger of defeat and occupation".

To attempt to eschew such a situation was simply to recognize one of the new international facts of life: "the recent phenomenal development of the heretofore latent Russian military and economic strength—a development which seems certain to prove epochal in its bearing on future politico-military international relationships, and which has yet to reach the full scope with Russian resources". While it is doubtful that Leahy's remarks represented a significant reversal of the nation's official attitude towards balance-of-power politics taken by Army Chief of Staff George C. Marshall and Admiral H. Stark in September 1941, as has been argued elsewhere,[47] they are significant in the sense that they indicate an official awareness of the limits of American power to influence events in postwar continental Europe, including the Balkans.

Meanwhile, President Roosevelt expressed his strong disapproval of the manner in which the British had handled the proposed Balkan arrangement. "I think I should tell you frankly", FDR cabled Churchill on 22 June, "that we were disturbed that your people took this matter up with us only after it had been put up to the Russians and they had inquired [at this late juncture] whether we were agreeable". More or less accepting the Foreign Office's explanation "that the proposal 'arose out of a chance remark' which was converted by the Soviet Government into a formal proposal", the President hoped that "matters of this importance can be prevented from developing in such a manner in the future".[48] The Prime Minister was quick to reply, pointing out in addition to the long-belabored observations that the Soviets were the only power that could do anything in Romania and that the Greek burden rested almost entirely on the British, that he had had no complaints of Roosevelt's recent private messages to Stalin with regard to the Poles. "I am not complaining at all of this", he assured the President, "because I know we are working for the general theme and purposes and I hope you will feel that this has been so in my conduct of the Greek affair". Appealing to FDR's political instincts, the Prime Minister conceded that, "It would be quite easy for me, on the general principle of slithering to Left, which is so popular in foreign policy, to let things rip when the King of Greece would probably be forced to abdicate" and the Communist-led elements "would work a reign of terror"; accordingly, the only way to prevent such a state of affairs was to persuade Moscow to quit boosting the Communists "and ramming it forward with all their force". It was in these circumstances, he concluded, "I proposed to the Russians a temporary working arrangement for the better conduct of the war. This was only a proposal and had to be referred to you for agreement".[49] Roosevelt seems to have grasped the message when several days later he replied to the Prime Minister saying, "It appears that both of us have inadvertently taken unilateral action in a direction that we both now agree to have been expedient for the time being". Nonetheless, he made clear, "It is essential that we should always be in agreement in matters bearing on our allied war matters".[50] And on that the incident seemed closed.

Several weeks later, upon receipt of news from Eden that the Kremlin had now found it necessary to give the question of a Balkan division "further consideration" and was, in fact, approaching the United States direct, Churchill virtually went through the ceiling. "Does this mean", he minuted the Foreign Secretary on 9 July, "that all we had settled with the Russians now goes down through the pedantic interference of the United States, and that Rumania and Greece are to be condemned to a regime of triangular telegrams in which the United States and ourselves are to interfere with the Russian treatment of Rumania, and the Russians are to boost up E.A.M. [the National Liberation Front] while the President pursues a pro-King policy in regard to Greece, and we have to make all things go sweet? If so, it will be a great disaster".[51] The following day, 10 July, Eden informed the War Cabinet that the proposed Anglo-Soviet spheres-of-action agreement with regard to Greece and Rumania had, in the foreign secretary's words, "broken down".[52] Puzzled by the actual meaning of State's response to the Soviet inquiry of 1 July—"Does this mean that the American have agreed to the three months' trial, or is it all thrown in the pool again"?[53]—and increasingly concerned by the prospect of Soviet interference in Greek affairs particularly the unheralded dispatch of a mission of Russian officers there in late July,[54] Churchill would have to await the changing tides of war before making another approach to the USSR on a Balkan settlement. Moreover, in the light of past experience with the Americans, it is hardly surprising that the next time the Prime Minister sought to play his hand in the Balkans, he would approach Stalin himself, after all, a man with whom Churchill "considered one could talk as one human being to another".[55] Until such time, and for all intents and purposes, the May Agreement had all but become a dead letter.[56]

By October 1944 the Prime Minister's time had come. For better and for worse the war situation had fundamentally been altered since spring. With respect to the latter the Red Army had now firmly established itself in Romania and Bulgaria and had only recently penetrated Yugoslavia and Hungary; by the same token, British influence in the region had been confined to Greece and Yugoslavia, principally in the form of military liaison missions with the guerilla organizations of those countries and, to a lesser extent, by hosting the Greek and Yugoslav governments in exile. Of particular urgency to Churchill was the threat to Greece posed by the possible Bulgarian retention of parts or all of Macedonia and Thrace occupied during the course of the war. The fact that Bulgaria now marched on the side of the Allies proved cold comfort, indeed, considering the Soviets were calling the tune. All of this is not to say, however, that Churchill would be travelling to Moscow without some bargaining power of his own. For as Sir Llewellyn Woodward has rightly observed, "If the Russians had made great advances in south-eastern Europe the Wester Powers had also won remarkable victories".[57] Since May the Second Front had been established, Paris and Brussels had both been liberated, and the frontier of the Reich breached. In fact, it began increasingly to appear that it would be the Western half of the Grand Alliance that would reach Berlin before the advancing Red Army. Furthermore, and as David Dilks has indicated in a related but different context, the Prime Minister could well boast that, at least "Until July 1944, the British Empire had more men in contact with the enemy world over, than had the United States".[58] Add to this Churchill's natural tendency, as he cabled Stalin on 4 October, to return "to Moscow under the much happier conditions created since August 1942, at which time, it will be recalled, it was the Prime Minister's mission to apprise the great Soviet leader that there would be no Second Front in 1942".[59] The great remaining question facing Churchill was, to paraphrase Halifax's words of the previous June, how "to get the Americans along with us". Predictably enough, the Prime Minister went straight to the President with whom he had just experienced the most cordial relations at the Second Quebec Conference (11-19 September) and at Hyde Park, American resistance to eleventh-hour Balkan military operations to the contrary notwithstanding.

On 29 September Churchill advised FDR that he and Eden were seriously considering flying to Moscow, the two great objects of the exercise being, "first, to clinch his [Stalin's] coming in against Japan and, secondly, to try to effect a friendly settlement with Poland. There are other points too about Greece and Yugoslavia which we could also discuss". And lest there be any misunderstanding, the Prime Minister reassured the President, "[W]e should keep you informed of every point".[60] Churchill followed up several days later, requesting Roosevelt to send Stalin "a message…saying that you approve of our mission", and that the United States Ambassador in Moscow would be available to take part in the proceedings.[61] The Prime Minister again wanted the President's blessing and almost got it. In a draft reply prepared by Admiral Leahy and approved without change by the White House, Roosevelt, to quote the most reliable source, "merely wished Churchill 'good luck', saying he understood perfectly why the trip had to be made".[62] At this point, according to Robert Sherwood, presidential adviser Harry Hopkins, having "learned that Roosevelt was dispatching a cable to Churchill in which he…in effect wash[ed] his hands of the whole matter [Balkans], with the implication that he was content to let Churchill speak for the United States as well as for Great Britain", intercepted the message and directed that it not be sent, a decision, to set the record straight, after Hopkins had phoned the President.[63] Sensitive both to Ambassador Harriman's September warnings from Moscow that the time had come to make clear to the Soviets "what we expect of them as the price of our good will"[64] and to Churchill's well-known inclination to make a Balkan deal, Hopkins persuaded Roosevelt it would be a mistake to send vague messages to Churchill and Stalin which would probably have the opposite effect of detaching the administration from the results of their meeting— whether on the Polish, Balkan or any other controversial issue. With the elections a month away and having just burned his fingers with the so-called Morgenthau Plan, to return all good Germans to the farm, the President agreed to sending Churchill and Stalin a different kind of message.

"I can well understand the reasons why you feel that an immediate meeting between yourself and Uncle Joe [Stalin] is necessary before the three of us can get together", FDR responded to Churchill on 4 October. "The questions which you will discuss there", he continued, "are ones which are, of course, of real interest to the United States, as I know you will agree. I have therefore instructed Harriman to stand by and to participate as my observer, if agreeable to you and Uncle Joe, and I have so informed Stalin". Finally, the President concluded unequivocally, "While naturally

Averell [Harriman] will not be in a position to commit the United States—I could not permit any one to commit me in advance—he will be able to keep me fully informed and I have told him to return to me as soon as the conference is over". All in all, the meeting in Moscow should prove "a useful prelude" to another meeting with the Big Three after the elections.[65] Churchill replied the next day, thanking Roosevelt for his thoughts on the matter and for his good wishes. Inasmuch as it was now apparent that he would not be receiving Roosevelt's blessing in advance, the Prime Minister then sought to protect his own freedom of manoeuvre: "I am very glad that Averell [Harriman] should sit in at all principal conferences; but you will not I am sure, wish this to preclude private tête-à-têtes between me and UJ [Stalin] or Anthony [Eden] and Molotov, as it is often under such conditions that the best progress is made", though he went on to reassure the President once again that "you can rely on me to keep you constantly informed of everything that affects our joint interests apart from the reports Averell will send".[66]

Roosevelt's message to Stalin, who seemed "somewhat puzzled" by it all, having supposed Churchill was coming in accordance with agreements reached at Quebec,[67] expressed similar sentiments with regard to the Prime Minister's wishes to have an early conference and similar instructions with regard to allowing Ambassador Harriman to stand in as his observer. Perhaps preoccupied more with preserving his options in future than he ought to have been, the President underscored his personal concern with the coming talks. "You, naturally, understand", he observed, "that in this global war there is literally no question, political or military, in which the United States is not interested. I am firmly convinced that the three of us, and only the three of us, can find the solution to the still unresolved questions. In this sense, while appreciating the Prime Minister's desire for the meeting, I prefer to regard your forthcoming talks with Churchill as preliminary to a meeting of the three of us, which so far as I am concerned, can take place any time after the elections here".[68] Again, the British had failed to carry the Americans along in advance, but this time there would be absolutely no doubt, both in Moscow and London, where the United States stood.

Interestingly, the very diplomat who had assisted in the drafting of these messages to Stalin and Churchill, Charles E. Bohlen, chief of the Division of Eastern European Affairs, was simultaneously pressing for an unequivocal statement of the administration's position in the Balkans in the absence of which Washington would only have itself to blame for any subsequent misunderstanding. "This Government", he contended in State, "[was] to some extent at fault because neither of our principal allies had yet a clear picture as to what the US will do and how much responsibility it will assume in Eastern Europe". Furthermore, Bohlen indicated that inasmuch as the Soviets tend to be more inclined to "accept comprehensive plans presented to them by others" rather than draw up their own, perhaps the time had come to raise "the question as to whether we might not present to the Russians a plan for dealing with this area".[69] By this time, however, Churchill was already in Moscow presenting a plan of his own.

At the outset of his meeting with Stalin in the evening of 9 October, Churchill had "hoped they might clear away many questions about which they had been writing to each other for a long time", to which Stalin replied "that he was ready to discuss anything". Turning from a discussion of the Polish Question whose ramifications would ultimately dominate the conference proceedings until the departure of the British delegation on the eighteenth, Churchill declared, "Britain must be the leading Mediterranean Power and...hoped Marshal Stalin would let him have first say about Greece in the same way as Marshal Stalin [would have the first say] about Rumania". Without once alluding to the May Agreement, Stalin concurred, pointing out that "if Britain were interested in the Mediterranean then Russia was equally interested in the Black Sea". It was further agreed that the two Powers should share equal interests in Hungary and Yugoslavia. The sticking point however was Bulgaria, which posed the single greatest threat to the British position in Greece. According to the records of the meeting, "The Prime Minister suggested that where Bulgaria was concerned the British interest was greater than it was in Rumania", where London's influence on the Soviet-controlled Allied Control Commission was admittedly nominal. Stalin, who suggested that the Prime Minister claimed too much for Britain in the area, countered that Bulgaria was after all a Black Sea country and, by extension, a matter of Russian concern. In response to Stalin's query, "Was Britain afraid of anything"? Eden who until now had remained silent retorted "that Britain was not afraid of anything". He also reminded the Soviet leader "that Britain had been at war with Bulgaria for three years [in contrast to recent Soviet-Bulgarian belligerency] and wanted a small share of the control of that country".[70] The Bulgarian armistice issue together with a change in the ratio of Soviet predominance in Hungary (80%-20%) was eventually settled by Eden and Molotov in the course of discussion over the next two days.[71] Thus a bargain of sorts had been struck over a division of Anglo-Soviet responsibilities in the Balkans; what it meant, exactly, was of course another matter.

From another level of analysis it is interesting to note the missing President's influence on the participants' maneuverings. When it came to phrasing the division of responsibilities Churchill, with the recent American experience fresh in his mind, thought it "better to express these things in diplomatic [more euphemistic] terms and not to use the phrase 'dividing into spheres', because the Americans might be shocked". Still, "as long as he and the Marshal understood each other he could explain matters to the President", no doubt at a time and place of the Prime Minister's choosing. At this juncture, Stalin interrupted his guest "to say that he [too] had received a message from President Roosevelt", indicating FDR's desire both to have the American Ambassador stand in as his observer and to regard the talks themselves as of a preliminary nature. Lest Stalin arrive at a false impression, Churchill advised the Soviet leader that he of course agreed with the President's wishes, observing that he and the President had no secrets. Nonetheless, he did not think Harriman, whose presence would be welcomed at a "good number of their talks", should be allowed to come between them in their private talks—presumably such as the one in progress. Stalin confessed he did not like Roosevelt's message as "it seemed to demand too many rights for the Unites States leaving too little for the Soviet Union and Great Britain who, after all, had a treaty of common assistance".[72] Actually, as Stalin must have surely known, the President's message demanded nothing of the kind; if anything, and once the President's electoral sensitivity has been factored out, the message comes closer to John Lukac's image of America's "supreme unconcern" in the region.[73]

Towards the end of their conversation, the Prime Minister made two final points that were undoubtedly for the Marshal's consumption. First, and in connection with the proposed Allied occupation of Germany, he considered it unlikely that the Americans would stay in Germany, and by extension Europe, for "very long", the implication being that European problems would have to be settled between themselves. Second, and with no thought of subtlety this time, Churchill personally wanted Stalin to know, to quote from the concluding comments in the record "that the British had as many division fighting against Germany in Italy and France as the United States and we had nearly as many as the United States fighting against Japan". Apparently, Churchill was anxious to assure his host that British credentials to speak for the solution of European problems were at least as good as the Americans, who, in any case, were not expected to remain.[74]

What precisely, then, did the Prime Minister hope to accomplish by the percentage agreement, such as it was? Unfortunately, and although the documentary record suggests numerous clues, there is no definitive answer to this question. In an official joint communique to Roosevelt of their first meeting Churchill together with Stalin merely informed the President: "We have to consider the best way of reaching an agreed policy about the Balkan countries including Hungary and Turkey", apparently omitting the concluding phrase, "having regard to our varying duty towards them", as reported by Harriman.[75] But was there in fact "an agreed policy"? In an unsent letter to Stalin dated 11 October, the British leader perhaps came nearer the truth when he noted that, "The percentages which I have put down are no more than a method by which in our thoughts we can see how near we are together, and then decide upon the necessary steps to bring us into full agreement"; and though "they could not be the basis of any public document, certainly not at the present time, they might however be a good guide for the conduct of our affairs".[76] A day later, 12 October, the Prime Minister wrote to colleagues in London further elaborating his thoughts on the percentages. "The system of percentages", he expanded, "is not intended to prescribe the number sitting on [the Allied Control] Commissions for the different Balkan countries, but rather to express the interest and sentiment with which the British and Soviet Governments approach the problems of these countries and so that they might reveal their minds to each other in some way that could be comprehended". More significantly, Churchill added, "It is not intended to be more than a guide, and of course in no way commits the United States, nor does it set up a rigid system of spheres of interest. It may however help the United States to see how their two principal Allies feel about these regions when the picture is presented as a whole".[77] To this picture, echoed Eden to the British undersecretary of state, Sir Orme Sargent, "Too much attention should not be paid to percentages which are of symbolic character only and bear no exact relation to number of persons of British and Soviet nationality to be employed [in the Control Commissions]".[78] To the Americans, who were at this stage fairly much in the dark, Churchill projected an altogether different, but confident image of the Balkan talks.

"Everything is most friendly here", the Prime Minister cabled Harry Hopkins on 11 October, "but the Balkans are in a sad tangle". In fact, he went on in a manner to justify the continual exclusion of the American Ambassador from the Balkan proceedings thus far, "We have so many bones to pick about the Balkans at the present time that we would rather carry matters a little further a deux in order to be able to talk more bluntly than at a larger gathering".[79] On the same day, the Prime Minister indicated to the President that, "It is absolutely necessary we should try to get a common mind about the Balkans, so that we may prevent civil war breaking out in several countries when probably you and I would be in sympathy with one side and U.J. [Stalin] with the other. I shall keep you informed of all this, and nothing will be settled except preliminary agreements between Britain and Russia, subject to further discussion and melting-down with you. On this basis I am sure you will not mind our trying to have a full meeting of minds with the Russians".[80] A week later on the eve of his departure from Moscow, and still in no mood to offer more information than was absolutely necessary, the British leader apprised FDR that "arrangements made about the Balkans are, I am sure, the best that are possible". Specifically, the Prime Minister continued: "Coupled with our successful military action recently we should now be able to save Greece and, I have no doubt, that agreement to pursue a fifty-fifty joint policy in Yugoslavia will be the best solution for our difficulties in view of Tito's behaviour and changes in the local situation, resulting from the arrival of Russian and Bulgarian forces under Russian command to help Tito's eastern flank. The Russians are insistent on their ascendancy in Rumania and Bulgaria as the Black Sea countries".[81] Characteristically the Soviet had even less to say.

"During the stay of Mr Churchill and Mr Eden in Moscow", Stalin cabled President Roosevelt on 19 October, "we have exchanged views on a number of questions of mutual interest". Doubtless aware that both Ambassador Harriman and the Prime Minister had already passed on their estimates of the most important

Moscow conversations, the Soviet leader sought to impart his own. "On my part", he observed with some economy of expression, "I can say that our conversations were extremely useful in the mutual ascertaining of views on such questions as the attitude towards...policy in regard to the Balkan states", among other things. Furthermore, Stalin stated, "During the conversations it has been clarified that we can, without great difficulties, adjust our policies on all questions standing before us, and if we are not in a position so far to provide an immediate necessary decision of this or that task...nevertheless, more favourable perspectives are opened. I hope that these Moscow conversations will be of some benefit from the point of view that at the future meeting of the three of us, we shall be able to adopt definite decisions on all urgent questions of our mutual interest".[82] Stalin's blue pencil tick upon Churchill's half-sheet of paper to the contrary notwithstanding, it is difficult to assess with certitude what if anything the Kremlin had hoped to achieve by the percentage agreement. Perhaps Stalin, not unlike FDR, was more concerned with keeping his Balkan options open more than anything else, at least until the dust of the Red Army had settled. There may be more than a little irony in the judgment of one Soviet history of the Second World War, which noted that with the exception of Greece, "The Red Army's successful offensive in the Southwestern theatre finally buried the plans of the British reactionary circles to forestall the Soviet military presence in the Balkans". In this sense, Stalin's adherence to the percentage agreement would seem but part of a calculated effort in which to buy time ultimately to bury "the plans of the British reactionary circles to forestall the Soviet military presence in the Balkans".[83] And who can deny that the Marshal was an expert at buying time?

Gradually informed of the thrust of the percentage agreement, though, like the principals, by no means certain of its actual meaning,[84] President Roosevelt chose to respond to the critical joint message of his Grand Alliance partners of 10 October in muted tones. "I am most pleased to know", he replied on 12 October, "that you are reaching a meeting of your two minds as to international policies in which, because of our present and future common efforts to prevent international wars, we are still interested".[85] Politician to the core, FDR knew, as Herbert Feis once reminded us, that "it was nearly impossible to find happy solutions for many European problems"; this being so, it is hardly surprising that "he wanted to remain as clear of them as he could, except for those involving

Germany".[86] Domestic political considerations aside, it would seem the President revealed his thoughts most clearly when he told Harriman, in a cable dated 11 October, "My active interest at the present time in the Balkans is that such steps as are practical should be taken to insure against the Balkans getting us into a future international war".[87] What practical steps Roosevelt had in mind would of necessity have to await the November elections. In the meantime, the State Department responded to the Moscow revival of spheres of influence politics with a program of its own.

In a memorandum passed on by Under-Secretary of State Edward Stettinius to President Roosevelt on 8 November, State declared that, "[W]hile the Government of the United States is fully aware of the existence of problems between Great Britain and the Soviet Union, this Government should not assume the attitude of supporting either country as against the other. Rather, this Government should assert the independent interest of the United States (which is also believed to be in the general interest) in favor of equitable arrangements designed to attain general peace and security on a basis of good neighborship, and should not assume the American interest requires it at this time to identify its interests with those of either the Soviet Union or Great Britain".[88] According to this view, American policy in the Balkans, among other places should be governed by the following general principles: self-determination, equality of commercial opportunity, freedom of press movement and ideas, freedom for American philanthropic and educational organizations to pursue their activities on a most-favored-nation basis, general protection of US citizens and their legitimate economic rights, and the proposition that territorial settlements should be left for postwar. However, what impression State's memorandum had on the President's thinking is unknown.

On the other side of the State Department spectrum were the views of George Frost Kennan who at the age of forty-one in 1945 was already the senior member of the American diplomatic corps in length of service in Russia. "I am aware of the realities of this war, and of the fact that we were too weak to win it without Russia's cooperation", the minister-councilor wrote to his friend Charles Bohen on the eve of the Yalta Conference.[89] "I recognize", he continued, "that Russia's war effort has been masterful and effective and must, to a certain extent, find its reward at the expense of other peoples in eastern and central Europe. But with all of this, I fail to see why we must associate ourselves with this political program, so hostile to the interests of the Atlantic community as a whole, so dangerous to everything which we need to see preserved in Europe. Why could we not make a decent and definite compromise with it— divide Europe frankly into spheres of influence—keep ourselves out of the Russian sphere and keep the Russians out of ours". For Kennan, who has remained consistent on this score from that time to this,[90] such a policy "would have been the best thing we could do for ourselves and for our friends in Europe, and the most honest approach we could have made to the Russians".[91] "Instead of this", exploded the father of containment, so-called, "what have we done"?

> Although it was evident that the realities of the after-war were being shaped while the war was in progress we have consistently refused to make clear what our interests and our wishes were, in eastern and central Europe. We have refused to name any limit for Russian expansion and Russian responsibilities, thereby confusing the Russians and causing them constantly to wonder whether they are asking too little or whether it was some kind of a trap. We have refused to face political issues and forced others to face them without us. We have advanced no positive, constructive program for the future of the continent: nothing that could encourage our friends, nothing that could appeal to people on the enemy's side of the line.

Though sympathetic with some of Kennan's arguments, Bohlen was quick to note that the foreign policy he spoke of could not be made in a democracy. "Only totalitarian states", concluded Roosevelt's interpreter and recently appointed State's liaison with the Executive, "can make and carry out such policies. Furthermore, I don't for one minute believe that there has been any time in this war when we could seriously have done very differently than we did".[92] Again, it is not known for certain what kind of impression such ideas had on the President's own thinking.

What is known for certain is that the subject of Balkan percentages was not again raised at the subsequent meeting of the Big Three at Yalta in February 1945 or at any other time. Militarily, the Soviet Union had further strengthened its stranglehold over eastern and central Europe. In the place of the October percentage agreement, the broad outlines of which were known to the Americans, the Allies with Roosevelt at the forefront now focused on the Declaration on Liberated Europe as the best way of dealing with the future of those countries liberated by the Red Army.

Broadly speaking, the Three Powers jointly declared "their mutual agreement to concert during the temporary period of instability the policies of their three governments in assisting the people liberated from the domination of Nazi Germany and the peoples of the former axis satellite states to solve by democratic means their pressing political and economic problems".[93] Stalin's decision to sponsor unilaterally a minority government in Romania in March, not to mention continuing differences over the composition of the Polish government, suggested both to Roosevelt and the State Department that what the Kremlin really thought about was what Stalin once called "the algebra of declarations" as opposed to "practical arithmetic"; to Churchill, it must have appeared as nothing less than the first fruits of "the pedantic interference of the United States" with his own preferred plans for the division of Europe.

Throughout the story of the percentage agreements, President Roosevelt emerges as a figure torn by the realities of the war perceived by the Churchills and Kennans on the one hand and the high ideals of the postwar perceived by the Hulls and Longs on the other hand. Surrounded by officials obsessed with fears that the division of eastern Europe into spheres of influence would lead to yet another "war for survival", faced with a fourth Presidential election campaign, knowing there were no happy solutions to problems in the region but certain that they would have to be dealt with at some time, it is not surprising to find Roosevelt pursuing seemingly contradictory policies.[94]

FDR's death in April left his successor in much the same position, but with even fewer options to choose from. In early May Truman listened carefully to the presentation of Major General Crane and Brigadier General Schuyler, chief American representatives-designate on the Allied Control Commission in Bulgaria and Romania respectively. The new President, according to an account by Acting Secretary of State Joseph Grew,[95] was told that the Soviets were determined to rule both countries "through Communist governments in a completely totalitarian way". From the standpoint of the American elements on the Control Commission, "Rumania and Bulgaria were test cases and if the Soviets were able to get away with their programs in those countries they would be encouraged to try the same game in every other country in Europe, as far as they could penetrate". Not unlike Kennan who several months earlier argued that American missions in eastern Europe were little more than "prize exhibits to the inhabitants that Russian policies and actions have the support of the United States and that there is no use in their looking to us for support or sympathy",[96] "the President asked why under these conditions, it would not be better to withdraw our representatives entirely". To this, the Secretary replied that "I did not think we ought to allow the matter to go by default and that there were some advantages in retaining our representatives at least for the present".[97] One can only imagine what advantages Secretary Grew had in mind at this very late date. The time for such thinking had long passed.[98] The Cold War was fast emerging.

## NOTES

1. Churchill's recollection is found in his *The Second World War,* vol 6: *Triumph and Tragedy* (Boston, 1953), pp. 226-28.

2. The Balkan agreement talks are located in "Records of Meetings at the Kremlin, Moscow, October 9-October 17, 1944", Prime Minister's Operational papers (PREMIER 3), File 343, Folder 2, pp. 4-17, Public Record Office, London (hereafter referred to as Kremlin Meetings). Copies of the half sheet of paper on which the Prime Minister jotted down the spheres of predominance he had in mind in the evening of question are in "Spheres of Influence in the Balkans" (PREMIER 3/66/7) (hereafter materials from this source will be referred to as Balkan File). For further discussion of this particular source material, see Joseph M. Siracusa, "The Meaning of TOLSTOY: Churchill, Stalin, and the Balkans, Moscow, October 1944," *Diplomatic History* 3 (Fall 1979): 443-63. (See Appendix #1)

3. Winston S. Churchill, A Speech to the House of Commons, 27 October 1944, in *The War Speeches of the Rt. Hon. Winston S. Churchill,* compiled by Charles Eade, 3 vols. (London, 1952), 3: pp. 244-45.

4. Remi Nadeau has even suggested that "secret deals are not negated by the public silence of the participants". See *Stalin, Chuchill and Roosevelt Divide Europe,* (New York, 1990), p. 119.

5. William Hardy McNeill, *America, Britain and Russia: Their Cooperation and Conflict, 1941-1946,* vol 3 of *Survey of International Affairs, 1939-1946,* ed. by Arnold Toynbee (London, 1953), p. 495.

6. Herbert Feis, *Churchill, Roosevelt, Stalin: The War They Waged and the Peace They Sought* (Princeton, NJ, 1957), pp. 441-68; John Lewis Gaddis, *The United States and the Origins of the Cold War, 1941-1847* (New York, 1972), pp. 90-91; Lynn Etheridge Davis, *The Cold War Begins: Soviet-American Conflict and Eastern Europe* (Princeton, NJ, 1974), pp. 156-59.

7. Daniel Yergin, *Shattered Peace: The Origins of the Cold War and the National Security State* (Boston, 1977), p. 61.

8. Albert Resis, "The Churchill-Stalin Secret 'Percentages' Agreement on the Balkans, Moscow, October 1944." *American Historical Review* 83 (Apr. 1978): 371, 374.

9. Bruce R. Kuniholm, *The Origins of the Cold War in the Far East: Great Power Conflict and Diplomacy in Iran, Turkey and Greece* (Princeton, NJ, 1980), pp. 117, 125.

10. Ibid., pp. 385-86. Also see Vojtech Mastny, *Russia's Road to the Cold War: Diplomacy, Warfare, and the Politics of Communism, 1941-45* (New York, 1979), pp. 207-12.

11. Eduard Mark, "American Policy Towards Eastern Europe and the Origins of the Cold War, 1941-1946: An Alternative Interpretation," *Journal of American History*, 68, no. 2 (Sept. 1981): 313-336.

12. Geir Lundestad, *The American Non-Policy Towards Eastern Europe 1943-1947* (Tromso, 1978); and *East, West, North, South: Major Developments in International Politics, 1945-1996* (Oslo, 1997), p. 16.

13. Warren F. Kimball, *Churchill and Roosevelt: The Complete Correspondence*, vol. 3 (Princeton, 1984), p. 349.

14. October 11, 1944, Roosevelt to Harriman, FRUS, IV, p. 1009.

15. Ibid.

16. Lloyd C. Gardner, *Spheres of Influence: The Great Powers Partition Europe, from Munich to Yalta* (Chicago, 1993).

17. Joseph S. Nye Jr., "Yalta Looks Better Than Ever From Here," *New York Times Book Review*, 3 Oct. 1993.

18. Remi Nadeau, *Stalin, Churchill and Roosevelt Divide Europe* (New York, 1990).

19. Sir Llewellyn Woodward, *British Foreign Policy in the Second World War*, 5 vols. (London, 1971), 3: pp. 146-53.

20. Sir John Wheller-Bennett and Anthony Nicholls, *The Semblance of Peace: The Political Settlement after the Second World War* (London, 1972), p. 198.

21. Elisabeth Barker, *British Policy in South-East Europe in the Second World War* (London, 1976), pp. 146-7.

22. W. Averell Harriman and Elie Abel, *Special Envoy to Churchill and Stalin, 1941-46* (New York, 1975), p. 358; and letter from Harriman to the author, 30 Oct. 1978.

23. Charles E. Bohlen, *Witness to History, 1925-1969* (New York, 1973), p. 170.

24. Anthony Eden, *The Memoirs of Anthony Eden, Earl of Avon*, vol. 3: *The Reckoning* (London, 1971), pp. 482-83.

25. *The Diaries of Sir Alexander Cadogan, 1938-1945*, ed. by David Dilks (New York, 1971), p. 672.

26. Quoted in *British Foreign Policy Towards Wartime Resistance in Yugoslavia and Greece*, ed. by Phyllis Auty and Richard Clogg (London, 1975), pp. 247-48.

27. Churchill, *Triumph and Tragedy*, p. 208.

28. Churchill Minutes to Foreign Secretary, 4 May 1955, Balkan File.

29. Quoted in Barker, *British Policy in South-East Europe in the Second World War*, p. 141.

30. Foreign Office to British Embassy in Moscow, 25 May, 1944, Balkan File (author's italics).

31. Cordell Hull, *The Memoirs of Cordell Hull*, 2 vols. (London, 1948), 2: pp. 1452-53; and Report to Congress on Moscow Conference, 18 Nov. 1943, Congressional Record, 78th Congress.

32. Mastny suggests that as early as the Teheran Conference, in late 1943, Stalin was acutely alerted to disagreements between the Western powers. Mastny, *Russia's Road to the Cold War*, pp. 123-4.

33. Halifax to Foreign Secretary, 31 May 1944, Balkan File.

34. Memorandum of Conversation, by the Secretary of State, 30 May, 1944, Department of State, *Foreign Relations of the United States, Diplomatic Papers: 1944* (Washington, 1965), 5: pp. 112-13 (hereafter referred to as FRUS).

35. Eden Minute to Prime Minister, 30 May 1944, Balkan File.

36. Prime Minister to President Roosevelt, 31 May 1944, No. 687, Balkan File.

37. Halifax to Foreign Secretary, 31 May 1944, Ibid.

38. *The War Diary of Breckenridge Long: Selections from the Years 1939-1944*, ed. by Fred L. Israel (Lincoln, NE, 1966), p. 352.

39. President Roosevelt to the British Prime Minister, No. 557, 11 June 1944, FRUS: 1944, 5: pp. 117-18.

40. Prime Minister to President Roosevelt, No. 700, 11 June 1944, Balkan File.

41. President Roosevelt to Prime Minister, No. 700, 12 June 1944, in The Messages between Franklin D. Roosevelt and Winston S. Churchill, 1939-1945 (Microfilm edition), Franklin D. Roosevelt Library, Hyde Park, NY (hereafter this source will be referred to as Roosevelt-Churchill Correspondence).
42. Foreign Office to British Embassy in Moscow, 20 June 1944, Balkan File.
43. Foreign Office to British Embassy in Moscow, 8 July 1944, Ibid. (author's italics).
44. British Embassy in Washington to Foreign Office, 27 July 1944, Ibid.
45. Papers of William D. Leahy, Diary 1944, 15 December 1944, Manuscript Division, Library of Congress, Washington DC.
46. Excerpt from Letter to Admiral Leahy (to Secretary Hull), 16 May 1944, FRUS: The Conferences at Malta and Yalta, 1945 (Washington, 1955), pp. 106-108.
47. See Davis, The Cold War Begins, p. 142; as well as Robert E. Sherwood, Roosevelt and Hopkins: An Intimate History, rev. ed. (New York, 1950), pp. 410-11.
48. President Roosevelt to Prime Minister, No. 565, 22 June 1944, Balkan File.
49. Prime Minister to President Roosevelt, No. 712, 23 June 1944, Ibid.
50. President Roosevelt to Prime Minister, No. 570, 27 June 1944, Ibid.
51. Churchill Minute to Foreign Secretary, 9 July 1944, Ibid.
52. Eden to the War Cabinet, 10 July 1944, Ibid.
53. Churchill Minute to Foreign Secretary, 1 August 1944, Ibid.
54. See Barker, British Policy in South-East Europe, p. 142.
55. Churchill, Triumph and Tragedy, p. 214.
56. The one exception occurred on 23 September 1944 when in response to information that a British force was about to depart for Greece, Soviet authorities surprisingly "confirmed" the May Agreement. See Barker, British Policy in South-East Europe, p. 144.
57. Woodward, British Policy in the Second World War, 3: p. 148.
58. Dilks, Diaries of Sir Alexander Cadogan, p. 632.
59. Churchill, Triumph and Tragedy, p. 221; for earlier mission to Moscow, consult FRUS: 1942 (Washington, 1961), 3: 618-24.
60. Prime Minister to President Roosevelt, No. 789, 29 Sept. 1944, Roosevelt-Churchill Correspondence.
61. Prime Minister to President Roosevelt, No. 790, 3 October 1944, Ibid.
62. Bohlen, Witness to History, p, 168.
63. Sherwood, Roosevelt and Hopkins, 832-34; and Action Sheet attached to No. 790. Also see Bohlen, Witness to History, pp. 169-170.
64. Harriman to Hopkins, 10 September 1944, FRUS: 1944, (Washington, 1966), 4: 988-90.
65. President Roosevelt to the Prime Minister, No. 626, 4 October 1944, FRUS: Malta and Yalta, pp. 7-8 (author's italics).
66. Prime Minister to President Roosevelt, No. 791, 5 Oct. 1944, Roosevelt-Churchill Correspondence.
67. Stalin to President Roosevelt, No. 231, 8 Oct. 1944. Correspondence between the Chairman of the Council of Minister of the USSR and the President of the USA and the Prime Minister of Great Britain during the Great Patriotic War of 1941-1945 (New York, 1965), p. 163.
68. President Roosevelt to Harriman, FRUS: Malta and Yalta, p. 6.
69. State Policy Committee Meeting, 13 Oct. 1944, quoted in Davis, The Cold War Begins, p. 154.
70. Kremlin Meetings, 9 October 1944, 4-9.
71. Ibid., 10-11 October 1944, 10-17. Useful background on the Bulgarian issue is found in "Anglo-Soviet Political Conversations at Moscow, October 9—October 17, 1944", (PREMIER 3/434/4), pp. 55-62. See table on percentage changes in Kuniholm, The Origins of the Cold War in the Near East, p. 115.
72. Kremlin Meetings, 9 Oct. 1944.

73. John Lukacs, *A New History of the Cold War*, 3rd ed. (Garden City, NY, 1966), pp. 47-8; and "The Night Stalin and Churchill Divided Europe," *New York Times Magazine*, 5 Oct. 1969, p. 36.

74. Kremlin Meetings, 9 Oct. 1944. At the Yalta Conference in February 1945, FDR confirmed Churchill's estimate when he stated "that he did not believe that American troops would stay in Europe much more than two years". *FRUS: Malta and Yalta*, p. 617.

75. Prime Minister Churchill and Marshal Stalin to President Roosevelt, 11 Oct. 1944, No. 794, Roosevelt-Churchill Correspondence; and Ambassador Harriman to President Roosevelt, 10 Oct. 1944, *FRUS: 1944*, 4: pp. 1006-07.

76. Prime Minister's Draft of an Unsent Letter to Stalin, 11 Oct. 1944, Balkan File. Apparently, Ambassador Harriman dissuaded Churchill from sending this letter, Harriman and Abel, *Special Envoy to Churchill and Stalin*, p. 358; and Churchill, *Triumph and Tragedy*, p. 231.

77. Memorandum by the Prime Minister to the Foreign Office, 12 Oct. 1944, Balkan File.

78. Eden to Deputy Under-Secretary of State for Foreign Affairs, Sir Orme Sargent, 12 Oct. 1944, Balkan File.

79. Prime Minister to Harry Hopkins, 11 October 1944, Ibid.

80. Prime Minister to President Roosevelt, No. 795, 11 Oct. 1944, Roosevelt-Churchill Correspondence.

81. Prime Minister to President Roosevelt, No. 799, 18 Oct. 1944, Ibid.

82. Marshall Stalin to President Roosevelt, 19 Oct. 1944, *FRUS: Malta and Yalta*, p. 9.

83. *Great Patriotic War of the Soviet Union, 1941-1945: A General Outline* (Moscow, 1974), p. 342. Also see Nikolai V. Sivachev and Nikolai N. Yakolve, *Russia and the United States*, trans. Olga A. Titelbaum (Chicago, 1979); and V. Trukhanovshy, *British Foreign Policy during World War II* (Moscow, 1970), especially, pp. 406-408.

84. By 13 October, State had had a fairly clear picture of the percentages worked out in Moscow though it is doubtful that there was much understanding regarding their meaning. See the American Ambassador in Turkey (Steinhardt) to the Secretary of State, 13 October 1944, *FRUS: 1944*, 4: pp. 1015-16.

85. Quoted in Churchill, *Triumph and Tragedy*, p. 231.

86. Feis, *Churchill, Roosevelt, Stalin*, p. 451.

87. President Roosevelt to Ambassador Harriman, 11 Oct. 1944, *FRUS: 1944*, 4: p. 1009.

88. Stettinius to President Roosevelt, 8 Nov. 1944, ibid., pp. 1025-26.

89. Letter from George Frost Kennan to Charles E. Bohlen, 26 January 1945, Paper of Charles E. Bohlen, Manuscript Division, Library of Congress, Washington DC (hereafter referred to as the Kennan Letter).

90. For example, see *The Cloud of Danger: Current Realities of American Foreign Policy* (Boston, 1977).

91. Kennan Letter.

92. Letter from Charles E. Bohlen to George Frost Kennan, undated, Bohlen Papers.

93. Declaration on Liberated Europe, *FRUS: Malta and Yalta*, pp. 971-73.

94. Also see Kuniholm, *The Origins of the Cold War in the Near East*, pp. 123-25.

95. Memorandum of Conversation, 2 May 1945, Papers of Joseph Grew, Houghton Library, Harvard university (hereafter referred to as Grew Memorandum).

96. Kennan letter.

97. Grew Memorandum. Revealing here is Cyril E. Black's, "The Start of the Cold War in Bulgaria: A Personal View," *Review of Politics* 41 (1979): 163-202.

98. Interestingly, others such as Foy Kohler suggest that it was not until 1947-1948 that the "eastern block states were definitely lost to the west". FRUS: 1949 (Washington, 1976), 5: p. 3 (author's italics).

# CHAPTER 2

# THE AUTHOR OF CONTAIMENT: THE STRANGE CASE OF GEORGE F. KENNAN & FRANK ROBERTS

"My reputation was made. My voice now carried."[1] Such was George F. Kennan's own response to the since-famous reception of the *Long Telegram* in Washington in February 1946. Kennan noted that the "effect produced in Washington by this elaborate pedagogical effort was nothing less then sensational". "It was" Kennan explained, "one that changed my career and my life in very basic ways".[2] Yet, he mused, he could not really understand the magnitude of its impact after the failure of earlier work to "evoke even the faintest tremble from the bell at which they were aimed".[3] He attributed the unexpected reaction to the fact that Washington's state of receptivity was strongly aroused, but oddly, has had little to add in explaining his own inspiration of his influential warning from Moscow. His silence in the matter, uncharacteristic of the man, is intriguing. The reason may in part be found in the following detailed comparison of the work of Kennan with that of his British counterpart in Moscow, Frank Roberts.

Kennan, by his own admission, was a man largely isolated from many of his American colleagues. It has thus been useful to examine the development of this American's relationship with Frank Roberts as well as that of the British government. During this precarious moment in history, the British Empire was looking towards the United States to come into accord with its own policy regarding the potentially hostile Soviet Union. Clearly, the American administration was unsure on which path to direct its foreign policy course. President Harry Truman was undoubtably receptive to the efforts of former Prime Minister Winston Churchill and, later, Prime Minister Clement Attlee to convince the United States to adopt a more confrontational stance towards the Soviet Union. To influence the course of American policy seems to have been part of a foreign policy plan of the British designed to protect its dwindling power from the perceived threat of the Soviet Union. Later, when discussing the collapse of the Council of Foreign Minister talks in Germany in 1948, Attlee made an interesting admission to Australian Prime Minister Ben Chifley. He denied that London was acting at Washington's behest and explained that on the contrary Britain was taking the lead in the matter "in order to ensure the crystallization of an American policy which is in our common interest and is thoroughly co-ordinated".[4] This raises then an interesting question. To what extent was this British policy relevant to the relationship between George Kennan and Frank Roberts during their time spent in Moscow? This brings us back to the unusually strange matter of the similarities between Kennan's *Long Telegram* and Roberts's *Despatches of March 1946*. In describing George Kennan at Princeton University in 1991, Secretary of State James Baker suggested Kennan had "articulated the logic and concept of containment".[5] More recently, former Secretary of State Henry Kissinger wrote that "Rarely does an embassy report by itself reshape Washington's view of the world, but what later came to be known as the 'Long Telegram' emphatically did".[6] Yet one suspects that Kennan's ticket to immortality, with the suggestion of containment as a policy possibility, should have been shared.

Both Roberts and Kennan shared a strong belief that an inherent fear for national security was at the basis of Soviet policy decisions. The *Long Telegram* stated that "at the bottom of the Kremlin's neurotic view of world affairs is a traditional and instinctive Russian sense of insecurity. Originally this was insecurity of a peaceful agricultural people trying to live on a vast exposed plain in a neighborhood of fierce nomadic peoples".[7] In a similar view Roberts in *Despatch 189* writes: "There is one fundamental factor affecting Soviet Policy dating back to the small beginnings of the Muscovite State: This is the constant striving for security of a state with no natural frontiers and surrounded by enemies.... National security is in fact at the bottom of Soviet, as of Imperial Russian, policy, and explains much of the high handed behaviour of the Kremlin and many of the suspicions genuinely held there concerning the outside world".[8] Both diplomats moreover indicated that a lack of Soviet development, compared to the West, only added to the insecurity. Roberts points out that "even today the Soviet Union, despite its prestige in the world, is more backward than not only Britain or the United States, but than most other European countries".[9] Kennan, for his part, observed that "as Russia came into contact with the economically advanced West, fear increased of the more competent, more powerful and more highly organised countries in the area".[10]

*Despatch 189* by Roberts deviates from Kennan's *Long Telegram*, in the initial paragraphs, by virtue of the fact that it deals extensively with Britain's own special relations with Russia. This started on a friendly footing in the mid-sixteenth century and passed through strained relations in the nineteenth century with the Tsarist System, which Britain regarded with the same ideological aversion as the present tyranny. This history was recently culminated by their joint action, based on their mutual hostility to Hitler. By paragraph five, however, one finds their views again converging. Both diplomats assess the Soviets' attitude to the outside world from official Russian sources and acknowledge the strength and success of the party line in a country where such a small percentage of the population were actually members of the Communist Party. Roberts notes "that this attitude is shown in the ideological line laid down for the Soviet public by the Communist Party, since this not only conditions the thinking of the Soviet public but also guides the activities of the Communist parties throughout the world".[11] Kennan mentions that "the Party line only represents the thesis which the official propaganda machine puts forward with great skill and persistence to a public often remarkably resistant in the stronghold of its innermost thoughts. But the party line is binding for outlook and conduct of the people who made up the apparatus of power—and it is exclusively with these that we have to deal".[12]

Roberts then moves on to speak of "the tone of the party propaganda, which particularly on the thoughtful and more authoritative publications such as the *Bolshevik*, *World Economy and Peace*, and *Party Organisations*, is not only critical of, but hostile to the outside world. The great bulk of information allowed to reach the Soviet public concerning Britain or the United States is mostly contemptuous in tone. These news items are weighted and selected in order to convey the desired impression of a civilization inferior to that of the Soviet Union and containing within itself the seeds of its own destruction. The Untied States is painted as a land torn with strikes, with an acute Negro [sic] problem and with the working class exploited by selfish capitalists".[13] Kennan takes a similar tack: "All Soviet propaganda beyond the Soviet security sphere is basically negative and destructive".[14] Added to this is the next extract which echoes the sentiment of Roberts, though structured differently: "We have here a political force committed fanatically to the belief that with the United States there can be no modus vivendi, that is desirable and necessary that the internal harmony of our society be disrupted, our traditional way of life be destroyed, the international authority of our state be broken, if Soviet power is to be secure".[15]

In Paragraph six of his despatch, Roberts speaks of "the Western democracies, weak and disunited though they may be shown as the main dangers in a continued capitalist encirclement of the Soviet Union,...and now that the German and Japanese menace has been removed, the former Allies of the Soviet Union are represented as potential, if not actual enemies".[16] Kennan portrays a similar fear as one of the basic features of the Soviet postwar outlook being put forward by their propaganda machine, adding the

> USSR still lives in antagonistic 'capitalist encirclement' with which in the long run there can be no peaceful co-existence. As stated by Stalin in 1927 to a delegation of American workers: 'In the course of further development of international revolution there will emerge two centers of world significance: a socialist center, drawing to itself the countries which tend toward socialism, and a capitalist center, drawing to itself the countries that incline toward capitalism. Battle between these two centers for command of world economy will decide the fate of capitalism and of communism in the entire world.[17]

Both diplomats continued their pattern of agreement when further delving into these Soviet-held beliefs. Roberts relates the understanding "that the capitalist world is however shown as profoundly divided both between the states and within individual states. In fact, in the orthodox Marxist view, these capitalists are bound to quarrel amongst themselves, more particularly over control of dwindling raw materials and over colonial territories still existing in the world".[18] Kennan matches this statement with the following: "The Capitalist world is beset with internal conflicts, inherent in the nature of capitalist society. These conflicts are insoluble by means of peaceful compromise. Greatest of them is that between England and the United States".[19]

The notion that the Soviet fear that they may be exploited to distract attention from internal capitalist problems was agreed upon by both men in the following extracts. On the one hand, Kennan states that "internal conflicts of capitalism inevitably generate wars.

Wars thus generated may be of two kinds: intra-capitalist wars between [the] two capitalist states, and wars on intervention against the socialist. Smart capitalists, vainly seeking escape from inner conflicts of capitalism, incline towards the latter".[20] On the other, Roberts observes that "above all there is a danger that some leaders of capitalist society might unite their countries in an attack upon the Soviet Union, if only to distract attention from their own internal problems".[21]

As a result of such a possibility both find unanimous approach in suggesting the practical steps taken by the Soviets as a result of the above apprehensions. Kennan describes an "internal policy devoted to increasing in every way the strength and prestige of the Soviet state, intensive military industrialization, maximum development of the armed forces, great displays to impress outsiders, continued secretiveness about internal matters continued to conceal weaknesses and to keep opponents in the dark".[22] Roberts, less dramatically, but equally forcefully, covers the same ground. "The Soviet Union must therefore be constantly on her guard, surrounded as she is by enemies. She must build up her industrial potential to the greatest possible extent and maintain a strong military establishment, even in time of peace. She must improve such backward aims in her Air Force and Navy and, above all, catch up with Western Democracies, over the harnessing of atomic energy".[23]

At this stage both assessments continue to elaborate on the official party line, which, as Roberts explains, preaches that in "the hostile capitalist world there are many good elements who may gain power and who, in any case, naturally sympathise with the Soviet Union and form of fifth column within individual states".[24] Kennan repeats this assessment and agrees with Roberts's conclusion, adding "it must be borne in mind that the capitalist world is not all bad. In addition to hopelessly reactionary and bourgeois elements, it includes certainly wholly enlightened and positive elements united in acceptable communistic parties or certain other elements (not described for factual reasons as progressive or democratic) whose rejections, aspirations and activities happen to be objectively favourable to interests of the USSR. These elements must be encouraged and utilized for Soviet purposes".[25]

Having examined the structure of the Soviet party line, both the Roberts *Despatch* and the *Long Telegram* then note that the premise on which it is based is not factual. Roberts points out that "Recent history has shown that the Western democracies, apart from writing against the Soviet Union, contribute all the aid in their power in the common struggle against fascism. Far from wishing to encircle the Soviet Union, Britain and America have made and are still making every effort to increase intercourse between their countries and peoples and those of the Soviet Union and to bring the Soviet Union fully into the world community. They have made concession after concession to encourage such co-operation, but so far with little response".[26] To be compared with these points are the following from Kennan: "Capitalist countries, other than those of Axis, showed no disposition to solve their differences by joining in a crusade against the USSR.... If not provoked by forces of intolerance and subversion the capitalist world of today is quite capable of living at peace with itself and with Russia".[27]

In paragraph nine, Roberts poses the question of the identity of the real power brokers in Russia, behind the propaganda. He suggests that the ultimate decisions are made within the confines of the limited Politburo,

> who have complete control of the military machine and of the ubiquitous and immensely powerful system of State security. The natural assumption is that Stalin is, in fact, a dictator as absolute as Hitler in Germany. There is little doubt that the last word rests with him: but we have so often found that views expressed by him in private conversation are belied by subsequent events, that it would seem either that he is exceptionally crafty in dealing with foreign statesmen or that he is himself dependent upon the collective decisions of his colleagues in the Politburo. The explanation may even be deeper in the information or lack of information which reaches him about the outside world.[28]

The speculation is further increased by his discussion on the possible roles of men such as Malendov and Beriya as well as Molotov. The following is also particularly relevant when compared directly with the proposals of Kennan. "Some well informed students of the Soviet Union have speculated that there may be a growing circle of ambitious Red Army men and industrial executives who knowing nothing of the outside world, are ready to risk a trial strength with their former Allies, in pursuing an adventurous foreign policy".[29] In the ensuing paragraph Roberts attempts to assess whether these men actually believe the view presented by the official party line. His comments again bear a striking resemblance to Kennan's words, soon to follow. "It would, I think, be safer to assume that brought up in the pure Marxist doctrine from earliest manhood and for the most part ignorant of the outside world, and having no real contacts even with leaders of other nations, they do in fact believe their own dogma".[30]

Kennan, again for his part, puts forward the idea that collaborators on the party line may be "too ignorant of the outside world…and have no difficulty making themselves believe what they find comforting and convenient to believe".[31] He also presents "the unsolved mystery as to who, if anyone, in the Soviet Union actually receives accurate and unbiased information about the outside world".[32] He suggests that he is himself "reluctant to believe that Stalin himself receives anything like an objective picture of the outside world",[33] viewing the government in terms of a conspiracy within a conspiracy. Unlike Roberts, who attempts to follow through the dilemma and place specific names on areas for disquiet, Kennan is quite content to generalise without specifics: "The very disrespect of Russians for the objective truth—indeed their disbelief in its existence—leads them to view all stated facts as instruments for furtherance of one ulterior purpose or another".[34] Even allowing for such differences in personal approach and analytical skill, the similarities of analysis are striking.

Roberts and Kennan both come to an agreement as to the problems associated with attempting to approach the Soviets in the normally accepted diplomatic patterns and conventions. The following is from Kennan: "The inability of foreign governments to place their case squarely before Russian policymakers—the extent to which they are delivered up in their relations with Russia to the good graces of obscure and unknown advisors, whom they never see and cannot influence—this to my mind is the most disquieting feature of diplomacy in Moscow, and one which Western statesmen would do well to keep in mind if they would understand the nature of difficulties encountered here".[35] Roberts contributes the following: "However well or ill informed the Kremlin may be on the situation in the outside world, it is certainly incapable of conducting international relations of the give and take, which is normal and indeed essential between other States".[36]

The aggressive attitude of the Soviet leaders in international relations was a warning issued by both the British and American diplomats. Kennan notes that "the Russians will participate officially in international organisation where they see the opportunity of extending Soviet power or of inhibiting or diluting the power of others".[37] Roberts views the Soviet Union as approaching a relationship whereby she "endeavours to extract the maximum advantage for the Soviet Union, if possible without any return and, having obtained what she wants, moves on to her next predetermined move".[38] At this point in the comparison it is important to note that the further one moves through Roberts' *Despatch 189*, the more similarities with Kennan's *Long Telegram* appear to leap from the pages. However, with this observation one comes to a sense of unease that the conclusion may not just be a comparison of contemporary works. One, in fact, may have been its intellectual predecessor. But which?

In paragraphs 14 and 15, Roberts refutes the suggestion that there is much in common between the regime and peoples of Nazi Germany, compared with the current Russian situation. He first concedes that the Russian leadership does believe that "the end justifies the means" and that they are head of "a system chosen to spread throughout the world".[39] However he suggests that the apprehension which arises from the above mellows in the light of the following facts. "The peoples of the Soviet Union are not naturally hostile to the outside world, nor eager to dominate other peoples."[40] He makes a comparison with "the master race of Germany destined to dominate the world and who fully sympathise with the ruthless and ambitious policies of their leaders."[41] By contrast he portrays the Russians as undisciplined and, frankly, lazy and needing continual motivation to hold their eminence on the world stage.

Kennan, in his telegram, had also been expressing similar apprehensions concerning the Soviets. He too concedes that "the Soviet people are by and large friendly to the outside world, eager for experience of it, eager to measure against it the talents they are conscious of possessing, eager, above all, to live in the peace and fruits of their own labour".[42] He then proceeds the following: "Soviet power, unlike that of Hitlerite Germany, is neither schematic nor adventuristic. It does not work by fixed plans. It does not take unnecessary risks. Impervious to logic of reason it is highly sensitive to the logic of force. For this reason it can easily withdraw—and usually does—when strong resistance is encountered at any point. Thus if the adversary has sufficient force and makes clear his readiness to use it, he rarely has to do so. If situations are properly handled, there need be no prestige engaging showdowns".[43] Surely this was the beginning of containment policy. But the question remains: Was Kennan alone in pushing his remedy.

Further investigation of Roberts suggests otherwise. In paragraph 17 of *Despatch 189* Roberts lists five reasons why comparisons of Nazi and Soviet regimes are incompatible. The second point is the most startling: "The rulers of Russia are infinitely more flexible than those of Germany. However much they may be wedded to Marxist doctrine, this allows them considerable latitude in regard to tactics and timing. Whereas the Germans set themselves a definite goal to be achieved within a given time regardless of opposition and changes in the international situation, the Russians are capable of re-adjusting their projects if faced with opposition or unexpected difficulties. They do not charge into brick walls even when they have the necessary strength to break them down, but prefer to wait and find some means of either getting round or climbing over the wall".[44]

Having assessed the potential of the current Soviet international menace, both diplomats then proceed to examine more directly the internal position and stabilization of the regime in Russia. Roberts notes that "there is no doubt that the present Soviet regime is fully accepted by the overwhelming majority of Soviet peoples. Large sections of the population now have a stake in the regime and all those under 40 know of nothing else".[45] While sounding a note of caution, Kennan is basically in agreement with the following: "In Russia, the party has now become a great and—for the moment—highly successful apparatus of dictatorial administration, but it has ceased to be a source of emotional inspiration".[46]

The depth of Roberts assessment can be seen in the diplomats' individual attempts to estimate the comparative strengths of the Soviet and Western spheres. Kennan bluntly writes: "Gauged against the Western world as a whole, the Soviets are still by far the weaker force".[47] Roberts, however, includes the following: "the internal position inside the Soviet Union, and in particular, the economic structure, is at present much weaker than might be imagined if one listened only to Soviet propaganda.... The advent of the atomic bomb has shown that the Soviet military machine is by no means invincible and the rulers of Russia know very well the inadequacy of the Red navy and air forces. They also know that there are strong forces throughout the world—American capitalism,

British social democracy and the Catholic Church among them—which would form strong centers of opposition to any attempt by the Soviet Union in the immediate future to dominate the world".[48]

Current Russian national policy was also given a similar overview by both diplomats. Roberts suggests the attitude that "Basically, the Kremlin is now pursuing a Russian policy which does not differ, except in degree from that pursued in the past by Ivan the Terrible, Peter the Great or Catherine the Great. But, what would, in other lands, be naked imperialism or power politics, is covered by the more attractive garb of Marxist-Leninist ideology, which in its turn, moulds the approach to world problems of statesmen, whose belief in their own ideology is as profound as that of the Jesuits in their own faith during the Counter Reformation".[49] Kennan confirms how the Marxist dogma, after the establishment of the Bolsheviks, "became a perfect vehicle for the sense of insecurity with which the bolsheviks, even more than previous Russian rulers were afflicted".[50] He sees it as "only the steady advance of uneasy Russian nationalism, a centuries old movement, in which conceptions of offence and defence are inextricably confused. But in the new guise of international Marxism, with its honeyed promised to a desperate and war torn outside world, it is more dangerous and insidious than ever before".[51]

The nature of the Soviets' long-term policy goal was also covered in the *Despatch* and *Long Telegram*. While they do not follow the same sequence, a selection of points and comparative quotes illustrate their unity of thought. Roberts, in paragraph 18, describes a Soviet Union making every effort to be the "most powerful state in the world".[52] This is to be achieved in several ways. Firstly, by maintaining and even modernising its armed forces at a time when other nations were demobilising. Secondly, by basing its search for security as "a constant expanding process" to advance Soviet power into, for example "the domination of Persian Azerbaijan to protect the oil in Baku, which leads on naturally to the domination of Persia as a whole, to the encouragement of a puppet Kurdish republic, to the isolation of Turkey and eventually to infiltration into the whole Arab world".[53] Kennan, in the first two paragraphs of a section devoted to the Projection of Soviet Outlook in Practical Policy, takes a similar stance. He speaks of maximising the armed forces and intensive military industrialization. This is combined with the following: "efforts will be made to advance official limits of Soviet power. For the moment, these efforts are restricted to certain neighbouring points conceived of here as being of immediate strategic necessity, such as Northern Iran, Turkey, and possible Bornholm."[54] As with Roberts, Kennan also goes on to note that Soviet power is advancing in European countries, through the power of increasing Communist Party pressure. In the same paragraph, Roberts enlarges on "the connected objective to weaken capitalist or social democratic countries in every way".[55] He mentions from the British point of view, the establishment and encouragement of national liberation fronts throughout the colonial world especially India and also the Middle East. To this he adds Russian attempts to undermine Britain's established position in Western Europe, Greece, Scandinavia and the Iberian Peninsula. He also notes the following Russian objective. "Everything possible will be done to keep the Americans and ourselves apart".[56]

Kennan gives a similar dimension to Russian activities on the international stage. It is naturally more general in tone and from the American point of view. "On the unofficial plan particularly violent efforts will be made to weaken the power and influence of the Western Powers on colonial, backward or dependent peoples. On this level, no holes will be barred. Everything possible will be done to set the major Western Powers against each other".[57] He mentions specifically that a rift will be encouraged between the British and American camps as well as with the Continentals. "Where suspicions exist they will be fanned, where not, ignited".[58] In Roberts, under the same headings, we have the following quote: "Although the Communist International no longer exists, the Communist parties everywhere will be supported and used to further Soviet interests and ultimately to take over the Government".[59] Kennan also finds "a concealed Commintern [i.e. The Third International] tightly coordinated and directed from Moscow".[60] Both diplomats concede that the Soviets will also make use of non government international organisations including groups such as Youth Leagues, Women's Organisations, Trade Unions, etc.

In concluding *Despatch 189*, Roberts offers several assumptions on which to base Britain's decisions with regard to future relations with the Soviets. He presents the Soviet regime as "dynamic and still expanding".[61] He notes that her long-term ambitions are dangerous to vital British interests as presently seen necessary. However, he emphasises "that security is the first consideration with the Soviet Union and that she will not endanger the realisation of her long term projects by pressing immediate issues to the point of serious conflict, except as a result of miscalculation of forces".[62] He concludes that it is therefore possible, though difficult, to reconcile British and Soviet interests in any problem which they are likely to face, granted the right mixture of strength and patience and avoidance of sabre rattling or the raising of prestige issues.

Similarly, Kennan reviews the Soviet regime as vigorous in character and expansionist by nature. He notes that while with the United States, there can be no permanent "modus vivendi", he believes that the problem is within our power to solve—and without recourse to any general military conflict.[63] If situations are properly handled, there need be no prestige engaging showdowns.[64] Kennan also presses for the Western World's need for "cohesion, firmness and vigor".[65]

A comparison of Roberts' *Despatch 189* with George Kennan's *Long Telegram* leaves little doubt on the consistently similar views shared by both of the British and American diplomats on the assessment of the nature of and direction to be taken by an apparently elusive postwar Soviet dictatorship. However this is not the end of the comparison. Roberts wrote a second *Despatch No 190*, on the 18th March 1947, to cover what he considered to be the most important question of all—the direction of British Foreign Policy, allowing for the assessment of the facts presented in *Despatch No 189*.

In paragraph 2, Roberts discusses the many approaches which Britain had tried with the Soviet Union since the Revolution. He speaks of "a brief attempt at the beginning of the revolution to work with the new regime in order to keep Russia in the war".[66] The result was a failure. Following this effort was a "period of isolation during which there were no diplomatic relations between the Soviet Union and the greater part of the outside world".[67] He then speaks of it becoming clear "that the Soviet regime had come to stay and diplomatic relations were opened, but it was not until the thirties, when the common German danger brought the Soviet Union into the League of Nations in the pursuit of collective security that anything approaching normality existed between London and Moscow".[68] "Then came the German attack upon the Soviet Union, the Anglo-Soviet Alliance of 1942, the growth of The Big Three cooperation and...the creation of the United Nations Organisation."[69] Roberts speaks of a painful but slowly improving period of Soviet-British relations in which the Soviets achieved the majority of concessions. He adds that "they probably hoped and expected that this would continue after the war, and the present crisis in our relations is largely due to a realisation on both sides that the time for one-sided appeasement and concessions is past".[70]

By paragraph 3, on the basis of the assessment, Roberts prescribes the following: "I would, however, suggest that the first essential is to treat the problem of Anglo-Soviet relations in the same way as major military problems were treated during the war. It calls for the closest coordination of political strategy for a very thorough staff study embracing every aspect of Soviet policy—not forgetting the ubiquitous activities of the Communist parties directed, if not controlled in detail from Moscow".[71] It is impossible at this point to resist placing quotes from Kennan's *Long Telegram* alongside Roberts's *Despatch*: "The problem of how to cope with this force is undoubtedly the greatest task our diplomacy has ever faced and probably the greatest it will ever have to face. It would be the point of departure from which our political general staff, working at the present juncture, should proceed. It should be approached with the same thoroughness and care as the solution of a major strategic problem in war and if necessary with no smaller outlay in planning effort".[72]

In paragraph 5 Roberts further notes that

[P]arallel with [this] should go a campaign to educate the British public with whom all decisions of policy ultimately rest. In the case of other important countries, the British public, or at influential sections of it, should have real knowledge on which to base their judgements. In the case of the Soviet Union alone they are dependent upon either Soviet propaganda or anti-Soviet prejudices which are all equally dangerous counsellors. In so far as normal contacts do not exist between the Soviet and British publics and are unlikely to be permitted by Soviet Government, and as even press correspondents in Moscow can only send out news censored by Soviet authorities and already coloured by their own fears, lest frankness might forfeit them a subsequent visa for the Soviet Union, the responsibility for educating the British public must rest with His Majesty's Government and the editors in London to an extent which could be abnormal in dealing with other countries.[73]

Kennan's advice to the Washington administration is again along a similar vein. "We must see that our public is educated to the realities of the Russian situation. I cannot over-emphasise the importance of this. The press cannot do this alone. It must be done mainly by Government, which is necessarily more experienced and better informed on the practical problems involved. In this we need not be deterred by the ugliness of the picture. I am concerned that there would be far less hysterical anti-Sovietism in our country today if the realities of the situation were better understood by our people. There is nothing as dangerous or as terrifying as the unknown.... Our only stake lies in what we hope rather than what we know; and I am concerned we have a better chance of realizing these hopes if our public is enlightened and if our dealings with the Russians are placed entirely on a realistic and matter of fact basis".[74]

Again, back to Roberts: "The most essential factor in our long term strategy is, however, to ensure that our own country, the Commonwealth, the Colonial Empire and those countries particularly in Western Europe and the Near and Middle East, whose fortunes are so closely bound up with ours, should be healthy political and economic organisers pursuing progressive policies, raising the standard of being of their peoples and removing the causes of social strife. At the same time we can offer civil and personal liberties which are unknown in the Soviet Union and would be the enemy of its inhabitants. In fact we should act as the champion of a dynamic and progressive faith and a way of life with an appeal to the world at least as great as that of the Communist system of the Kremlin".[75]

In the *Long Telegram*, Kennan also presses the need for an internal strength in American society to meet the Soviet challenge: "Much depends on the health and vigor of our own society. World communism is like a malignant parasite which only feeds on diseased tissue. This is the point at which domestic and foreign policies meet. Every courageous and incisive measure to solve the internal problems of our own society, to improve self-confidence, discipline, morale and community spirit of our own people, is a diplomatic victory over Moscow, worth a thousand diplomatic notes and joint communiques". "We must formulate and put forward for other nations a much more positive and constructive picture of the sort of world we would like to see than we have put forward in the past. It is not enough to urge people to develop political processes similar to our own. Many foreign people, in Europe at least are tired and frightened by experiences of the past and are less interested in abstract than in security. They are seeking guidance rather than responsibilities. We should be better able than the Russians to give them this. And unless we do, the Russians certainly will".[76]

In the closing paragraphs of his *Despatch*, Roberts turns his attention to tactics rather than strategy. The opinions that he expresses are notable, not just for their decisive and logical approach, but also for the fact that they permeate Kennan's *Long Telegram*. Roberts notes that "the day has also long gone when we might hope by unilateral gestures or concessions on our side gradually influence Soviet policy and so to inspire similar gestures and concessions from the Soviet side. In dealing with the Soviet Union as indeed with the Old Russian Empire we should base ourselves firmly on the principle of reciprocity and give nothing unless we receive a counter-advantage in return. This in turn implies great firmness in dealing with big matters and small alike, coupled, however, with a friendly approach with perfect politeness and with formal correctness, which we may no longer consider necessary in our dealings with other countries in this democratic age". "In all our dealings with the Soviet Union we should certainly bear in mind the absolute need for earning and maintaining respect. This means that we must be strong and look strong. But this strength should never be paraded unnecessarily and it should always take account of Soviet susceptibilities and prestige. Above all we should never rattle the sabre and make it difficult for the Russians to climb down without loss of face".[77]

The following comes from Kennan's report. While the working of the words varies considerably, the sentiment and emphasis are clearly recognisable. "Our final step must be to apprehend and recognise for what it is the nature of the movement with which we are dealing. We must study it with the same courage, detachment, objectivity and the same determination, not to be emotionally provoked or unseated by it, with which the doctor studies the unruly and unreasonable individual".[78] "We must have courage and self-confidence to cling to our own methods and conceptions of human society"[79] and "if situations are properly handled there need be no prestige engaging showdowns".[80] Just as with Roberts, Kennan sees relations with the Soviet Union best conducted within formal guidelines. He notes that "Soviet official relations will take what might be called a 'correct' course with individual foreign governments, with great stress being laid on the prestige of the

Soviet Union and its representatives and with punctilious attention to protocol, as distinct from good manners".[81]

Having noted the undeniable similarities between the analysis of both Kennan and Roberts, it is necessary at this point to discuss the relationship between the two diplomats and allow them to explain for themselves the similarities between the two documents. In his memoirs Kennan only briefly mentioned his relationship with Roberts. In a footnote on the chapter discussing the *Long Telegram*, Kennan recalled, "I knew him not only as a diplomatist of outstanding experience and ability but as a loyal colleague and valued friend".[82] In a letter to the author, dated 17 March 1980, he overflowed with kind words about his opposite number in the British Embassy. He largely reiterated his earlier comments. "We were, and are, good friends, and I have always had high respect for him." "He was [and is] a true diplomatic professional, discreet and reserved. I remember him as an intelligent, highly competent, loyal, helpful colleague."[83] However, Kennan's reply to the author appears also to encompass a certain degree of vagueness regarding some aspect of his working relationship with Roberts. "I can only say that we were opposite numbers in the British and American embassies at Moscow in the 1945-46 period (as I remember it) and had many occasions to consult about the problems of the respective relationships of our two governments with the Soviet Union".[84] This was a vital period in Kennan's life, a turning point, yet he infers that Roberts's influence was indirect. This is most likely an attempt by Kennan to dispel suggestions that there was a certain degree of collaboration between the two diplomats on this issue.

Frank Roberts, in a letter to the author dated 4 June 1980, exhibited a more relaxed and measured tone. He also commented upon a happy relationship between himself and George Kennan. Roberts, writing from his retirement home at Kensington Court Palace, graciously noted that he had already seen Kennan's reply to the author's query, stating that his "reply can only echo the nice letter he [Kennan] sent to you on March 17th".[85] Roberts's correspondence is relaxed and in parts non-commital—in the best diplomatic sense. He described Kennan as a "great expert on the Russian scene" and continued that he had "learned to respect very highly George Kennan's courage and integrity of character, as I have always done since".[86] He has also suggested that their close working relationship was based on the fact that Kennan's "far deeper knowledge of the Soviet Union was perhaps at that time balanced to some extent by my wider experience in the wartime Foreign Office".[87]

Yet, Roberts's letter does provide clues to the important question of overlap in attitudes within their respective areas of diplomatic expertise. "We were working very closely together as were our governments at the time—we took a very similar view on the problems affecting Soviet relations with the West and we gave similar advise to our respective governments."[88] He speaks of similar situations: both were running their embassies while awaiting new ambassadors, both were asked by their governments to provide recent interpretation of Soviet foreign policy, both were widely acclaimed and both promoted as a result of their analysis. In a short chapter in his memoirs relative to the two documents Roberts added that the conclusions they reached were bound to be similar because "we were living in the same place, studying and reacting to the same policies of the same person, Stalin, and we were in constant consultation with each other". He further added "I should have been surprised if they had been different in essentials".[89]

In a similar argument Kennan stated that "we faced, after all, almost identically the same problems, and reacted similarly to them".[90] Kennan recalled that he "had many occasions to consult about the problems of the respective relationships of our governments with the Soviet Union" and could recall no differences of opinion between the two.[91] Yet he is quick to comment that he would not attribute all his views to Roberts, adding that he does "not recall seeing any of his [Roberts's] despatches from that period",[92] and unsurprisingly makes no mention of the despatches in his memoirs. However, the similarities remain.[93]

As a result of the close interaction between the two embassies, there was clearly a planned and directed sounding board action between Roberts and Kennan. Both parties have admitted to considerable contact and discussion during this critical juncture. Kennan has insisted, though, that he was the senior partner, stating "In our discussions of Soviet policy and behaviour I fear, to my shame, that I did most of the talking, and he—most of the listening". Yet neither document suggests this superiority. The earlier postal date on the *Long Telegram* is unimportant. Who sent what cable first is not really the question.

Yet it has been argued by others that there are no foundations for the suggestion of a collaboration theory. Sean Greenwood has suggested that it is not the similarities but the differences which bring an answer to the suspicions of collaboration. He has argued that Frank Roberts had his own distinct message. He emphasised British interests and policy and also stressed the importance of Anglo-American relations which deviated from the essence of Kennan's telegram. In his memoirs Frank Roberts also accentuates these differences. "Mine did differ in the sense that the British and American positions were different and that I was writing not only about the position in the Soviet Union, as George Kennan had been, but also about Soviet policy towards the British".[94] Greenwood suggested that the differences in emphasis and style are discreet enough to dissipate suspicions of teamwork. "For all their similarities to the 'Long Telegram' and to the context in which it was written, Frank Roberts's despatches had their own distinctive message and were aimed at a rather different audience".[95] This is definitely one way to look at it.

An interesting, yet little known incident which encourages theories of close collaboration on this issue has been provided by Roberts himself in his recently published memoirs. Although he provides no dates, he does suggest that he had read and summarised the *Long Telegram* for London *before* being asked to submit his own ideas. "George showed me his *Long Telegram* and allowed me to send a summary back to London. London then asked me for my own views".[96] Roberts described Kennan's *Long Telegram* as an accurate summary, written "with his usual thoroughness, honesty and great knowledge of this country".[97] The British Foreign Office was impressed by Kennan's report and were therefore eager to see the conclusions Roberts reached. Roberts does not make clear whether he had read the *Long Telegram* before the State Department, nor does he give any explanation as to why Kennan allowed him to summarise the top secret telegram for Whitehall.

So how do Kennan, Roberts and the documents they produced fit into the larger picture of postwar Anglo-American relations? Certainly the widespread attention that the *Long Telegram* received in Washington worked to the advantage of the British. It had long become clear to many British diplomats and members of the Foreign Office that world leadership had passed to the United States. Yet, "they expressed hope that the US would seek their more experienced and worldly guidance".[98] British observer Bernard Gage, wrote in 1945, "In due course it will no doubt be borne upon Americans that we, with our long experience, can be of some assistance to them in the proper application of their power".[99] So began the long British campaign to convince the American government of the importance of strengthening Anglo-American ties and bringing American foreign policy, particularly regarding the Soviet Union, into line with the British. By mid-1945 Foreign Office officials had abandoned all faith in Soviet goodwill. They had in fact already reached many of the conclusions Kennan had long before the release of the *Long Telegram*.[100]

In the closing stages of the Second World War, this advice was falling upon deaf ears. Franklin Roosevelt had been attempting to establish a three power 'triangularity' structure in international affairs, based on accommodation and goodwill towards the Soviets. Roosevelt had his own views about Britain's return to Empire. He feared greater Anglo-American collaboration would be interpreted by the Soviet Union as an anti-Soviet bloc and therefore constitute a threat to world peace. Yet, British Prime Minister Winston Churchill did not share this sentiment. Henry Ryan wrote, "Churchill's government, if successful, would have created in the international arena a new power, one made up of two nations. It could appropriately be called 'Anglo-America'".[101] Britain considered Roosevelt's 'triangularity' proposal misguided and therefore dangerous to the West. It also posed other problems for Britain. Britain did not have the strength to maintain its corner of the triangle, and if isolated in its third of the relationship, would shrink to an inferior rank of international powers. This was a motivating concern in British foreign policy. Churchill saw the only way to preserve Great Britain's place in the big power society was to tighten its links with the United States. "What Great Britain could not be, Anglo-America could".[102] In a letter to Ernest Bevin, four months before the famous 'Iron Curtain' speech, Churchill wrote:

> The long-term advantage to Britain and the Commonwealth is to have our affairs so interwoven with those of the US in external and strategic matters, that any idea of war between the two countries is utterly impossible, and that in fact, however the matter may be worded, we stand or fall together.[103]

In the postwar period it became imperative for the British to reverse their declining relevance if they were to maintain their relative position among the other players. Closer collaboration with the United States was the principal means they chose to pursue this end. Thus it became important to align American policies with their own on issues of vital significance, particularly the threat of the Soviet Union.

The growing belligerency of the Soviet Union set the very scene to which George Kennan would contribute. The State Department had called on Kennan to make his interpretative report in the wake of Stalin's provocative February 9th election speech. The State Department considered this statement by Stalin the most important and authoritative guide to the prevailing Soviet policy. This has been confirmed with the release of the so-called 'Novikov Telegram'. The cable from Soviet Ambassador to the United States, Nikolai Novikov, to Soviet Foreign Minister Molotov, dated 27 September 1946, has been regarded as a parallel to the *Long Telegram* and one of the landmark documents of the early Cold War period, one which Molotov appears to have taken great heed.[104] The essence of Soviet outlook is summed up in Novikov's opening sentence, "[T]he foreign policy of the United States, which reflects the imperialist tendencies of American monopolistic capital, is characterized in the postwar period by a striving for world supremacy".[105]

As early American attempts to mediate with the Soviet Union faltered, the British offer of collaboration on the Soviet issue became more appealing. The British sought to contain Soviet expansion and influence, yet they lacked the power necessary. Therefore they sought to influence American relations with the Kremlin both during and after the war.[106] An increase in US-Soviet hostilities suited Britain in various ways, particularly by making the US more favourably disposed towards Britain in general, a point British diplomats were well aware of.[107] Lord Halifax referred to this relationship as the well-established principle that "our stocks in the United States appreciate as those of the Soviet Union decline and vice versa".[108] British diplomats agreed that the greater the US perceived the Soviet threat to be, the better that British interests were suited. To this end Churchill and the Foreign Office made a deliberate attempt to convince both the American administration and the American people that a "firm, reasonable, steady-minded confrontation of the Soviet Union was the only way to assure peace".[109] This was no more evident than in Churchill's "Iron Curtain" speech, delivered in Fulton, Missouri on 5 March, 1946.

The "Iron Curtain" speech was an attempt by former Prime Minister to bring to the attention of both the American administration and society the goals of postwar Britain. In this speech he addressed the importance of close Anglo-American ties in maintaining world peace, emphasising that this collaboration would in no way conflict with the newly established United Nations Organisation. He also drew attention to the points of conflict and differences with the Soviet Union. Lord Halifax reported that the speech had "given the sharpest jolt to American thinking of any utterance since the end of the war".[110] While this perhaps may be slightly exaggerated, the speech did, like the *Long Telegram*, significantly contribute to a hardening of the Western position towards the Soviet Union.

Delivered less then two weeks after the arrival of the *Long Telegram*, Churchill's speech was likewise surrounded by controversy regarding the input by American officials. Henry Ryan suggests that while Whitehall was unsure of what Churchill had prepared to say at Fulton, the American administration were well aware.[111] Secretary of State James F. Byrnes and Admiral William Leahy were aware of the contents of the speech about one week before it was made. Churchill told Attlee and Bevin that both had seen and approved the speech. While President Truman had not technically read the speech, he was fully briefed of its contents. Churchill commented: "He welcomed the outline I gave him of my message".[112] Byrnes later added, "Anticipating that the Soviets would charge the British and Americans with 'ganging up' on them, he [Truman] could truthfully say he had not read the speech prior to its delivery".[113]

Historians have since concluded that Truman, in conjunction with Churchill used the suggestions implied in the "Iron Curtain" speech to gauge popular opinion and from there devise a course of action. "In addition, the speech seems certainly to have been a 'trial balloon' for Truman, who could dissociate himself from the ideas expressed if they aroused undue hostility in whatever quarter".[114] Ironically, however, while the speech was successful in assisting the US to adopt a confrontational position, it did little to promote the notion a "fraternal association of English speaking peoples". "It would seem that Britain, partly by design and partly by default, had promoted the United States to adopt a policy of containment".[115]

So, to what extent was this British determination to influence American policy evident in the relationship between Roberts and

Kennan? Kennan received much support and encouragement from his British colleague Roberts, who described him as "a great expert on the Russian scene".[116] Kennan's views naturally commanded a great deal of respect from the Foreign Office. Roberts wrote in his memoirs, "I was in closer contact with my own government at home then he was with his. So each had something to offer the other".[117] In the earlier stages of his work in Moscow, it seems Kennan was receiving from Roberts the support he did not receive from his American colleagues and in return he was telling the American government exactly what the British wanted to hear. C. Ben Wright described Kennan as a "long-life Anglophile; he had more in common with his British colleagues than he did with his own countrymen".[118] Perhaps this goes some of the way to explaining Kennan's decision to allow Roberts and Whitehall to preview the confidential Long Telegram.

"The effect produced in Washington by this elaborate pedagogical effort was nothing less then sensational. It was one that changed my career and my life in very basic ways." This was how Kennan described the effect of the *Long Telegram* upon Washington. Since then, Kennan and his history have become an influential field of study in its own right. Kennan has been described as "the intellectual spokesman for the Cold War consensus in the US" and the "chief ideologist of containment".[119] John L. Gaddis described the *Long Telegram* as "to this day the single most influential explanation of postwar Soviet behaviour, and one which powerfully reinforced the growing tendency within the US to interpret Moscow's actions in a sinister light".[120] Henry Kissinger wrote, "Kennan sketched the American dream of a peace achieved by conversion of the adversary". He continued by describing the subsequent "X Article" as a "lucidly written, passionately argued literary adaptation of his *Long Telegram*, Kennan [had] raised the Soviet challenge to the level of philosophy of history".[121] Surely this is an exaggerated description of the impact of the *Long Telegram* and the role of George Kennan in the scheme of Truman's foreign policy. Kennan himself only met the President once or twice in this period and had strong doubts that Truman ever really read anything he wrote. Still, Kennan's contribution to Washington's understanding of the Soviet threat was a major factor in the diplomatic origins of the Cold War.[122]

## NOTES

1. George F. Kennan, *Memoirs 1925-1950* (Boston, 1967), p. 297.

2. Ibid.

3. Ibid. Also see David S. McLellan, "Who Fathered Containment? A Discussion," *International Studies Quarterly* 17:2 (1973): 205-26; Robert L. Messer, "Paths Not Taken: The United States Department of State and Alternatives of Containment, 1945-1946," *Diplomatic History* 1:4 (1977): 297-319; and Richard J. Powers, "Who Fathered Containment?" *International Studies Quarterly* 15:4 (1971): 526-43. The outgoing ambassador, W. Averell Harriman told this writer that he saw Kennan's despatch when it arrived and encouraged other policymakers to read it; Harriman doubted that even Kennan knew he had commended it to others. Interview with W. Averell Harriman, Georgetown, Washington DC, 25 Apr. 1977.

4. Cable No. 72 Attlee to the United Kingdom High Commissioner, Canberra 2 February 1948, (Public Record Office, London) PM operational papers, PREMIER 8/787.

5. James Baker, "America and the Collapse of the Soviet Empire: What has to be Done," *United States Information Service*, Dec. 16, 1991.

6. Henry Kissinger, "Reflections of Containment," *Foreign Affairs* 73 (May/June 1994): 114.

7. Kennan's *Long Telegram*, reprinted in Joseph M. Siracusa, ed., *The American Diplomatic Revolution: A Documentary History of the Cold War* (Sydney, NY, 1976), p. 190. (See Appendix.)

8. Frank Roberts, *Despatch 189*, March 17, 1946, FO 371/56763 N4156/38 (Public Record Office, London), p. 1. (See Appendix.)

9. Ibid.

10. Kennan, *Long Telegram*, p. 190.

11. Roberts, 189, p. 2.

12. Kennan, *Long Telegram*, p. 189.

13. Roberts, 189, p. 2.

14. Kennan, *Long Telegram*, p. 196.

15. Ibid., p. 195.

16. Roberts, 189, p. 2.

17. Kennan, *Long Telegram*, p. 188.

18. Roberts, 189, p. 2.

19. Kennan, *Long Telegram*, p. 188.

20. Ibid.

21. Roberts, 189, p. 3.

22. Kennan, *Long Telegram*, p. 191.

23. Roberts, 189, p. 3.

24. Ibid.

25. Kennan, *Long Telegram*, p. 188.

26. Roberts, 189, p. 3.

27. Kennan, *Long Telegram*, p. 189.

28. Roberts, 189, p. 3.

29. Ibid., p. 4.

30. Ibid., p. 4.

31. Kennan, *Long Telegram*, p. 191.
32. *Ibid.*
33. Ibid.
34. Ibid.
35. Ibid.
36. Roberts, 189, p. 4.
37. Kennan, *Long Telegram*, p. 192.
38. Roberts, 189, p. 4.
39. Ibid., p. 5.
40. Ibid.
41. Ibid.
42. Kennan, *Long Telegram*, p. 189.
43. Ibid., p. 195. For Kennan's further refinement of this concept see "The Sources of Soviet Conduct," *Foreign Affairs* 25:4 (1947): 566-82. Also see John L. Gaddis, "Containment: A Reassessment," *Foreign Affairs* 56:4 (1977): 873-87; Eduard M. Mark, "The Question of Containment: A Reply to John Lewis Gaddis," *Foreign Affairs* 56:2 (1978): 430-41; and C. Ben Wright, "Mr 'X' and Containment," *Slavic Review* 35:1 (1976): 1-36.
44. Roberts, 189, p. 6.
45. Ibid.
46. Kennan, *Long Telegram*, p. 196.
47. Ibid.
48. Roberts, 189, p. 6.
49. Ibid.
50. Kennan, *Long Telegram*, p. 190.
51. *Ibid.*
52. Roberts, 189, p. 6.
53. *Ibid.*
54. Kennan, *Long Telegram*, p. 191.
55. Roberts, 189, p. 6.
56. Ibid.
57. Kennan, *Long Telegram*, p. 191.
58. Ibid.
59. Roberts, 189, p. 7.
60. Kennan, *Long Telegram*, p. 193.
61. Roberts, 189, p. 8.
62. *Ibid.*
63. Kennan, *Long Telegram*, p. 195.
64. Ibid., p. 196.
65. Ibid.
66. Frank Roberts, *Despatch 190*, 18th March, 1946, FO 371/56763 N4157/38 (Public Records Office, London), p. 1.
67. Ibid.
68. Ibid.
69. Ibid.
70. *Ibid.*

71. Ibid.

72. Kennan, *Long Telegram*, p. 195.

73. Roberts, 190, p. 2.

74. Kennan, *Long Telegram*, p. 196.

75. Roberts, 190, p. 2.

76. Kennan, *Long Telegram*, p. 197. Years later Kennan is still hoping to make America a better place. See George F. Kennan, *Around the Cragged Hill: A Personal and Political Philosophy* (New York, 1993), pp. 232-59.

77. Roberts, 190, p. 2.

78. Kennan, *Long Telegram*, p. 196.

79. Ibid., p. 197.

80. Ibid., p. 196.

81. Ibid., p. 193.

82. G. Kennan, *Memoirs*, p. 289.

83. George Kennan, Letter to J. Siracusa, 17th March, 1980.

84. Ibid.

85. Frank Roberts, Letter to J. Siracusa, 4th June, 1980.

86. Ibid.

87. Introduction by Sir Frank Roberts in Sean Greenwood, "Frank Roberts and the 'Other' *Long Telegram*: The View from the British Embassy in Moscow, March 1946," *Journal of Contemporary History* 25:1 (1990).

88. F. Roberts, Letter to J. Siracusa.

89. Frank Roberts, *Dealing With Dictators, The Destruction and Revival of Europe, 1930-1970* (London, 1991), p. 108.

90. G. Kennan, Letter to J. Siracusa.

91. Ibid.

92. Ibid.

93. In defence of Kennan, C. Ben Wright, "Letter to the Editor," *SHAFR Newsletter* 23:1 (Mar. 1992), argued that the diplomatic establishment in Moscow during the 1930s and 1940s was close and, although it was certainly not monolithic, it did share many of the same perceptions about Russian history, Stalin, and Soviet foreign policy. He suggested that there is, therefore, no need to explain the similarities and that the "parallels" were an obvious and natural outcome. Also see John Lewis Gaddis, *We Now Know: Rethinking Cold War History* (New York, 1992), p. 20.

94. Roberts, *Dealing With Dictators*, p. 108.

95. Greenwood, "Frank Roberts and the 'Other' *Long Telegram*," p. 119.

96. Roberts, *Dealing with Dictators*, p. 108.

97. Greenwood, "Frank Roberts and the 'Other' *Long Telegram*," p. 110.

98. Peter Boyle, "The British Foreign Office View of Soviet-American Relations", *Diplomatic History* 3 (1979): 308.

99. Quoted in ibid.

100. Ibid., p. 310.

101. Henry Ryan, *The Vision of Anglo-America, The US-UK Alliance and the Emerging Cold War, 1943-1946* (Cambridge, 1987), p. 2.

102. Ibid. For a discussion on how Churchill gambled and lost, see John Charmley, *Churchill's Grand Alliance: The Anglo-American Special Relationship, 1940-1957* (London, 1995).

103. See Ibid., p. 4.

104. Kenneth Jensen, ed, *Origins of the Cold War, The Novikov, Kennan, and Roberts 'Long Telegrams' of 1946* (Washington, DC, 1991), p. ix.

105. Quoted in Ibid., 3, emphasis replicates that of M. Molotov.

106. Terry Anderson, *The US, Great Britain and the Cold War 1944-1947* (Columbia, 1981), p. 176.

107. P. Boyle, "The British Foreign Office View," p. 317.

108. Quoted in Ibid.

109. Ryan, *The Vision of Anglo-America*, p. 7.

110. Boyle, "The British Foreign Office View", p. 314.

111. See Ryan, "A New Look at Churchill's 'Iron Curtain' Speech," *The Historical Journal* 22:4 (1979).

112. Attlee papers, University College, Oxford, box 4, Churchill file.

113. J.F. Byrnes, *All In One Lifetime* (New York, 1958), p. 349.

114. Ryan, "A New Look at Churchill's 'Iron Curtain' Speech," p. 910.

115. Anderson, *The US, Great Britain and the Cold War*, p. 179.

116. Roberts, *Dealing With Dictators*, p. 92.

117. Ibid.

118. C. Ben Wright, "Letter to the Editor," SHAFR *Newsletter* 22 (Sept. 1991): 59.

119. Walter Hixon, *George F. Kennan—Cold War Iconoclast* (New York, 1989), pp. ix, x.

120. J.L. Gaddis, *The Long Peace: Inquiries Into the History of the Cold War* (New York, 1987), p. 39.

121. Kissinger, "Reflections of Containment," p. 120-21.

122. Wilson Miscamble's comment that the *Long Telegram* "helped construct the intellectual supports for the already developing disposition of firmness towards the Soviet Union", is perhaps more to the point. See Wilson D. Miscamble, *George F. Kennan and the Making of American Foreign Policy, 1947-1950* (Princeton, NJ, 1992), p. 27. Also see Melvyn P. Leffler, *A Preponderance of Power: National Security, the Truman Administration, and the Cold War* (Standford, 1992), p. 108.

# CHAPTER 3

# NSC 68 AND
# THE H-BOMB DECISION

On 31 January 1950, several months after America's atomic monopoly had been broken and in line with the President's decision to determine the technical feasibility of a thermonuclear weapon, Harry S. Truman directed Secretary of State Dean Acheson and Secretary of Defence Louis Johnson "to undertake a re-examination of our objectives in peace and war and of the effect of these objectives on strategic plans, in the light of the probable fission bomb capability and possible thermonuclear capability of the Soviet Union".[1] Moreover, the terms of reference[2] continued:

> It must be considered whether a decision to proceed with a program directed toward feasibility prejudges the more fundamental decision (a) as to whether, in the event that a test of a thermonuclear weapon proves successful, such weapons should be stockpiled, or (b) if stockpiled, the conditions under which they might be used in war.

Truman, acutely sensitive to the potential pressure to produce and stockpile such weapons in the event that tests proved affirmative, regarded the question of "use policy" in the broadest possible terms. Specifically, the President noted, "The question of our policy can be adequately assessed only as a part of a general re-examination of this country's strategic plans and its objectives in peace and war", a position that also took into consideration the incipient arms race with the USSR as well as related social, psychological and political questions.

None could doubt the gravity of the exercise. "The outcome", concluded Truman, "would have a crucial bearing on the further question as to whether there should be revision in the nature of agreements, including the international control of atomic energy, which we have been seeking to reach with the USSR". The final joint State-Defense report, "United States Objectives and Programs for National Security", was submitted to the President on 7 April 1950. Five days later, on April 12, Truman referred the document to the National Security Council for consideration, with the additional request that the NSC provide him "with further information on the implications of the conclusions contained therein".[3] Thus was born Policy Paper Number 68 of the National Security Council—NSC 68.

Since then, and well beyond its ultimate declassification in early 1975,[4] NSC 68 has continued to attract the attention of historians, political scientists, and scholarly commentators of every political persuasion. The net effect has been the elevation of NSC 68 to a position of landmark significance in the annals of modern American foreign policy, even though there was by no means agreement on what the significance was supposed to be. Preceded by occasional hints and "leaks", the first important treatment of the subject appeared in 1962 with the publication of Paul Y. Hammond's pioneering essay, "NSC 68: Prologue to Rearmament". Unable to quote directly from the still-classified document, Hammond interviewed instead the principals involved and produced what would for a generation become the standard account of the formulation and evolution of NSC 68. The purpose of NSC 68, according to Hammond was straightforward and unequivocal. "The object of the study", he wrote, was to take a new look at the general strategic picture, and to reappraise it...an attempt...at a rational projection of strategic policy requirements from the national strategic situation".[5] In 1966, correspondent Cabell Phillips, who apparently had access to at least some of the document, defined NSC 68 as a "posture that set up certain basic assumptions about the new world order and our role in it", the assumption of which served "to indicate and to underpin the specific steps that had to be taken in Korea".[6] In the same year, and based on the partial text of NSC 68 published in Phillips's study, Walter LaFeber went a step further in its interpretation and pronounced it "one of the key historical documents of the cold war", inasmuch as "it asked the United States to assume unilaterally the defence of the free world at a tremendous price with no hesitation",—nothing less, the same author would reassert ten years later, than "the American blueprint for waging the Cold War during the next twenty years".[7] Gaddis Smith was quite correct in proclaiming NSC 68 "the most famous unread paper of its era".[8]

Since its declassification in 1975, NSC 68 has remained a compelling focus of study. It has invited comment from scholars who have differed, sometimes dramatically, on its significance and its role in the evolution of American nuclear strategy. Ernest R. May argued that NSC 68 "laid out the rationale for US strategy during much of the cold war", providing the "blueprint for the militarization of the cold war from 1950 to the collapse of the Soviet Union at the beginning of the 1990s".[9] Journalist-turned diplomat Strobe Talbott described the prescription of NSC 68 as strong medicine. He saw the document as "a highly classified manifesto that was intended to grab its few readers by the scruff of the neck and shake them, so that they would then go out and rouse the nation".[10] Yet did NSC 68 establish new goals or constitute a major departure in postwar American foreign policy? In his autobiography Paul Nitze admitted that NSC 68 was not a sharp departure in US policy. It largely reaffirmed what was already approved in NSC 20/4. The major change was an increased level of effort, with emphasis on strengthening US military capabilities in the face of significantly increased Soviet capabilities.[11] Melvyn Leffler echoed Nitze's comments by arguing that NSC 68 did not propose any alternative goals and all that was 'new' about it was the call for conventional rearmament and strategic superiority. Furthermore, according to Leffler, it initiated no great debate because it did not provide any new analysis on the Soviet threat.[12] Similarly, Samuel F. Wells argued that NSC 68 did not represent a dramatic departure from American policy as it restated much of the objectives that were set out in NSC 20/4 in 1948. However, he continued, the call for an increased and tougher stand was somewhat more hostile and urgent. "Viewed as a call to action rather than policy analysis, NSC 68 is an amazingly incomplete and amateurish study."[13] Far from amateurish, Wilson Miscamble described NSC 68 as a "paradigmatic document", although, he continued, it was not a new position but rather reinforced Acheson's stance at the at the conclusion of the H-bomb debate that the basis of America's policy should be to create a "situation of strength".[14] Elsewhere NSC 68 has been described as "a selling job, not a precise delineation of US commitments".[15]

Yet, others have argued that NSC 68 did indeed constitute a change in policy or a least provide a new basis for policy towards the Soviet Union. John Gaddis treated NSC 68 as "a qualitative break from the past", and as such, constituted "the most elaborate effort made by United States officials during the early cold war years to integrate political, economic and military consideration into a comprehensive statement of national security policy".[16] Daniel Yergin has argued that NSC 68 was as significant in postwar history as the Truman Doctrine or Kennan's Long Telegram. In an attempt to explore the perplexing questions regarding the Soviet Union, he continued, NSC 68 "expressed the fully formed cold war mind set of American leaders, and provided rationalisation not only for the H-bomb but also for a much expanded military establishment".[17] For the very fact that it did urge recognition of an accelerated program of rearmament as opposed to earlier US initiatives which used economic and political means to halt Soviet expansion, Steven Rearden argued that NSC 68 was "an unprecedented departure from previous US policy". In what he described as an "emotional but still analytical paper", Rearden continued, NSC 68 "signalled the eclipse of idealism and the acceptance of a new code of behavior that would deeply intensify American interest and involvement in events abroad".[18] In any event, the overall characterisation of NSC 68 from Hammond to the present as "one of the key historical documents of the Cold War" has with few exceptions generally been accepted by academia.[19]

Interestingly, policymakers of the period most intimately concerned with the composition and implementation of NSC 68 seem neither as certain nor as consistent as their critics. Paul H. Nitze, the principal author of the document and George F. Kennan's successor as Director of the State Department's Policy Planning Staff, is a case in point. Harvard-educated and an investment banker who worked throughout the Great Depression for Dillon, Read and Company in New York, Nitze travelled to Washington in 1940 as an assistant to the Under Secretary of the Navy, James Forrestal, the former President of Dillon, Read. During World War II, Nitze served consecutively as financial director of the Co-ordinator of Inter-American Affairs; as head of the Board of Economic Warfare's Metal and Materials branch; the Foreign Economic Administration's director of Foreign Procurement and Development; and finally, vice-chairman of the United States Strategic Bombing Survey from 1944 to 1946. Before stepping into Kennan's role at the Policy Planning Staff, the erstwhile investment banker served both as deputy-director of the Office of International Trade Policy in 1946 and as deputy to the Assistant Secretary for Economic Affairs from 1947 to 1949. In the matter of NSC 68, Nitze contended that it is true that the ostensible object of the exercise was to provide an argument for lifting the budget ceiling of the defence establishment, which had been set at \$13.5 billion for fiscal Year 1950.[20] But it is also true that the actual objective was to provide a solid argument for the production and stockpiling of thermonuclear weapons in the event they proved feasible.[21] At other times, Nitze's meaning was less clear.[22]

Much the same applies to Dean Acheson. During the course of an historical seminar arranged for his former colleagues at Princeton in 1953, the Secretary of State appeared unequivocal about the meaning and significance of NSC 68:

> [It is] one of the great documents in our history. I don't believe that there is going to be one that will stand up to it. I don't think what John Adams and other people produced about Monroe Doctrine, or anything else, is going to be anywhere equal to the analysis of this paper in terms of American survival in the world.[23]

Yet in his memoirs, a number of years later, Acheson remembered it differently. What had been "one of the great documents in our history" had now been relegated to the lesser status of "a formidable document", the purpose of which was merely "to so bludgeon the mass mind of 'top government' that not only could the President make a decision but that the decision could be carried out".[24] Charles E. Bohlen, one of the State's leading Kremlinologists who was one of the few asked to comment on the original draft, spoke little of NSC 68 in his memoirs and recalled that he did not have an opportunity to study it fully until he returned from Paris to Washington in 1951.[25] Along these same lines, Averell Harriman had no particular recollection of NSC 68, despite Acheson's personal briefing on the matter.[26]

Related to policymakers' differing perceptions of what NSC 68 was supposed to accomplish, is the equally intriguing question of the relationship of the document and its final implementation to the outbreak of the Korean war. It should be recalled that it was not until 30 September 1950,—several months after the North Korean invasion of South Korea and at the 68th Meeting of the National Security Council,—that President Truman finally "approved the Conclusions of NSC 68 in the statement of policy to be followed over the next four or five years, and directed their implementation by all appropriate executive departments and agencies of the US Government".[27] Nor was it until 14 December 1950, shortly after the introduction of Chinese "volunteers" into the conflict and at the

75th Meeting of the NSC, that the President approved a number of measures aimed at realizing the broad goals of NSC 68 "as a working guide for the urgent purpose of making an immediate start".[28] In this and in other ways a close examination of subsequent materials casts a somewhat different light on the conventional interpretation surrounding the issue of implementation. Herbert Feis, for example, entertained deep-seated doubts as to how far NSC 68 would have gone without the outbreak of the Korean War. Feis, who regarded the document as "the most ponderous expression of elementary ideas not very coherently expressed", recalled at Acheson's Princeton seminar:

> I don't think it [NSC 68] would have gotten very far without the attack, in Korea, despite the fact that it was signed [sic], just because it was being...nibbled to death by the ducks...the people in budget were cutting at it, people who were responsible for raising tax money were cutting at it....[29]

Atomic physicist, J. Robert Oppenheimer, also troubled by this relationship, asked the seminar point-blank, "What would have happened to it if the attack had not occurred in Korea?" No answer was forthcoming until one State official concerned with "selling" NSC 68 to the public conceded that "We were sweating over it, and then...thank God, Korea came along". Acheson was compelled to agree. Korea, he admitted, had absolutely nothing to do with NSC 68 "except to prove our thesis", creating "the structure which made action". None of the other participants, including Nitze (who has since had second thoughts on the subject)[30] disagreed at the time.

Scholars, however, are less than unanimous on the issue. Wells concluded that had Korea not intervened, "there is strong evidence to suggest that no major increase in defense spending would have won administration approval".[31] Less confident, Gaddis claimed that it would have been possible to increase defense expenditure without war, but it seems that the key to its success was the Korean war.[32] Similarly cautious, May conceded that had Korea not intervened, the budgetary struggle over the proposal may not have gone in favour of NSC 68. However he is quick to continue that while defense spending may not have tripled so promptly, "Truman would nevertheless have found it difficult, perhaps impossible, not to spend substantially more money for ready military power".[33] Yet Rearden has argued that even without Korea, there is strong evidence to suggest that Truman would have passed NSC 68. He suggested that withholding approval would have damaged the prestige and credibility of Acheson, possibly his most trusted and closest advisor, who had been intimately involved with the project. Although Rearden does concede that while financial increases were virtually assured, the Korean war insisted they were to the extent that Acheson had wanted.[34]

Such evidence, on the face of it, seriously challenges the traditional image of NSC 68 in the literature of the subject, the bulk of which until very recently portrayed the acceptance of the premises of NSC 68 as almost "instantaneous and complete", a veritable blueprint for waging the Cold War, "a policy in search of an opportunity".[35] Within this framework, then, this chapter will attempt to suggest NSC 68's actual place in the foreign policy debate that informed the first phase of what Walt Rostow once referred to as "the American diplomatic revolution" that occurred in Washington in the late 1940s and whose consequences shaped so much of American society.[36] Specifically, an attempt will be made to provide a reappraisal of the origin, meaning, and impact of NSC 68.

The intellectual origins of NSC 68 may best be traced back to the nation's first and, until recently, unheralded postwar national security review—the National Security Council 20 Series proposed by Secretary of Defense James Forrestal in July 1948. Against the background of budget preparations for Fiscal Year 1950, in the midst of a growing inter-service rivalry for limited funds, and assuming the Soviet Union to be the most likely enemy of the United States for some time to come, Forrestal reminded Truman that "Since the entire reason for the maintenance of military power in this country is the safeguarding of our national security, their size, character, and composition should turn upon a careful analysis by which such dangers can best be met within the limitations of our resources".[37] Forrestal contended that the Soviet threat should be faced squarely. On the one hand, continued the Secretary, "If the dangers are great, immediate and of military character, this fact should be clearly reflected in our military budget and our military strength adapted accordingly"; on the other hand, "If the risks are small, if they are distant rather than immediate, or if they are primarily of a non-military character, military estimates should be adjusted to accord with this situation". As a consequence of his own reading of international affairs and with the implications of the Soviet-inspired Berlin Blockade undoubtedly foremost in his mind, Forrestal held it "imperative that a comprehensive statement of national policy be prepared, particularly as it relates to Soviet Russia, and that this statement specify and evaluate the risks, state our objectives and outline the measures to be followed in achieving them". Pursuant to this request, the nation's first Secretary of Defense suggested that the initial statement of this character be prepared by State as a point of departure for further discussion within the National Security Council. While waiting to hear from the President, Forrestal passed on the memorandum, "Appraisal of the Degree and by the Character of Military Preparedness Required by the World Situation", to the NSC for its information and for preliminary consideration; and on 12 July 1948, it was distributed to members of the Council, taking on the designation of NSC 20.[38]

Truman responded to Forrestal, first, in a brief note dated July 13, with the observation that while he thought his memorandum most interesting, "It seems to me that the proper thing for you to do is to get the Army, Navy and Air people together and establish a program within the budget limits which have been allowed. It seems to me that is your responsibility".[39] Two days later, this time in the form of a letter, the President again responded to his Secretary's proposal of a national security review. Though personally approving of such a study, which had in fact been placed on the NSC agenda for July 15, Truman did not personally believe that the preparation of the initial 1950 budget estimates could be delayed or based wholly on this particular effort.[40] Within one month the Policy Planning Staff of the Department of State complied with Forrestal's request and produced a paper, "United States Objectives with Respect to Russia", and submitted it to the NSC for its information. Largely the work of George F. Kennan, NSC 20/1, as it came to be called, was the first of four papers that, taken together, comprised the nation's first significant postwar national security review.

Subtle, tough-minded, and cerebral, NSC 20/1 was pure Kennan. In an analysis devoted to the inner workings of the Kremlin, Kennan perceived America's basic objective with regard to Soviet Russia to be twofold: first, *"to reduce the power and influence of Moscow to limits in which they* [sic] *will no longer constitute a threat to the peace and stability of international society"*; and, second, *"to bring about a basic change in the theory and practice of international relations observed by the government in power in Russia"*.[41] If these objectives could be realized, Kennan argued, then the problem that the United States faced in its relations with the Soviet Union would be reduced to more normal dimensions. The father of Containment, so-called, was not hopeful, however, for, according to Kennan, as long as Soviet leaders continued to be "animated by the concepts of the theory and practice of international relations which are not only radically opposed to our own but are clearly inconsistent with any peaceful and mutually profitable development of relations between that government and other members of the international community", little, if anything, could be expected from them.[42] In fact, given "the relationship of antagonism", he added pessimistically, "war is an ever-present possibility and no course which this Government might adopt would appreciably diminish this danger".[43] This is not to say of course that Kennan regarded war as inevitable, for he did not. What he regarded as inevitable was, in his words, "the possibility of war, as something flowing logically and at all times from the present attitude of the Soviet leaders; and we have to prepare realistically for that eventuality".[44] Observing the stated desire of the Truman administration to achieve its objectives within a peaceful framework, Kennan highlighted the possibility of having to take a tougher stand. "Should we at any time", he argued, "come to the conclusion (which is not excluded) that this is really impossible and that relations between communist and non-communist worlds cannot proceed without eventual armed conflict, then the whole basis of this paper would be changed and our peacetime aims...would have to be basically altered".[45] Under what conditions and in what circumstances that time would come, was left unclear.

The second paper in the NSC 20 Series was submitted to the National Security Council by Kennan's Policy Planning Staff on August 25, 1948. Briefer and less philosophical than its predecessor, NSC 20/2 sought, essentially, "to clarify the factors bearing on the question as to the nature which the US defense effort should assume in the light of Soviet policies and attitudes (with particular relation to the question whether US defense preparations should be pointed to meet an expected conflict at a given probable time or whether they should be planned on a basis which they could and would be permanently maintained)".[46] Within this context, the report dealt at length with an analysis of the various factors militating *for* and *against* the likelihood of direct Soviet military action in the immediate period ahead. Among the factors indicating planned Soviet action, according to Kennan, was the belief of Soviet leaders that "their military strength will never again stand in so favorable relationship to the military strength of the western powers"; this, together with the adverse prospect of European recovery, might well tempt the Kremlin "to resort to armed action in the West and to ensure an immediate extension of communist power in that region, as a means of defending Soviet power in Eastern Europe".[47] There were, on the other hand, a number of factors that could well give the Soviets pause. Among these the most prominent were Soviet uncertainty as to "dealing a decisive blow to the North American military-industrial potential in the initial phase" of conflict, "the war-weariness of the Soviet peoples", and the Kremlin's strong traditional preference for political means as opposed to direct military action.[48] Thus, in line with contemporary Central Intelligence estimates,[49] the Policy Planning Staff concluded "that the Soviet Government is not now planning any deliberate armed action of this nature and is still seeking to achieve its aims predominantly by political means, accompanied—of course—by the factor of military intimidation".[50] Nonetheless, the report made allowance for error and miscalculation leading to war. As Soviet tactics tended to heighten the danger that military complications could lead to hostilities, the prospect of war had therefore to "be regarded, if not as a probability, at least as a possibility, and one serious enough to be taken account of fully in our military and political planning".

A second major aspect of NSC 20/2, and one perhaps that sheds the greatest light on NSC 68, examined the extent to which Soviet intentions were apt to be influenced by the successful development of an atomic capability in the USSR. Significantly, Kennan's Policy Planning Staff asserted at the time that political factors alone would probably "militate against use of the atomic weapon by the Soviet Government and against major urban and industrial areas in other countries, *except by way of retaliation for attacks made on Russia*".[51] According to State Department estimates, it was thought doubtful that the Soviet Union would choose to resort to atomic warfare in Western Europe, its basic aim principally being that of a concealed political domination over the area rather than its destruction. Echoing the theme of deterrence inherent in the President's Air Policy Commission Study (the Finletter Report) released earlier in the year, NSC 20/2 maintained persuasively that "If the Soviet leaders felt that there would be a strong probability of retaliation, this would be an important factor in dissuading them from taking the initiative in the use of atomic weapons against western cities".[52] From another level, however, the report added, the mere existence of America's atomic monopoly had heretofore probably been the principal contributing factor to continued Soviet intransigence in the field of international control of atomic energy and other related matters. The reason and remedy—in contrast to the grimmer pictures yet to be painted in NSC 68—bear repeating in full:

> To the Soviet mind it is unthinkable that we, [the United States] enjoying this factor of military superiority are not taking it into account our plans and attempting to exploit it for political purposes. They therefore must assume that our international positions, particularly in matters of the control of atomic energy, are predicted on this superiority and contain a margin of excessive demand, which would not be there if a better balance existed in the power of disposal over the weapon. *For this reason, they may actually prove to be more tractable in negotiation when they have gained some measure of disposal over the weapon, and no longer feel that they are negotiating at so great a disadvantage.*[53]

In this sense, then, reasoned Kennan, "It is *not* probable that the pattern of Soviet intentions...would be appreciably altered in the direction of greater aggressiveness by the development of the atomic weapon in Russia".[54]

In any event, NSC 20/2 recommended a high level of American readiness as the only safeguard against potential Soviet hostilities. It could hardly be otherwise. For, according to the prevailing American Cold War paradigm, "In dealing with a Government so highly centralized, so incorrigibly conspirational in its methods, so hostile traditionally towards its world environment, and so unpredictable in foreign affairs, it is necessary that we keep ourselves in a state of unvacillating mental (and military) preparedness". Nothing in the foreseeable period ahead appeared likely to alter the situation. "We must reckon", continued Kennan on a final note, "that the necessity for the maintenance of armed forces as a deterrent will continue undiminished as long as the Soviet power, as we know it today, continues to be dominant in Russia, and probably longer". Translated in political terms, "the only safe deduction", concluded Kennan, "would be that for at least the next five or ten years we will require such an establishment as would make it possible for us to wage war if it should be forced upon us".[55]

Prepared by the staff of the National Security Council with the advice and assistance of representatives of the Department of State,

the Army, the Navy and the Air Force, the National Security
Resources Board, and the Central Intelligence Agency, the third and
last paper in the NSC 20 Series was submitted to the National
Security Council for its consideration on November 2, 1948. Titled
"US Objectives with Respect to the USSR to Counter Soviet Threats
to US Security", NSC 20/3 contained a summary of observations
and conclusions flowing from the analyses prepared beforehand. At
its twenty-seventh meeting on November 23, 1948, the NSC
adopted NSC 20/4—and not only recommended the conclusions
contained therein but directed that "the report be disseminated to all
appropriate officials of the US Government for their information and
guidance". The President responded favourably the following day
and on November 24, 1948, NSC 20/4 with its doctrine of
Containment writ large became the official policy of the Truman
Administration.[56]

The assumption that underlay the final analysis again clearly
revealed the hand of Kennan and the Policy Planning Staff. "The
will and ability of the leaders of the USSR to pursue policies which
threaten the security of the United States", NSC 20/4 began,
continued to "constitute the greatest single danger to the US within
the foreseeable future", the ultimate objective of the Kremlin being
nothing less than "the domination of the world".[57] Though the
immediate goal of Soviet leaders appeared to be the political
conquest of Western Europe, the Soviet Union would not feel secure
until the non-communist nations had been so reduced in strength and
numbers that communist influence was dominant throughout the
world. Seen in this light the immediate purpose and the ultimate
objective of the Soviet leaders could only be seen to be inimical to
the safety of the United States and would continue to be so
indefinitely. Militarily, the Soviet ability to wage war grew
unabated. "In present circumstances", warned NSC 20/4 ominously,
"the capabilities of the USSR to threaten US security by the use of
armed power are dangerous and immediate".[58] Though not in a
position to deliver a decisive blow either against the US or the
Western Hemisphere, the Soviet Union was nevertheless thought
fully capable of serious submarine warfare and of a limited number
of one-way bomber sorties. Within a matter of years, it was
estimated, the Soviet war machine would be in a better position from
which to attack the United States. "Present estimates indicate", the
top secret document averred, "that the current Soviet
capabilities…will progressively increase and that by no later than

1955 the USSR will probably be capable of serious air attack against the United States with atomic, biological and chemical weapons, of more extensive submarine operations (including the launching of short-range guided missiles), and of airborne operations to seize advance bases".[59]

But theorizing about "the year of maximum danger" was one thing; assessing with any degree of certainty whether or not or when the Kremlin's present political strategy would in point of fact shift to that of armed conflict, was another. Thus NSC 20/4 concluded that "While the *possibility* of planned Soviet actions which involve this country cannot be ruled out, a careful weighing of the various factors points to the *probability* that the Soviet Government is not now planning any deliberate armed action calculated to involve the United States and is still seeking to achieve its aims primarily by political means, accompanied (of course) by military intimidation".[60] America's foreign policy mandate was clear: the reduction of the power and influence of the USSR to manageable limits and effecting a basic change in the Soviet conduct of international relations so as to bring it more in line with the purpose and principles envisaged in the United Nations Charter. It would remain the task of NSC 68, in the words of its main author Paul H. Nitze, "in getting from general objectives (of the NSC 20 Series) to the details of what the problem was and how to get from where you were to where you want to go".[61]

There is no question that Nitze drew heavily on the analyses of his predecessor on the Policy Planning Staff of the Soviet political and military threat. Numerous references throughout NSC 68 underscored the continuing relevance and validity of the conclusions reached in the NSC 20 Series in general and in NSC 20/4 in particular. The Soviet threat was still perceived to be that "of the same character as that described in NSC 20/4". What had radically altered in a period of approximately one year was Washington's perception of "the immediacy of the danger". "The growing intensity of the conflict which has been imposed upon us", wrote Nitze, "requires the changes of emphasis and additions that are apparent; coupled with the probable fission bomb capability and possible thermonuclear bomb capability of the Soviet Union, the intensifying struggle requires us to face the fact that we can expect no lasting abatement of the crisis *unless and until a change occurs in the nature of the Soviet system*".[62] This was a theme that would appear over and over again.

Before all else, the newly-appointed Director of the Policy Planning Staff sought to delineate the motives of the Kremlin and in doing so develop a thesis that would carry the burden of the arguments and subsequent recommendations enumerated in NSC 68. Working from the central premise of the NSC 20 Series, that "Communist ideology and Soviet behaviour clearly demonstrate that the ultimate objective of the leaders of the USSR is the domination of the world", Nitze tried to order the Kremlin's priorities. At this point he came in direct collision with Charles E. Bohlen, the Russian expert from the State Department. While Bohlen agreed that "American military power be increased so as to be more commensurate with commitments forced on us in the world", he did not agree to the extent that Nitze had proposed, nor did he believe that extensive budget increases would be adopted. However, his major confrontation with Nitze pertained to Nitze's efforts to prioritise Soviet objectives. Bohlen insisted that the "fundamental design of those who control the USSR is (a) the maintenance of their regime in the Soviet Union, and (b) its extension throughout the world to the degree that is possible without serious risk to the internal regime".[63] His objection was that NSC 68 gave too much emphasis to Soviet ambitions for expansion. Nitze countered that the Soviet Union's doctrinaire leaders were largely governed by fears of American atomic power,[64] or so it seemed. Bohlen wrote Nitze that NSC 68 "simplifies the problem". As with Kennan, Nitze attributed Bohlen's differences to his ignorance of military capability. Yet Nitze did concede to some extent. He made changes that he considered to be purely cosmetic, but which Bohlen had insisted upon. Nitze wrote, "The fundamental design of those who control the Soviet Union and the influential communist movement, is to retain and solidify their absolute power, first in the Soviet Union and second in areas now under their control". However to effect this goal, he continued, "requires the dynamic extension of their authority and the ultimate elimination of any effective opposition to their authority". After much debate with Bohlen[65] he elaborated:

> The design...calls for the complete subversion or forcible destruction of the machinery of government and structure of society in the countries of the non-Soviet world and their replacement by an apparatus and structure subservient to and controlled from the Kremlin. To that end Soviet efforts are now directed toward the domination of the Eurasian land mass.

It followed, then, that the United States, as the principal center of power in the non-Soviet world and the bulwark of opposition to Soviet expansion, "is the principal enemy whose integrity and vitality must be subverted or destroyed by one means or another if the Kremlin is to achieve its fundamental design".[66]

At the heart of the Cold War, Nitze argued, lay the underlying, fundamental conflict in the realm of ideas and values. "There is", he wrote, "a basic conflict between the idea of freedom under a government of laws, and the idea of slavery under the grim oligarchy of the Kremlin, which has come to a crisis under the polarization of power (created by the aftermath of World War II)...and the exclusive possession of atomic weapons by the two protagonists". In Nitze's clearly defined perception of the world, freedom was seen as subversive of slavery although the reverse was not necessarily true. In a free society, the individual has "the positive responsibility to make constructive use of his freedom in the building of a just society", and welcomes diversity. A free society, Nitze continued "derives its strength from its hospitality even to antipathetic ideas". In a real sense, it is "a market for free trade in ideas, secure in its faith that free men will take the best wares, and grow to a fuller and better realization of their powers in exercising their choice". Nitze, adhering to the concept of the presumed indivisibility of war and peace that had been popular among anti-appeasers in the 1930s, postulated that in current circumstances a defeat of free institutions anywhere constituted a defeat everywhere, the most recent case having been the destruction of Czechoslovakia in February, 1948. Acknowledging that in the material sense Czechoslovak capabilities were already at the disposal of the Soviets, Nitze lamented that "when the integrity of Czechoslovak institutions was destroyed, it was in the intangible sense of values that we registered a loss more damaging than the material loss (which) we had already suffered".[67] Such sentiments characterized the Cold War mentality for much of the next generation.

Perhaps more important than the Soviet threat to American values, according to Nitze, was the growing Soviet threat to the nation's capability to protect its material environment. "Thus", he went on to explain, "we must make ourselves strong, both in the way we affirm our values in the conduct of our national life, and in the development of our military and economic strength". The United States must lead the way "in building a successfully functioning political and economic system in the free world", accepting without hesitation "the responsibility of world leadership". The strategy, which treated the USSR as an ideology in the possession of a state, was eminently simple: "It is only by developing the moral and material strength of the free world that the Soviet regime will become convinced of the falsity of its assumptions and that the pre-conditions for workable agreements can be reached". In other words, "by practically demonstrating the integrity and vitality of our system the free world widens the area of possible agreement and thus can hope gradually to bring about a Soviet acknowledgment of realities which in sum will eventually constitute a frustration of the Soviet design". Short of this goal, however, Nitze conceded that "it might be possible to create a situation which will induce the Soviet Union to accommodate itself, with or without the conscious abandonment of its design, to coexistence on tolerable terms with the non-Soviet world".[68]

The Soviet Union could only be checked by employing a policy of containment, the rough intellectual outlines of which had been developed by George Kennan during and immediately after the war. As interpreted by Nitze, containment meant essentially a policy that sought "by all means short of war to (1) block further expansion of Soviet power, (2) expose the falsities of the Soviet pretensions, (3) induce a retraction of the Kremlin's control and influence, and (4) in general, to foster the seeds of destruction within the Soviet system [so] that the Kremlin is brought at least to the point of modifying its behaviour to conform to generally accepted international standards".[69] A key feature of containment envisaged the United States dealing with the Soviets from the position of strength. "In the concept of 'containment', "noted Nitze, "the maintenance of a strong military posture is an ultimate guarantee of national security and as an indispensable backdrop to the conduct of the policy of containment". To Nitze, there was no substitute for the maintenance of superior force: "Without superior aggregate military strength, in being ready and mobilizable, a policy of 'containment'—which is in effect a policy of calculated or gradual coercion—is no more than a bluff".[70] Negotiations were not to be ruled out, however, for "a diplomatic feeze...tends to defeat the very purpose of 'containment' because it raises tensions at the same time that it makes Soviet retraction of moderated behaviour more difficult"; conversely, it tends "to inhibit our initiative and deprive us of opportunities for maintaining a moral ascendancy in our struggle with the Soviet system".[71] Moreover, he thought it desirable not to challenge Soviet prestige directly, for this would keep open "the possibility for the USSR to retreat before pressure with a minimum loss of face and to secure political advantage from the failure of the Kremlin to yield or take advantage of the openings we leave it". This was one negotiating technique that policymakers of various political persuasions could generally agree upon as most likely to produce results.

The greatest factor, or course, in Washington's changed perception of "the immediacy of the danger" ahead was the recent Soviet acquisition of the atomic bomb. NSC 68 "estimated that within the next four years, the USSR will attain the capability of seriously damaging vital centers of the United States, *provided it strikes a first blow and provides further that the blow is opposed by no more effective opposition than we now have programmed*".[72] Interestingly, and generally overlooked by students of NSC 68, is the almost casual manner in which the new presidential review of national security replaced Kennan's previous assumption that it was "*not* probable that the pattern of Soviet intentions...would be appreciably altered in the direction of greater aggressiveness by the development of the atomic weapon in Russia" with Nitze's presumption of a Soviet first-strike mentality. Furthermore, though Nitze persisted in the belief that the present American atomic retaliatory capability was probably adequate to deter the Soviets from launching a direct military attack against the United States, he warned that the time was fast approaching when it would not be so. "When it calculates", wrote Nitze of the Soviet Union, "that it has a sufficient atomic capability to make a surprise attack on us, nullifying our atomic superiority and creating a military situation decisively in its favor, the Kremlin might be tempted to strike swiftly and with stealth: Taking a page straight out of Pierrepont B. Noyes' apparently influential and prophetic story of a once-great civilization destroyed by atomic weapons, first published in 1927,[73] Nitze contended that the mere existence of more than one superpower was in itself inherently destabilizing. "The existence of two large atomic capabilities in such a relationship", observed Ronald Reagan's future arms control negotiator, "might well act, therefore, not as a deterrent", as generally thought, "but as an incitement to war"; put another way, Nitze had come to fear Soviet fear.[74] In these circumstances the United States had little choice but to increase both its atomic and, if feasible, its thermonuclear capabilities[75] as rapidly as possible. In addition, such measures as greatly increased warning systems, air defenses, and a civil defense program would be required.

While Nitze reported to the Policy Planning Staff in January 1950 that he believed that the possibility of Soviet aggression had increased and the chance of war was "considerably greater than last fall",[76] his predecessor, George F. Kennan did not. Before leaving for South America in February 1950, Kennan prepared a final memorandum to Acheson and the PPS. "There is little justification for the impression that the 'cold war', by virtue of events outside of our control, has suddenly taken some drastic turn to our disadvantage". The fall of China was "the culmination of processes which have long been apparent." The Soviet acquisition of the A-bomb "likewise adds no new fundamental element to the picture". Neither, he believed, did the H-bomb. "In so far as we feel ourselves in heightened trouble at the present moment, that feeling is largely of our making".[77] The point of departure between Kennan and Nitze was over the deterrence value of the atomic bomb in light of the Soviet acquisition. Nitze believed that Soviet atomic capabilities would increase Soviet risk taking as well as compromising US willingness to risk nuclear war over limited issues. Kennan argued that the Soviets would not attack unless provoked and took offence to the increasing military nature that the containment policy was taking. "What is necessary to win a war", Kennan stressed, "is not the same as what is necessary to deter an aggressor from waging war".[78] Yet Kennan's insistence on the continuity of Soviet foreign policy did not gather many adherents in the State Department. Kennan later complained of Nitze, "Paul was in one sense like a child.... He loved anything that could be reduced to numbers. He was mesmerized by them.... He had no feeling for the intangibles-values, intentions. Where there was talk of intentions, as opposed to capabilities, he would say, 'How can you measure intentions? We can't be bothered to get into psychology; we have to face the Russians as competitors, militarily".[79] Apparently Nitze was not prepared to gamble on Kennan's interpretation of Soviet foreign policy. The military-orientation of NSC 68 marked the discarding of Kennan's views by Nitze.

In the area of international control of atomic energy, Nitze perceived the prospect of improvement as negligible. Nitze, an expert on strategic bombing and already a keen student of nuclear strategy, entertained serious reservations that any kind of international control agreement could really prevent the production and employment of atomic weapons in a prolonged war. Equally important and years before satellite surveillance, it was doubted whether any system could be designed that would give certainty of notice of violation in the absence of good faith. "Finally", NSC 68 observed on the virtue of what came to be called linkage, "the absence of good faith on the part of the USSR must be assumed until there is concrete evidence that there has been a decisive change in Soviet policies".[80] And even here, it was highly problematical whether such a change could take place without the much sought change in the nature of the Soviet system itself. Accordingly, Nitze warned against apparent Soviet willingness to negotiate agreements on the control of atomic energy, for it would surely "result in a relatively greater disarmament of the United States than of the Soviet Union, even assuming considerable progress in building up the strength of the free world in conventional forces and weapons."[81] In fact, he went on, "It might be accepted by the Soviet Union as part of a deliberate design to move against Western Europe and other areas of strategic importance with conventional forces and weapons"; as a result, "the United States would find itself at war, having previously disarmed itself in its most important weapons, and would be engaged in a race to redevelop atomic weapons". Such was the dilemma of distrust.

The Soviet possession of atomic weapons, reasoned Nitze, had the dual effect not only of putting a premium on a more violent and ruthless prosecution of the Kremlin's design of world conquest, "especially if the Kremlin is sufficiently objective to realize the improbability of our prosecuting a preventive war", but also of putting "a premium on piecemeal aggression against others, counting on our unwillingness to engage in atomic war unless we are directly attacked".[82] Thus what advantages had presumably accrued to America's atomic monopoly had now been dissipated; the Soviets, too, could play the game.

As is well-known, NSC 68 distinguished four possible courses of action open to the United States: (a) continuation of current policies, with current and currently projected programs for carrying out these policies; (b) isolation; (c) "preventative" war; or (d) a rapid build-up of political, economic, and military strength in the free world.

Nitze postulated that "on the basis of current programs the United States has a large potential military capability but an actual capability which, though improving, is declining relative to the USSR, particularly in light of the probable fission bomb capability and possible thermonuclear bomb capability". Moreover, he continued, "a review of Soviet policy shows that the military capabilities, actual and potential of the United States, together with the apparent determination of the free world to resist further Soviet expansion, have not induced the Kremlin to relax its pressure generally or to give up the initiative of the cold war". In fact, the opposite seemed to be true because "the Soviet Union has consistently pursued a bold foreign policy, modified only when its probing revealed a determination and an ability of the free world to resist encroachment upon it". Unfortunately, Nitze conceded, "the relative military capabilities of the free world are declining, with the result that its determination to resist may also decline and that the security of the United States and the free world as a whole will be jeopardised". Consequently, "from the military point of view, the actual and potential capabilities of the United States, given a continuation of current and projected programs, will become less and less effective as a war deterrent". Thus, Nitze went on to emphasize, "improvement of the state of readiness will become more and more important not only to inhibit the launching of war by the Soviet Union but also to support a national policy designed to reverse the present ominous trends in international relations".[83]

Particularly threatening in this regard was the Soviet development of an atomic capability. Nitze held that the Soviet Union's acquisition of the atomic bomb, together with Communist successes in China, "led to an increasing confidence on its part and to an increasing nervousness in Western Europe and the rest of the free world", especially as Washington could not be sure of the strengths or weaknesses of the other free countries reacting to it. Keeping in mind Russia's atomic option Nitze also suggested that the free world was inadequately equipped to check Soviet or Soviet-inspired conventional forces in a small war. "The free world", he wrote, "lacks adequate means to thwart such expansion locally". Accordingly, "the United States will therefore be confronted more frequently with the dilemma of reacting totally to a limited extension of Soviet control or of not reacting at all (except with ineffectual protests and half measures)". The continuation of such trends, Nitze concluded would most likely "lead...to a gradual withdrawal under the direct or indirect pressure of the Soviet Union until we discover one day that we have sacrificed positions of vital interests".[84] Nitze recognized that a return to isolationism was a possible second course of action. "There are those", he wrote, "who advocate a deliberate decision to isolate ourselves".[85] He concluded that isolation did in fact evidence "some attractiveness as a course of action, for it appears to bring our commitments and capabilities into harmony by reducing the former and by concentrating our present, or perhaps even reduced, military expenditures on the defense of the United States". Nitze argued that such thinking overlooked what he called "the relativity of capabilities".[86] For instance, he observed, "with the United States in an isolated position, we could have to face the probability that the Soviet Union would quickly dominate most of Eurasia, probably without meeting armed resistance"; at that juncture, the USSR "would thus acquire a potential far superior to our own and would promptly proceed to develop this potential with the purpose of eliminating our power, which would, even in isolation, remain as an obstacle to the imposition of its kind of order in the world". Put another way, Nitze in a manner reminiscent of George Kennan, remarked "there is no way to make ourselves inoffensive to the Kremlin except by complete submission to its will", a position that ultimately condemned "us to capitulate or to fight alone on the defensive, with drastically limited offensive and retaliatory capabilities in comparison with the Soviet Union". If the United States followed such a policy, Nitze would come to favor a preemptive strike against the Soviet Union and its satellites, "in a desperate attempt to alter decisively the balance of power". Yet according to NSC 68, it was "unlikely that the Soviet Union would wait for such an attack before launching one of its own". In any case, if such a surprise attack were successful it would hardly be worth the candle as "the United States would face appalling tasks in establishing a tolerable state of order among nations after such a war and after Soviet occupation of all or most of Eurasia".

Nitze then proceeded to expand on a preventive war as the third course of action open to America. Noting that "some Americans favor a deliberate decision to go to war against the Soviet Union in the near future", Nitze believed that it went "without saying that the idea of 'preventive' war—in the sense of a military attack not provoked by a military attack upon us or our allies—is generally unacceptable to Americans".[87] Conceding the plausibility of a case for a first strike, Nitze countered that there were other factors to consider. For example, it was doubtful that a surprise attack could alone "force or induce the Kremlin to capitulate and that the Kremlin would still be able to use the forces under its control to dominate most or all of Eurasia". In the process, he added, "this would probably mean a long and difficult struggle during which the free institutions of Western Europe and many freedom-loving people would be destroyed and the regenerative capacity of Western Europe dealt a crippling blow". Aside from this, Nitze went on to say:

> A surprise attack upon the Soviet Union, despite the provocativeness of recent Soviet behaviour, would be repugnant to many Americans. Although the American people would probably rally in support of the war effort, the shock of responsibility for a surprise attack would be morally corrosive. Many would doubt that it was a "just war" and that all reasonable possibilities for a peaceful settlement had been explored in good faith. Many more, proportionately, would hold such views in other countries, particularly in Western Europe and particularly after Soviet occupation, if only because the Soviet Union would liquidate articulate opponents. It would, therefore, be difficult after such a war to create a satisfactory international order among nations. Victory in such a war would have brought us little if at all closer to victory in the fundamental ideological conflict.

Having thus made a case against a preemptive strike, Nitze emphasized that the Soviets should be left in no doubt that the United States would not hesitate to use any weapons at its disposal in a critical situation.[88]

Confident that the United States had a large unactualized military capability, though persuaded it alone could not provide the resources, Nitze chose the last course, the case for "A more rapid build-up of political, economic, and military strength and thereby of confidence in the free world than is now contemplated...the only course which is consistent with our fundamental purpose".[89] Specifically, he added, "The frustration of the Kremlin design requires the free world to develop a successfully functioning political and economic system and a vigorous political offensive against the Soviet Union", which, "in turn, requires an adequate military shield under which they can develop". Above all, "It is necessary to have the military power to deter, if possible, Soviet expansion, and to defeat, if necessary, aggressive Soviet or Soviet-directed actions of a limited total character". Only such a program, concluded NSC 68 hopefully, could "postpone and avert the disastrous situation which, in light of the Soviet Union's probable fission bomb capability and possible thermonuclear bomb capability, might arise in 1954 on a continuation of our present programs"; accordingly, "by acting promptly and vigorously in such a way that this date is, so to speak, pushed into the future, we would permit time for the process of accommodation, withdrawal and frustration to produce the necessary changes in the Soviet system".[90] Thus ended the presidential reexamination of American objectives in peace and war. The only question remaining was how best to implement it.

Contrary to the view that President Truman and the National Security Council officially "approved"[91] the document for implementation in April 1950, NSC 68 had as yet a long road to travel. Comments on the draft were requested from atomic physicists Chester Barnard, Henry Smyth, J. Robert Oppenheimer, James B. Conant, Ernest Lawrence, and under Secretary of State Robert Lovett. Only Oppenheimer and Conant raised serious objections to the draft. While he accepted the need for an increased defense effort, Oppenheimer called for a shift away from "complete dependence on the atomic bomb" and expressed concern at the high level of government secrecy regarding technical information. He also exhibited concern at the unanswered questions regarding the stockpiling and control of nuclear weapons and the interpretation of the Soviet Union, questioning if it actually was such a clear distinction between "jet black and pure white". James Conant, President of Harvard University, believed that the US had set its sights "much too high" arguing instead for some kind of accommodation with the Soviet Union and its satellites. He also called for greater emphasis on land forces and tactical air power rather than strategic air power.[92] Nitze considered Oppenheimer and Conant's concerns as "peripheral issues" and believed that Conant's suggestion to put one million troops in Europe to avoid reliance on atomic weapons to be unrealistic considering Conant proposed to keep the troops there indefinitely.[93]

Perhaps the most difficult obstacle was newly appointed Secretary of Defense, Louis Johnson. The President was determined to hold down the defense budget at 12.5 billion. The ambitious Johnson had been appointed with that brief and he considered fulfilment of that to be his means of obtaining the Democratic Presidential nomination when Truman stepped down. Nitze recalled that Johnson had objected to the review all along, "probably because he knew that such a review would undermine his credibility by exposing critical deficiencies in our military posture".[94] While the Secretary of State had been appraised daily on the goup's work, the Secretary of Defense claimed in a meeting on March 22nd that he had only just received the report and refused to participate in the meeting claiming to be the victim of a State Department conspiracy against him. Later, however, Johnson saw little option but to add his approval to the report after recognizing that most of the Pentagon and many of the physicists backed Nitze. Nitze recalled, "Johnson may have suffered from numerous defects of character, but he knew when he was beaten; in this instance he tried to make the best of the situation by adding his approval to the report and by recommending that Mr Truman accept it".[95]

State Department representatives most concerned with securing Congressional support of the broad analysis contained in NSC 68 had initially hoped, in the words of one of them, to make "public a large part of it, taking it out of the Top Secret category, and making it general knowledge".[96] Or, as Nitze put it: "the essential issue was whether the President would authorize us to make available to the public a vetted version of the argumentation which was in the paper, because it was perfectly clear that you weren't going to get even a seventeen or eighteen or twenty billion dollar appropriation and the kind of a program which could be financed thereby, unless you made available to the public at least the substance, having excluded the really secure elements of the argumentation which were in the paper, and we couldn't get the President's approval of that...". Truman, for reasons of his own, retained for himself sole responsibility for any disclosure of the document. "It is requested", noted the Executive Secretary of the NSC of the President's request, "that this report be handled with special security precautions in accordance with the President's desire that no publicity be given this report or its contents without his approval".[97] In retrospect, Truman's decision to keep the entirety of NSC 68 from Congress was probably a mistake. Nitze has himself estimated that only a single paragraph in NSC 68—the American intelligence community's crude four-year projection of the Soviet Union's fission bomb production capability—fell into the category of "secret information"; and, even here, Oppenheimer believed it was "not a cardinal one percent".[98]

While Truman perhaps did not disagree with the intellectual framework of the report, he was primarily concerned with the fiscal issues. The budgetary implications of NSC 68 were deliberately unclear. Five days later Truman passed the unsigned report on to the NSC for further review, he wrote: "I am particularly anxious that the Council provide me with clear indication of the programs which are envisaged in the Report, including estimates of the probable costs of such programs".[99] Acheson recalled in his memoirs, "NSC 68 lacked, as submitted, any section discussing costs. This was not an oversight. To have attempted one would have made impossible all those concurrences and prevented any recommendation to the President".[100] Acheson wanted to get the President and the top bureaucracy "signed-on" before he went to the Congress and the people. Including a figure such as 40 billion dollars would have doomed the document. Nitze, who initially wanted to include this estimated figure, recalled a warning from Acheson, "Paul, don't put any such figure into this report. It is right for you to estimate it and to tell me about it, and I will tell Mr Truman, but the decision on the amount of money to be requested of the Congress should not be made until it has been costed out in detail".[101]

In the ad hoc interagency committee designed to assess the budgetary implications of NSC 68, representatives from the Bureau of Budget and Council of Economic Advisors inflicted serious attacks on the document. A deadlock was forming and it seemed that NSC 68 would not survive. Only the North Korean invasion of South Korea on 25 June 1950, ultimately solved the problem of how best to sell NSC 68. Without the communist attack, which was not altogether unanticipated,[102] it is probably safe to conclude, along with Herbert Feis, that the proposed rearmament program would have been nibbled to death by the bureaucratic ducks.

As noted, it was not until 30 September 1950 that the President and the National Security Council actually "adopted the Conclusions of NSC 68 as a statement of policy to be followed over the next four or five years". It was also agreed at that time that the implementing programs would be put into effect as rapidly as feasible, with the understanding that the specific nature and estimated costs of these programs were to be decided as they were more firmly developed.[103] During the next several months the NSC Staff, with the assistance of representatives of the relevant departments and agencies participating in the NSC 68 project, revised an earlier action paper that had also been prepared in September but had been deferred for further study. On December 14, 1950, at its 75th meeting, with Truman presiding, the National Security Council together with the Secretaries of the Treasury and of Commerce, the Economic Cooperation Administrator, the Director of the Bureau of Budget, and the Chairman of the Council of Economic Advisers approved the final draft on the subject (NSC 68/4) "as a working guide for the urgent purpose of making an immediate start".[104] And, again, Truman evidenced special caution with regard to the manner with which the report was to be handled.[105]

Briefly, "United States Objectives and Programs for National Security" or NSC 68/4 began with the assumption that "The invasion of the Republic of Korea by the North Korean Communists imparted (yet) a new urgency to the appraisal of the nature, timing, and scope of programs required to attain the objectives outlined in NSC 68".[106] Furthermore, it went on to say that the substantial intervention of Mao's "volunteers" in late November "had created a new crisis and a situation of great danger;" consequently, "Our military build-up must be rapid because the period of greatest danger is directly before us". The several programs described in NSC 68/4 were conceived as mutually dependent; and, in agreement with the underlying concept of NSC 68, they represented an effort to achieve, under the shield of a military build-up, an integrated political, economic, and psychological offensive design to counter the current threat to the national security posed by the Soviet Union. Among the report's numerous directives, none loomed larger than accelerating the nation's military build up. "It is evident", underscored the document, "that the forces envisaged earlier for 1954 must be provided as an interim program as rapidly as practicable with a target date of no later than June 30, 1952". Other goals dealt, inter alia, with such matters as civilian defense, stockpiling of strategic and critical materials, the uses of psychological warfare, intelligence activities, and the internal security situation. In this way, then, and at an estimated cost of hundreds of billions of dollars—projections reaching "a peak annual rate of 70 billion dollars during the second half of the Fiscal Year 1952, or about 25 per cent of total national output"[107]—the implementation of the conclusions reached in NSC 68 was soon to be realized.

In summary, this chapter suggests that the basic American strategic position taken toward the USSR in NSC 68 in 1950 had, with minor modifications, remained relatively unchanged from that taken in late 1948 in the wake of the Berlin crisis. The only appreciable, though most dramatic, change in those years—if the NSC 20 Series may serve as a guide—was the Truman Administration's shift in perception of the Soviet acquisition of the atomic bomb which, with its presumed first-strike character, led to the decision to pursue further the feasibility of a thermonuclear bomb, though no one knew for certain what it would cost let alone look like. Equally significant, the available evidence indicates that the case for the direct relationship between the recommendations contained in NSC 68 and the final United States commitment to the UN police action in Korea is, at best, tenuous. The views of policymakers such as Truman, General Omar N. Bradley, Chairman of the Join Chiefs of Staff, and Admiral Forrest P. Sherman, Chief of Naval Operations, as to the origin of the decision to draw the line against perceived communist imperialism make it probable that Korea was more likely an opportunity in search of a policy rather than vice versa.[108] Those who argue what might be called the "action significance"[109] of NSC 68 tend to fall into the classical historical trap of *post hoc, ergo proper hoc.* Finally, and in response to Ernest R. May's question, "Is NSC 68 a timeless example of reason-of-state reasoning, or is it a document peculiar to a democratic system, perhaps peculiar to the American system, clanging alarm bells so as to catch the attention of politicians and couching appeals in terms that tap deep-rooted emotions?", my money is on the latter.

## NOTES

1. NSC 68, A Report to the National Security Council, "United States Objectives and Programs for National Security," Apr. 14, 1950, p. 3, President's Secretary's File (PSF), Papers of Harry S. Truman, Harry S. Truman Library, Independence, Missouri (Hereaftercited as NSC 68). Also see, Harry S. Truman, *The Memoirs of Harry S. Truman: Years of Trial and Hope 1946-1953* (London, 1956), 2: p. 326; and "Report by the Special Committee of the National Security Council to the President," Jan. 31, 1950, Department of State, *Foreign Relations of the United States: 1950* (Washington, 1977), pp. 513-23. (Hereafter this source will be cited as *FRUS.*) The Soviet atomic bomb test, 29 Aug. 1949, was of the plutonium type. David Holloway, *Stalin and the Bomb: The Soviet Union and Atomic Energy, 1939-1956* (New Haven, 1994), pp. 196-223.

2. The "Terms of the Reference" were framed by Nitze. Interview with Paul H. Nitze, Center for National Security Research, Arlington, Virginia, Apr. 29, 1977. Also see, "Memorandum by the Director of the Policy Planning Staff (Nitze) to the Secretary of State," Jan. 17, 1950, *FRUS: 1950*, 1: pp. 13-17.

3. NSC 68/1. The National Security Council met again on April 20 and agreed that an ad hoc committee should be constituted to prepare a response to the President's directive. Minutes of the 55th Meeting of the National Security Council, PSF, Papers of Harry S. Truman, Truman Library.

4. NSC 68 was declassified by Secretary of State Henry Kissinger in his capacity as Assistant to the President for National Security on Feb. 27, 1975. An official version of the text of NSC 68—minus its terms of reference was published shortly thereafter in *Naval War College Review* 27:6 (May-June 1975): 53-108. May has argued that NSC 68 was declassified to rescue Nitze's 1975 nomination for assistant secretary of defense for international security affairs. Nixon sought to placate conservative Republicans who believed Nitze advocated unilateral disarmament under Kennedy. See Ernest R. May, ed, *American Cold War Strategy: Interpreting NSC 68* (Boston, 1993), p. 19; *New York Times*, 22 Mar. 1974.

5. Paul Y. Hammond, "NSC 68: Prologue to Rearmament," in *Strategy, Politics and Defense Budgets*, ed. by Warner R. Schilling, Paul Y. Hammond, and Glenn H. Synder (New York, 1962), p. 314. Also see Samuel P. Huntington's *The Common Defense: Strategic Programs in National Politics* (New York, 1961), pp. 47-64.

6. Cabell Phillips, *The Truman Presidency: The History of a Triumphant Succession* (New York, 1966), p. 308.

7. Walter LaFeber, *America, Russia, and the Cold War, 1945-1966* (1st ed., New York, 1967), pp. 90-91; and *America, Russia and the Cold War, 1945-1975* (3rd ed., New York, 1976), p. 97.

8. Gaddis Smith, *Dean Acheson* (New York, 1972), p. 161.

9. Ernest R. May, *American Cold War Strategy*, p. vii.

10. Strobe Talbott, *The Master of the Game, Paul Nitze and the Nuclear Peace* (New York, 1988), p. 55.

11. Paul H. Nitze (with Ann M. Smith and Steven L. Rearden), *From Hiroshima to Glasnost, At the Centre of Decision—A Memoir* (London, 1989), p. 97.

12. Melvyn P. Leffler, *A Preponderance of Power: National Security, the Truman Administration and the Cold War* (Stanford, 1992), pp. 356-359.

13. Samuel F. Wells, Jr., "Sounding the Tocsin: NSC 68 and the Soviet Threat," *International Security* 4 (Fall 1979): 138-39. Nitze critiques some of Wells' assumptions, "The Development of NSC 68," *International Security* 4 (Spring 1980): 170-176.

14. See Wilson D. Miscamble, *George F. Kennan and the Making of American Foreign Policy, 1947-1950* (Princeton, NJ, 1992), p. 309; See also "Peace goals Demands Firm Resolve," extemporaneous remarks by Secretary Acheson, 8 Feb. 1950, *Department of State Bulletin* (20 Febr. 1950): 272-74.

15. Walter Isaacson and Evan Thomas, *The Wise Men, Six Friends and the World They Made* (London, 1986), p. 497.

16. John Lewis Gaddis, *Strategies of Containment: A Critical Appraisal of Postwar American National Security Policy* (New York, 1982), pp. 90-92; Thomas H. Etzold and J.F. Gaddis, eds., *Containment: Documents on American Policy and Strategy 1945-1950* (New York, 1978), p. 383. Gaddis, "NSC 68 and the Problem of Ends and Means," *International Security* 4 (Spring 1980): 164, and recently *We Now Know: Rethinking Cold War History* (New York, 1997), p. 76.

17. Daniel Yergin, *Shattered Peace: The Origins of the Cold War and the National Security State* (Boston, 1977), p. 401.

18. Steven L. Rearden, *The Evolution of American Strategic Doctrine: Paul H. Nitze and the Soviet Challenge* (Boulder, 1984), pp. 1-8.

19. Also see Alexander L. George and Richard Smoke, *Deterrence in American Foreign Policy: Theory and Practice* (New York, 1974); Gregg Herkin, *The Winning Weapon: The Atomic Bomb in the Cold War, 1945-1950* (New York, 1980), p. 329; and William Appleman Williams, *Empire as a Way of Life* (New York, 1980), pp. 187-91.

20. Nitze later wrote that "Those who thought we must live within a 12.5 billion budget would in fact have been responsible for our having no alternative to a

doctrine of massive retaliation," see Paul H. Nitze, "The Development of NSC 68," p. 175.

21. Interview with Paul H. Nitze, Apr. 29, 1977. On the decision to accelerate the development of the thermonuclear weapon consult Richard G. Hewlett and Francis Duncan, *Atomic Shield: 1947-1952* (University Park, PA, 1969); Herbert F. York, *The Advisers: Oppenheimer, Teller, and the Superbomb* (San Francisco, 1976); George H. Quester, *Nuclear Diplomacy, The First Twenty-Five Years* (2nd ed., New York, 1973), p. 69; Warner R. Schilling, "The H-Bomb Decision: How to Decide Without Really Choosing," *Political Science Quarterly* 76 (Mar. 1961): 24-26; and David Alan Rosenberg, "American Atomic Strategy and the Hydrogen Bomb Decision," *Journal of American History* 66 (June 1979): 62-87.

22. See, especially, Nitze's "US Foreign Policy, 1945-1955," Foreign Policy Association, Headline Series (Mar.-Apr. 1956), 3-55; and "The Evolution of National Security Policy and the Vietnam War," in *Lessons of Vietnam*, ed. by W. Scott Thompson and Donaldson D. Frizzell (New York, 1977), pp. 2-7.

23. Princeton Seminars, Oct. 11, 1953 (evening session), Copy 1, Folder 1, Papers of Dean Acheson, Truman Library (hereafter cited as Princeton Seminar).

24. Dean Acheson, *Present at the Creation: My Years in the State Department* (New York, 1969), pp. 488-89. Interestingly, William P. Bundy who was assigned NSC duties (for the Central Intelligence Agency) in the summer of 1952 to work on a national security paper that picked up where the NSC 68 Series left off, believes that Acheson was nearer the truth of the matter in his memoirs than he was in 1953. Letter from William P. Bundy to the author, Nov. 30, 1978.

25. C. E. Bohlen, *Witness to History, 1929-1969* (New York, 1976), pp. 307-308.

26. Interview with W. Averell Harriman, Georgetown, Washington, DC, April 25, 1977; and Memo of Conversation between Acheson and Harriman, April 28, 1950, Papers of Dean Acheson, Box No. 65, Truman Library.

27. NSC 68/2, A Report to the National Security Council, "United States Objectives and Programs for National Security," Sept. 30, 195, attached noted by the Executive Secretary to the NSC, PSF, Papers of Harry S. Truman, Truman Library. (Hereafter cited as NSC 68/2.)

28. NSC 68/4, A Report to the President by the National Security Council, "United States Objectives and Programs for National Security," attached note by the Executive Secretary to the NSC, Dec. 14, 1950, Ibid., (Hereafter cited as NSC 68/4.)

29. Princeton Seminar, Oct. 11, 1953.

30. Nitze has subsequently discussed the impact that Alexander Sachs of Lehman Brothers had on his thinking with regard to his analysis in early 1950 that the Soviets would almost likely encourage the North Koreans to attack South Korea by June or July of that year. Nitze, "The Evolution of National Security Policy and the Vietnam War," p. 4; and Interview with Paul H. Nitze, 29 Apr. 1977.

31. Wells, "Sounding the Tocsin," p. 139.

32. Gaddis, "NSC 68 and the Soviet Threat Reconsidered," p. 166.

33. May, *American Cold War Strategy*, p. 15.

34. Rearden, *The Evolution of American Strategic Doctrine*, pp. 27-29.

35. See Yergin, *Shattered Peace*, p. 403; and LaFeber, *America, Russia and the Cold War, 1945-1975*, p. 100.

36. W.W. Rostow, *The American Diplomatic Revolution* (Oxford, 1946).

37. NSC 20, A Report to the National Security Council, "Appraisal of the Degree and Character of Military Preparedness Required by the World Situation", July 12, 1948, National Security Council Files (NSCF), Modern Military Records, Division, National Archives, Washington, DC.

38. Note by the Executive Secretary to the National Security Council, July 12, 1948, Ibid.

39. Memorandum for Forrestal from Truman, July 13, 1948, PSF, Papers of Harry S. Truman, Truman Library.

40. Letter from Truman to Forrestal, July 14, 1948, Ibid.

41. NSC 20/1, A Report to the National Security Council, "United States Objectives with Respect to Russia", August 18, 1948, 5, NSCF, Modern Military Records Division National Archives (Kennan's italics).

42. Ibid., p. 10.

43. Ibid., p. 19, (Kennan's italics).

44. Ibid., p. 29.

45. Ibid., p. 3.

46. NSC 20/2, A Report to the National Security Council, "Factors Affecting the Nature of the US Defense Arrangements in the Light of Soviet Policies," Aug. 25, 1948, II, NSCF, Modern Military Records Division, National Archives, (Hereafter cited as NSC 20/2).

47. Ibid., p. 3.

48. Ibid., pp. 1-2.

49. Central Intelligence Agency Estimates, "Possibility of Direct Soviet Military Action during 1948," Apr. 2, 1948; and "Possibility of Direct Soviet Military Action during 1948-1949," Sept. 16, 1948, Central Intelligence Agency Files, Modern Military Records Division, National Archives.

50. NSC 20/2, p. 4.

51. Ibid., p. 5 (author's italics).

52. Ibid. See *Survival in the Air Age: A Report by the President's Air Policy Commission* (Washington, DC, 1948), pp. 10-23.

53. Ibid., (author's italics).

54. Ibid., (author's italics); and "Memorandum by the Counsellor (Kennan)", Jan. 20, 1950, *FRUS: 1950*, 1: p. 35.

55. Ibid., pp. 6-8.

56. Memorandum for Executive Secretary to the President, November 23, 1948, PSF, Papers of Harry S. Truman, Truman Library.

57. NSC 20/4, A Report to the President by the National Security Council, "US Objectives with Respect to the USSR to Counter Soviet Threats to US Security", Nov. 23, 1948, p. 1, PSF, Papers of Harry S. Truman, Truman Library.

58. Ibid., p. 4.

59. Ibid., p. 5.

60. Ibid., p. 6 (author's italics). For a program of specific measures intended to implement NSC 20/4 see the ill-fated "Measures Required to Achieve US Objectives with Respect to Russia," March 30, 1949, *FRUS: 1949* (Washington, DC, 1976), 1: pp. 271-77; and for State's objections and subsequent removal of "Measures...," from the NSC agenda, Ibid., pp. 282-84, 296-98. Another study of NSC 20/4, in terms of establishing the forces and logistical requirements necessary to fulfil its broad outlines, is found in Anthony Cave Brown, ed., *Drop Shot: The US Plan for War with the Soviet Union in 1957* (New York, 1978).

61. Nitze, "The Evolution of National Security Policy and the Vietnam War," p. 3.

62. NSC 68, pp. 10, 60, (author's italics). In suggesting that "This demand for a change in the nature of the Soviet system represents the most notable new element stated in the national security objectives of NSC 68," Wells' conclusion of the significance of NSC 68 is wide of the mark. The problem, of course, is that

Wells failed to consult the earlier position papers in the NSC 20 Series. Wells, "Sounding the Tocsin," p. 132.

63. "Memorandum by Mr Charles E. Bohlen to the Director of the PPS," *FRUS: 1950*, 1: pp. 221-225.

64. Interview with Paul H. Nitze, 29 Apr. 1977.

65. Bohlen remained dissatisfied with the final document and complained in his memoirs that "NSC 68's misconception of Soviet aims misled, I believe, Dean Acheson and others in interpreting the Korean war". Bohlen reiterated that it had been a mistake to present Soviet policy "as nothing more than an absolute determination to spread the Communist system throughout the world". To Bohlen, the Soviet Union tended to behave as a national state in pursuit of traditional national interests, the spread of Communism being a secondary objective: "The main Bolshevik aim is to protect the Soviet system above all in Russia and secondarily in the satellite countries". Bohlen did not convince either Nitze or Acheson, however, with his views. Bohlen, *Witness to History, 1929-1969*, pp. 291, 307; Acheson, *Present at the Creation*, pp. 954-55; and Interview with Paul H. Nitze, 29 Apr. 1977.

66. NSC 68, p. 6.

67. NSC 68, pp. 7-9.

68. Ibid., pp. 9-10.

69. Ibid., p. 21.

70. NSC 68, pp. 21-22.

71. NSC 68, p. 22.

72. Ibid., pp. 37, 38 (author's Italics). Isaacson and Thomas, *The Wise Men*, p. 503, argued that Nitze put too much emphasis on Soviet capability, and too little on the Kremlin's intentions, and in doing so, overestimated Soviet strength. In the same vein, S. Talbott, *The Master of the Game*, p. 56, has described NSC 68 as "an early example of what came to be known as threat inflation."

73. Pierrepont B. Noyes, *The Pallid Giant* (New York, 1927), reissued in 1946 under the title *Gentlemen: You Are Mad*. Nitze regards Noyes' essay as the classical description of the nuclear arms race and the kind of mentality it breeds. Interview with Paul H. Nitze, 29 Apr. 1977.

74. NSC 68, p. 38. For his part, Stalin held the view that "America, though it screams war, is actually afraid of war more than anything," conversation between Stalin and Mao, Moscow, 16 Dec. 1949, Cold War International History Project (CWIHP) *Bulletin* (Winter 1996/1996): 5.

75. In many respects, according to Nitze, the rationale and analysis of NSC 68 flow directly from the following passage: "It appears to follow from the above that we should produce and stockpile thermonuclear weapons in the event they prove feasible and would add significantly to our net capability," NSC 68, Ibid., p. 39.

76. "Record of the Eighth Meeting of the Policy Planning Staff," *FRUS: 1950*, 1: p. 143.

77. "Draft Memorandum by the Counselor to the Secretary of State," *FRUS: 1950*, 1: pp. 160-167.

78. Quoted in Miscamble, *George F. Kennan and the Making of American Foreign Policy*, p. 312.

79. Talbott, *Master of the Game*, p. 57.

80. Ibid., p. 52.

81. Ibid., p. 47.

82. NSC 68, p. 35.

83. Ibid., pp. 48-49.

84. Ibid., pp. 45-50.

85. Ibid., p. 50.

86. Ibid., p. 52.

87. Ibid., pp. 52-53.

88. For some earlier thoughts on America's atomic use policy consult NSC 30, A Report to the National Security Council, "United States Policy on Atomic Warfare," Sept. 10, 1948, National Security Council Files, Modern Military Records Division, National Archives.

89. Ibid., p. 54.

90. Ibid., p. 59.

91. Repeated in Yergin, *Shattered Peace*, p. 403; May argues that "once the President studied the document and discovered how carefully Acheson and Nitze had built their base of support, he probably recognised that he was trapped," *American Cold War Strategy* p. 14.

92. See "Record of the Meeting of the State-Defense Policy Review Group," *FRUS: 1950*, 1: pp. 162-182.

93. Nitze, "The Development of NSC 68," p. 176.

94. Nitze, *From Hiroshima to Glasnost*, p. 91.

95. Ibid., p. 95.

96. Princeton Seminar, 11 Oct. 1953.

97. Note by the Executive Secretary, James S. Lay, Jr., to the National Security Council, Apr. 14, 1950 (attached to NSC 68).

98. See NSC 68, p. 19, for the paragraph in question. Interview with Paul H. Nitze, 29 Apr. 1977. For the exchange between Oppenheimer and Nitze consult Princeton Seminar, Oct. 11, 1953.

99. "The President to the Executive Secretary of the National Security Council", *FRUS: 1950*, vol. 1: p. 235.

100. Acheson, *Present at the Creation*, p. 374.

101. Nitze, *From Hiroshima to Glasnost*, p. 96.

102. NSC 8/1, A Report to the National Security Council. "The Position of the united States with Regard to Korea," Mar. 16, 1949, NSCF, Modern Military Records Division, National Archives. That North Korea attacked South Korea with Soviet complicity is no longer in doubt. See Jonathan Haslam, "Russian Archival Relevations and Our Understanding of the Cold War," *Diplomatic History* 21 (Spring 1997): 224-25; and CWIHP, *Bulletin* (Winter 1995/1996): 6-7. For a different view consult Bruce Cumings, *The Origins of the Korean War*, vol. 2, *The Roaring of the Cataract, 1947-1950* (Princeton, 1990).

103. NSC 68/2, attached note by the Executive Secretary.

104. NSC 68/4, note by the Executive Secretary. Since programs in NSC 68/4 were not definitive, Truman directed State and Defense "to undertake immediately a joint review of the politico-military strategy of their Government with a view to increasing and speeding up the programs outlined...as critical situation and submit to me appropriate recommendations, through the NSC, as soon as possible."

105. Ibid.

106. NSC 68/4, p. 1.

107. The various programs were described in NSC 68/3, A Report to the National Security Council, "United States Objectives and Programs for National Security," Dec. 8, 1950, NSCF, Modern Military Records Division, National Archives. Expenditures for national security rose to 22.3 billion dollars in FY 1952, and 50.4 billion dollars in FY 1953. Whereas the defense budget accounted for 5.2 per cent of the GNP in 1950, in 1953 it accounted for 13.5 per cent of a much expanded GNP. Huntington, *Common Defense*, p. 54.

108. Memoranda of Conversations held at Blair House, June 25, 1950, pp. 2-3; and June 27, 1950, p. 6, Papers of Dean Acheson, Truman Library. These views are also confirmed in *FRUS: 1950*, 7, pp. 125-270.

109. Suggested by William P. Bundy to the author, 30 Nov. 1978.

# CHAPTER 4

# FDR, TRUMAN AND INDOCHINA

American involvement in Vietnam was, by any standard of judgement, the most disastrous episode in the history of United States foreign policy.[1] The loss in national treasure and blood was staggering. From 1961 until the collapse of the Thieu regime in late April 1975, United States expenditures in Indochina amounted to a total in excess of $US141 billion or, to put it another way, $US7,000 for each of South Vietnam's 20 million people. The loss of life was equally staggering. From the time of the death in 1961 of Specialist 4 James Thomas Davis, of Livingston, Tennessee, the man later designated by President Lyndon Johnson as "the first American to fall in defence of our freedom in Vietnam", until the Paris Peace Accords of 1973, American casualties alone reached a figure of 350,000 with approximately 58,000 killed (40,000 in combat). Vietnamese casualties (North and South) reached a figure of more than two million, with more than 241,000 South Vietnamese combat deaths, and more than one million combined North Vietnamese and Viet Cong combat deaths. In addition to the known dead there are 300,000 North Vietnamese MIAs, in contrast with the famous 2,000 Americans still missing.[2]

The war, which was daily televised and made napalm and "free-fire zones" household words, witnessed a number of dubious precedents, including bombing tonnage (more than three times the tonnage dropped in World War II) and the first known use of weather warfare. There was always something surrealistic about it. Even the alleged attack by North Vietnamese PT-boats on American destroyers on the evening of 4 August 1964—the basis of the Gulf of Tonkin Resolution—never took place.[3]

At home as well as on the battlefield, the Vietnam imbroglio left its mark. The economy was racked by severe inflation, university campuses were politicised; a generation of unpardoned and unpardonable draft registers were exiled to Canada and other foreign lands; presidents were made and unmade; and the traditional security of the office of the Executive was shaken to its roots. In these and countless other ways the Vietnam experience affected the lives of all who survived it, from the president and his policymakers to the proverbial man in the street. In the Vietnam era, nearly 27,000,000 American men came of draft age; of that number there were 570,000 apparent draft evaders. Another 15,000,000 were deferred, exempted or disqualified, including Sylvester Stallone who spent his time as a coach at a private girls' school in Switzerland and then as an acting student at the University of Miami. (So much for Rambo!)[4]

At the height of the conflict, draftees were getting killed at twice the rate of enlistees, with the result that avoiding the draft became the preoccupation of an entire male generation or at least that part of it which had the means and wit to manipulate the Selective Service System to its advantage. The majority of men who fought and died in Vietnam were frequently society's losers, blacks, browns and rednecks, the very men who often got left behind in school and work. The war and the draft that served it tormented American society.

Despite the losses and the staggering enormity of pulverising civilian populations, cities, and even hospitals, the American people were more or less at a loss to explain American involvement in Vietnam. "Quite suddenly and surprisingly", wrote the liberal reformer Senator Eugene J. McCarthy in 1967, "we have found ourselves involved in the third largest war in our history and involved under terms and conditions which are different from any we have known in the past".[5] The millions of words scholars spilled on the legality of United States assistance to South Vietnam revealed precious little about the nature of the conflict.[6] A large number of historians and scholarly commentators agreed with McCarthy that the United States somehow drifted into war, the victim of false conceptions,[7] intellectual errors,[8] and arrogance.[9] Others of a more leftist persuasion criticized the drift thesis as liberal wishful thinking and counter-charged that the United States' presence in Southeast Asia was a product of design whether for reasons of imperial hegemony or a rational overhead cost to demonstrate to the Third World what was expected of it.[10] Focusing on responsibility and moral conduct, both advocates of the drift and their critics turned the Vietnam conflict into a theological debate which settled little.

The American people did not really need Robert S. McNamara to tell them belatedly something was terribly wrong. By May 1971, 61 per cent of the 1,502 persons interviewed by the Gallup Poll thought it had been a mistake for the United States to become involved in Vietnam. (The questions asked was, "In view of the developments since we entered the fighting in Viet Nam, do you think the United States made a mistake sending troops to fight in Viet-Nam?" 28 per cent answered, "No", and 11 per cent had no opinion.) The significance of the May poll lay in the fact that it marked a complete reversal of public opinion since Gallup first started asking the question in August 1965. (At that time only 24 per cent of those interviewed thought the involvement of American troops was a mistake; 61 per cent said it was not, while 15 per cent had no opinion.)[11]

In any case, taken individually or together none of these explanations (official and unofficial) seemed intellectually satisfying. There was as yet no conceptual framework with which to explain governmental actions. Then the Sunday 13 June 1971 issue of the *New York Times* appeared to have the answer. In a front page story, the American reading public was apprised by correspondent Neil Sheehan that a massive study of how the United States went to war in Indochina, conducted by the Pentagon three years previously, demonstrated that four administrations (Truman, Eisenhower, Kennedy and Johnson) had developed progressively a sense of commitment to a non-communist Vietnam, a readiness to fight the North to protect the South, and an ultimate frustration with this effort—all to a much greater extent than their public statements had acknowledged at the time. Covering the period from 1945 to May 1968, the latter date marking the start of the Paris peace talks after President Johnson had imposed limits on future military commitments and had revealed his decision to retire from public life, the *New York Times* version of the so-called Pentagon Papers reached a number of tentative conclusions. The most important of these were, first, that President Truman's decision to provide military assistance to France in her colonial war against the communist-led Vietminh had "directly involved" the United States in Vietnam and set the course of American foreign policy in the region for years to come; second, that President Eisenhower's decision to rescue South Vietnam from a communist coup and to undermine Ho Chi Minh's regime in the north had given the Administration a direct role in the ultimate breakdown of the Geneva settlement in 1954;

third, that President Kennedy, though spared from major escalation decisions by his death, had transformed a policy of "limited risk", which he had inherited, into a relatively "broad commitment" that left the Johnson Administration with the restricted options of either escalating or withdrawing; fourth, that President Johnson, though himself reluctant to make a final decision on the matter, had intensified the covert war against North Vietnam and had begun planning in the spring of 1964 to wage an overt war, a full year before he publicly revealed the depth of his involvement; and fifth, and finally, that the campaign of growing clandestine military pressures through 1964, together with the expanded bombing of North Vietnam, had been initiated despite the judgment of the federal intelligence community that such measures would probably not cause Hanoi to cease its support of the Vietcong and that the bombing had been deemed militarily ineffective within a short period of time. Such stories of dissimulation in high places and governmental deception of the public fell on fertile ground. For, at the time, the Nixon administration, with its obsession with secret diplomacy and studied indifference to public reaction to, say, the American incursion into Cambodia and later the Watergate affair, generally reinforced the image conveyed by the Pentagon Papers.

*The Pentagon Papers*, in whatever form they appeared (in addition to the *New York Times* edition, there were the four-volume Senator Gravel and the official twelve-volume Defense Department editions) failed to reconstruct the total framework in which America's Vietnamese policy evolved. For while the compilers had full access to Defense files and CIA materials, the Task Force had had only limited access to State Department cables and memoranda and none at all to those of the White House. Moreover, they were expressly forbidden to interview any of the principal participants, a defect that has partly been remedied.[12] Even the 548-page study of the Vietnam War ordered by then National Security Adviser Henry Kissinger in January 1969 added little to what was already well known. (Incidentally, the Kissinger study was subsequently made available to the *New York Times* in the spring of 1972, very likely to indicate to the *Times*'s editors that there was no hard feelings on the part of the Nixon administration in its abortive attempt to censor material in advance of publication.)

In any case, the principal thrust of this chapter is that an understanding of the origins and evolution of American involvement in Vietnam is utterly unintelligible considered apart from the climate of opinion and from the far larger foreign policy considerations and requirements of the United States during the last stages of World War II, the early Cold War period, and particularly the Korean War. In an examination of these factors, it will be argued that Franklin D. Roosevelt's Indochinese policy served on the whole both as a function of his overall policy to accelerate the liberation of colonial peoples (where possible) on one side and his efforts to punish the French by depriving them of their Southeast Asian colonial empire on the other side. Under Harry S. Truman, whose administration in time virtually overturned FDR's policies in the area, America's Vietnamese policy served as a function of HST's larger policy of containing first Soviet and then Sino-Soviet imperialism in Korea and Southeast Asia. From the impact of the Korean experience onward, successive American presidents—Eisenhower, Kennedy, Johnson, Nixon, and then Ford—increasingly came to view the Vietnam theatre as an internationalized testing ground of rival great powers and ideological claims and never seriously bothered to consider the political realities of that part of Asia, which were from time to time dimly perceived, separately from larger policy considerations. When the Nixon trips to Beijing and Moscow inaugurated a period of detente with America's erstwhile rivals, the nation's Vietnam policy stood alone for a season and appeared, at least to those who had forgotten their own history (or worse, never knew it), basically absurd if not evil. The official arguments that the United States presence there gave credibility to the nation's international commitments and determination to stand by those commitments (and subsequent arguments for continued economic and military assistance to South Vietnam) merely highlighted this absurdity.[13]

In what may properly be called the first phase of United States-Vietnamese relations, Vietnam (and Indochina generally) was seen by the Roosevelt Administration as one part of its overall strategy both to accelerate the decolonization of the Far East and to punish the French (de Gaulle?) by depriving them of their Southeast Asian empire, although by the end of World War II there remained the distinct possibility that France herself would be permitted to liberate her own colonies under specified conditions. FDR's determination to prevent the resumption of French colonial rule in Indochina and to establish in its place an international trusteeship that would ultimately gain its independence foundered in the end, in the words of Gary R.

Hess, on "Roosevelt's reluctance to risk a rupture in the wartime coalition and utilize fully his military and diplomatic power".[14] Still others have argued that under the combined pressure of the British and the French, FDR had totally abandoned his plans for a liberated Indochina by mid-1944; this thesis, however, has been much undermined by revelations in the declassified wartime messages between Roosevelt and Churchill, which provide evidence that as late as March 1945, the President and the Prime Minister shared very different views on the matter.[15] Both judgments, whatever their merits, seem to overlook the alternative hypothesis that FDR's apparent diplomatic weakness and, at least in this instance, principal strength lay in his ostensible vacillation; for until the Axis powers were completely defeated it would surely have been unreasonable on his part, a possibility perhaps overlooked by his critics, to take a fixed position on such peripheral issues. The central point here is that the general direction of President Roosevelt's policy, i.e., the liberation and ultimate independence of the Indochinese peoples, was constantly in the same direction, in much the same way he opposed spheres of influence.

"From time to time", recalled Secretary of State Cordell Hull of FDR's Indochinese policy, "the President had stated forthrightly to me and to others his view that French Indo-China should be placed under international trusteeship after the end of the war, with a view to its receiving full independence as soon as possible". As a correlative to this goal, FDR appeared to have been equally motivated by his desire to see the French punished for what he regarded as their moral turpitude in the face of danger. "The French dependency", continued Hull, "stuck in his mind as having been the springboard for the Japanese attack on the Philippines, Malaya, and the Dutch East Indies. He could not but remember the devious conduct of the Vichy Government in granting Japan the right to station troops there, without consultation with us but with an effect to make the world believe we approved".[16]

The occasions on which FDR discussed the possibility of an international trusteeship were both numerous and well-documented. Hull related that in March 1943 he attended a White House conference at which British Foreign Secretary Anthony Eden and Ambassador Lord Halifax heard the President indicate his hope to see an international trusteeship in the region. The British, who used their own opposition to the dissolution of the French Far Eastern empire as a "stalking horse" with regard to theirs, were furious. After finding some support from Under Secretary of State Sumner Welles, Eden cabled Churchill that "the President was being very hard on the French, from which the strongest opposition was to be expected. He [FDR] admitted this but said that France would no doubt require assistance for which consideration might be the placing of certain parts of her territory at the disposal of the United Nations".[17] One cannot help thinking that Eden must surely have suspected that FDR had counted on the British, too, to "require assistance for which consideration might be the placing of certain parts of her territory at the disposal of the United Nations".

At the Anglo-American conference (Trident) at Washington in May 1943, which was principally devoted to global strategy planning and the opening of a second front in Europe, Roosevelt personally called Churchill's attention to the fact, as he saw it, that the French had renounced their claims to Indochina in favour of the Japanese fully six months before Pearl Harbor. Then, according to the Wallace diary, FDR continued by saying, "I believe that after the Japs are driven out, the French have no longer any claim to French Indo-China and I am sure that the Chinese will not want French Indo-China". The Prime Minister retorted, "Of course, the Chinese will want it". Never one to refrain from twisting the lion's tail, Roosevelt characteristically replied: "Well, you are speaking for Britain which has been for centuries an imperialistic power and you have several generations of imperialist ancestors behind you. You have never refused a square mile anywhere that you could lay your hands on".[18]

In early October 1943, Hull attended another White House conference with Admiral William Leahy and State Department officials. At this time FDR reaffirmed the idea of an international trusteeship for Indochina, as well as the same probability for the Dutch East Indies; he also discussed the possibility, to quote Hull, that "the British might, as a gesture of generosity, return Hong Kong to China while China might, in turn, immediately declare Hong Kong a free port under international trusteeship". Such suggestions doubtless gave the British anxious moments. In January 1944, Ambassador Halifax called on the Secretary of State for clarification; two weeks later Hull notified FDR of the British inquiry; ten days later, on 24 January 1944, FDR informed Hull of a recent discussion with Halifax on the subject. "I", Hull quoted FDR as having said, "saw Halifax last week and told him quite frankly that it was perfectly true that I had, for over a year, expressed the opinion that Indo-China should not go back to France but that it should be administered by an international trusteeship". The President's estimate of the French was severe: "France has had the country—thirty million inhabitants—for nearly one hundred years, and the people are worse off than they were at the beginning". After noting that he had already secured the support of Chiang Kai-shek and Stalin, he added that he saw "no reason to play in with the British Foreign Office in this matter". Roosevelt contended further that "the only reason they seem to oppose it is that they fear the effect it would have on their own possessions and those of the Dutch. They have never liked the idea of trusteeship because it is, in some instances aimed at future independence"—a thought, one could imagine, of no small discomfiture to Prime Minister Churchill. After conceding that each case must be judged on its own merits, FDR concluded that the case of French Indochina was clear: "France has milked it for one hundred years. The people of Indo-China are entitled to something better than that".[19] From this basic assumption FDR never departed.

Nonetheless, and in spite of his preference for an international arrangement for Indochina, Roosevelt officially hesitated to discuss hard and fast plans relative to the implementation of the trusteeship. For, as late as November 1944, FDR still seemed uncertain about the political future of Southeast Asia. "We have made no final decision on the future of Indo-China. This should be made clear".[20] Yet, on the eve of that same Presidential election, Harry Hopkins could confidently predict that in contrast to the Republicans, who would have posed no serious obstacles to British territorial planning "you will find him [Roosevelt] right in on all these questions with his own views and you will have to pay attention to them".[21] Then, moving on to specific instances, Hopkins continued:

> Take Indo-China. I know what French rule has meant in Indo-China. It is going to be American and British boys who will die to take it back from the Japanese. Why would we let the French walk in again on their own terms when it is we and not they who will have made all the sacrifices?

Nonetheless, in early January 1945, FDR again demonstrated his reluctance to commit himself officially too soon to what was an obviously fluid situation. Consequently, he wrote in a memorandum to the Secretary of State, "I still do not want to get mixed up in any

Indochinese situation. It is a matter for postwar".[22] The President's logic seemed both unexceptional and unexceptionable. "From both the military and civilian point of view", he concluded, "action at this time is premature". Historical critics have understandably seized on such comments as sufficient proof of Roosevelt's indecisiveness and general weakness in planning for the postwar world. But in point of fact, it was only on details, implementation, etc., that FDR was prepared to keep his options open. Again, the thrust of his anti-French policy remained on course and in fact never failed to make a profound impact on those most concerned with the area.

For example, FDR indicated beyond peradventure that the French should have as little as possible to do with liberating Indochina. "The President orally expressed the view to Mr Stettinius", wrote James C. Dunn, the director of the Office of European Affairs, in March 1944, "that no French troops should be used in Indo-China. He added that in his view the operation should be Anglo-American in character and should be followed by the establishment of an international trusteeship over the French colony".[23] Moreover, United States armed forces were ordered not to interfere with the Japanese eviction of the remaining French troops there. General Chennault of the Fourteenth Air Force Group stationed in south China recalled that he had been under explicit orders "to proceed with 'normal action' against the Japanese provided it did not involve supplying French troops". Chennault recounted in his memoirs that "apparently it was American policy that French Indo-China would become a mandated territory after the war and not be returned to the French". The Roosevelt administration hoped that the postwar separation of Indochina from the French empire could more easily be achieved if the French were first ejected from the area. Chennault, the consummate soldier, carried out his orders despite his own reservations about their wisdom. "I carried out my orders to the letter", concluded Chennault, "but I did not relish the idea of leaving Frenchmen to be slaughtered in the jungle while I was forced officially to ignore their plight".[24] However, their plight was being closely observed by General de Gaulle.

In the context of the American Ambassador's being told that French troops still resisting the Japanese in Indochina had futilely appealed to American military authorities in China and that the United States government had refused to provide transport for an expeditionary force to Indochina, de Gaulle remarked that he was deeply disturbed by the American attitude. "This worries me a great deal", Ambassador Jefferson Caffery quoted the general as having said, "and it comes at a particularly inopportune time". Puzzled, de Gaulle then launched into what was to become a standard French diplomatic blackmail motif for the rest of the decade. "What are you driving at"? he earlier had demanded of Harry Hopkins. "Do you want us to become...one of the federated states of the Russian aegis"? Developing his case further, de Gaulle tied the issue of Indochina to the fate of France in Europe. "If the public here comes to realize that you are against us in Indo-China", he went on to say, "there will be terrific disappointment and nobody really knows to what that will lead. We do not want to become Communist; we do not want to fall into the Russian orbit, but I hope that you do not push us into it".[25] By January 1945, the French government insisted that the principle of its reestablishment in Indochina was no longer susceptible to discussion. French policymakers sought, with now almost complete disregard for American opinion, "to go forward with the integration of the colonies into an Empire system; that is to say, as fast as their education, etc., allows, they will advance toward complete equality with Metropolitan France—politically and otherwise".[26]

Despite the French repudiation of American influence in the region, probably further exacerbated by FDR's quarrel the previous year with General de Gaulle over the proposed postwar American use of bases in the French empire, Roosevelt continued to pursue his own plans for the eventual liberation and independence of Indochina. At a presidential press conference on 23 February 1945, in response to a reporter's query as to which nation would be liberating French Indochina, Roosevelt, off the record, reiterated his concern about Indochina and his discussion of the matter with Chiang Kai-shek and Stalin at Teheran. According to the President, Chiang and Stalin both agreed that Indochina should not be returned to the French. FDR's characterization of French rule was both characteristic and consistent: "They [the French] have been there over a hundred years and have done nothing about educating them. For every dollar they have put in, they have taken out ten".[27] After recalling the possibility of establishing an international trusteeship, Roosevelt then added:

> Stalin liked the idea. China liked the idea. The British don't like it. It might bust up their empire, because if the Indo-Chinese

were to work together and eventually get their independence, the Burmese might do the same thing to the King of England. The French have talked about how they expect to recapture Indo-China, but they haven't got any shipping to do it with. It would only get the British mad. Chiang would go along, Stalin would go along. As for the British, it would only make the British mad. Better to keep quiet just now.

Such comments and the reiteration of his views shortly after Yalta suggest Roosevelt's strongly held views on the subject, as well as his predictable cautionary note, "Better to keep quiet just now".

In March 1945, the month before he died, Franklin Roosevelt continued to evidence a growing and acute sensitivity to the needs and minimum political requirements of the colonial peoples of the Far East in general and those of Indochina in particular. "The President", wrote State Department adviser Charles Taussig of a recent discussion with FDR, "said he was concerned about the brown people in the East. He said that there are 1,100,000,000 brown people. In many Eastern countries they are ruled by a handful of whites and they resent it".[28] Having made a realistic estimate of the situation, FDR then noted prophetically that "our goals must be to help them achieve independence—1,100,000,000 potential enemies are dangerous". With regard to the Indochinese problem, Roosevelt was under no particular illusions about the rough sledding ahead with the French; but he was still confirmed in his belief "that French Indochina...should be taken from France and put under a trusteeship". In what might be considered his last thoughts on the subject, he conceded, however, that he might be persuaded to retreat somewhat, if the French were prepared to make a number of appropriate and formal concessions. "If we can get the proper pledge from France to assume for herself the obligations of a trustee, then...[he] would agree to France retaining these colonies with the proviso that independence was the ultimate goal...and you can quote me in the State Department". The President died a short time afterwards on 12 April.

At this juncture, traditional historical scholarship, as well as plainly partisan accounts, concluded that the Indochina trusteeship plan went to the grave with FDR, and that Harry S. Truman, faced with a new set of circumstances, mainly the threat of Soviet imperialism in Europe, either declined to meddle in French affairs or, worse, supported them. There is, of course, some truth in this judgment, for which the usual documentation may be cited.[29]

A number of American policymakers bitterly resented Truman's apparent reversal of FDR's plans for Indochina. On 29 May 1945, Patrick J. Hurley, the United States ambassador to China and the man most on the scene urgently cabled Washington for instructions, offering the observation that there seemed to be a shift away from the Administration's inherited anticolonial views. Complaining that "the French Ambassador and Military Missions have become exacting in their demand for American support...and war supplies as a matter of right", he went on to recall:

> In my last conference with President Roosevelt I informed him fully on the Indo-China situation. I told him that the French, British and Dutch were cooperating to prevent the establishment of a United Nations trusteeship for Indo-China. The imperialist leaders believe that such a trusteeship would be a bad precedent for the other imperialistic areas in Southeast Asia. I told the President also that the British would attempt with the use of our Lend Lease supplies and if possible our man power to occupy Indo-China and reestablish imperial control.[30]

At this point Hurley then related how he had earlier asked FDR for a written directive for General Wedemeyer, chief of staff to Chiang Kai-shek, and himself; the President had replied that at the coming San Francisco conference a United Nations trusteeship would be set up aimed at allowing the Indochinese to choose their own form of government. Specifically, continued Hurley, the behaviour of "the American Delegation at San Francisco seemed to support the theory of imperial control of colonies and dependent nations by the separate or combined imperialistic nations, not by a United Nations trusteeship", all of which "seemed to indicate a change in American policy." The one-time Secretary of War and lawyer from Oklahoma was furious and added his own judgment:

> If American policy is not opposed to imperialism in Asia it is in conflict with the Hull policy. It is in conflict with the principles of the Atlantic Charter. It is in conflict with the principles of the Iran Declaration. It is in conflict with the policy to which all the nations including the imperialistic nations gave support when they were asking the United States to join the fight for liberty and democracy. It is in conflict with the policy that the United States invoked as our reason for the defeat and destruction of Japanese imperialism.

In reply to Hurley's previous request that month for disclosure of any secret arrangements worked out at Yalta, the State Department responded on May 18: "No Yalta decision relating to Indo-China known to Department. Military and political papers now under consideration will be transmitted for your secret information when approved." No message was sent. On 6 June 1945, Hurley apprised State, in what must have been a sense of exasperation, "This morning I received definite information through another source that the State Department advised the War Department of a change in policy in regard to Indo-China".[31] It was thus painfully obvious to Hurley that Roosevelt's hope for an international trusteeship had been more or less jettisoned for the sake of Franco-American relations, in itself a policy shift of some complexity and one effected with obvious reluctance.

When fighting broke out between the French and the Vietnamese in 1946, the Truman administration found itself in a difficult position. On the one hand, it believed that "as a general principle, the United States should support the armed forces of France with military supplies; on the other hand, it does not...desire to strengthen the hand of the French Government in its current attempt to restore by force the pre-war position of France in Indo-China".[32] During the last months of 1945 and throughout 1946, Franklin Roosevelt's policy towards Indochina became gradually transformed in the hands of Truman into a policy that attempted to accomplish two things simultaneously: first, to contribute towards the liberation and ultimate independence of the Indochinese people, albeit now within a prescribed French framework; and, second, to coordinate Allied support against what was perceived as a Soviet threat to Western Europe, a not unreasonable perception given Soviet activities in Eastern and Central Europe. There can be no doubt with regard to the sincerity of the United States' intention to understand and improve, so far as it could, the conditions of the Indochinese peoples. In a State position paper dated 22 June 1945, Acting Secretary of State Joseph C. Grew pointed out that inasmuch as America had an interest in the Pacific, "there should be a progressive enlargement of the political responsibilities, both as individuals and as groups, of all the peoples of this region in order that they may be prepared and able to assume the responsibilities of natural freedom as well as to enjoy its rights".[33] Correlative to this desire was the concern and difficult task of how best to support colonial peoples without at the same time alienating the colonial powers whose support was needed in Europe, i.e., to construct a united front to check Soviet ambitions. The problem thus revolved around the question, How to secure the cooperation of France and Britain in Europe while supporting the increasingly insistent demands of their colonies for a greater share of political and economic freedom? The policy finally adopted, which by its nature was probably foredoomed, was to harmonize the two goals if possible but in the last instance to abandon the colonial peoples if necessary.

These judgments were based, again, on a relatively realistic analysis of political conditions in the area. The State Department accurately predicted in 1945 that "the Indochinese independence groups, which have been working against the Japanese, will quite probably oppose the restoration of French control". Independence sentiment was on the rise, and there could be little doubt that its advocates were prepared to fight and die for it. (This particular observation was supposed to have been one of the "great lessons" of United States involvement in Vietnam in the 1960s.) "It is believed", noted Grew, "that the French will encounter serious difficulty in over-coming this opposition and in reestablishing French Control". And again it was hoped that a large measure of self-government, generously bestowed by the French, presumably, would be the best immediate remedy. At the same time, and here was the rub, it became increasingly apparent that "French policy toward Indochina will be dominated by the desire to re-establish control in order to reassert her prestige in the world as a great power."

By the summer of 1945, then, the official policy of the United States was to recognize French sovereignty over Indochina, with the expectation that the French "would allow colonial peoples an opportunity to prepare themselves for increased participation in their own government with eventual self-government as the goal". In this manner, the Truman Administration, in part, attempted to execute FDR's last will and testament on Indochina. Within a short period of five years, however, American policymakers systematically abandoned the Indochinese to the tender mercies of the French and in so doing sacrificed Vietnamese aspirations and dreams to the larger considerations of Cold War policy, falling into the trap that critics of containment had predicted. So much for the mysterious law of unintended consequences.

As is well known, wartime United States-Vietnamese relations unofficially originated in late 1944, when the Vietminh assisted in the rescue of an American pilot shot down over Tonkin. After personally aiding in the return of the pilot to his base in South China, Ho Chi Minh shortly established contact with the Office of Strategic Services and was soon recruited to organize rescue teams for American flyers and was even provided with arms and munitions, presumably with the understanding that they were to be used against the Japanese and not the French. With the Japanese coup in March 1945, in which the Japanese eliminated the French opposition, the Vietminh received additional military supplies and radio equipment from the OSS. In May, several OSS units, which were apparently impressed with Ho's determination to realize independence, parachuted into Tonkin and proceeded for the next several months to work closely with the Vietminh.

In the wake of the Japanese surrender, Ho utilized the OSS to transmit messages to the State Department in what was to be the beginning of a futile effort to secure the aid and recognition of the United States. Ho Chi Minh early hoped and, to a degree, expected that America would take special interest in his country. Between October 1945 and February 1946, Ho addressed a series of messages to the Truman Administration, a fact generally unknown by the public for more than twenty-five years. In the summer of 1945, Ho requested that Vietnam be accorded the same status as the Philippines—i.e., tutelage followed by independence; in November 1945, he wrote Acheson requesting the invitations of a cultural exchange; and in February 1946, he wrote to President Truman to defend Vietnamese independence, pointing to the granting of independence to the Philippines.[34] Ho, who seemed to be confronted with a host of obstacles, worked hard in attempting to warm up the Americans. For example, in proclaiming Vietnamese independence on 2 September 1945, Ho invoked the spirit and indeed the very words of the United States Declaration of Independence: "All men are created equal; they are endowed by the Creator with certain inalienable rights; among them are Life, Liberty, and the pursuit of Happiness". Ho's borrowing was obviously open, intentional, and, unfortunately for the course of American history, of marginal impact.[35]

The last and perhaps the most significant appeal of Ho Chi Minh to the Truman Administration occurred in September 1946, while Ho was in Paris attempting to negotiate a modus vivendi with the French. According to George M. Abbott, First Secretary of the

United States Embassy, who spoke with him at the request of Ambassador Caffery, Ho "emphasized his admiration for the United States and the respect and affection for President Roosevelt which is found even in the remote villages of his country".[36] He made particular reference, continued Abbott, "to our policy toward the Philippines and pointed out that it was only natural that his people, seeing an independent Philippines on one side and India about to gain its freedom on the other, should expect France to understand that similar measures for Indo-China are inevitable". Ho also "took up the question of his supposed Communist connections which he, of course, denied", pointing out "that there are no Communist ministers in his government and that the Viet-Nam constitution opens with a guarantee of personal liberties and the so-called rights of man and also guarantees the right to personal property", although he admitted "that there are Communists in Annam...". Finally, Ho spoke to Abbott of the aid that he might acquire for his country. And then, what must seem in retrospect very odd behaviour for a presumably dedicated revolutionary, he went on to mention attractive investment opportunities to be found in Southeast Asia. "He explained", Abbott quoted Ho as having said, "that the riches of his country were largely undeveloped, [and] that he felt that Indo-China offered a fertile field for American capital and enterprise". To further interest the Americans, with their traditional preoccupation with a freely trading "open door" world, Ho made it clear that the French could no longer rely on all their previously held special privileges in the region, inasmuch as "he resisted and would continue to resist the French desire for a continuation of their former policy of economic monopoly". In any case, Ho's parting wish was the hope "that through his contacts with the Embassy the American public would be informed of the true situation in Indo-China". That Ho's message fell on deaf ears must surely be one of the larger ironies of history.

In a telegram sent 5 December 1946, before large-scale fighting broke out between the French and the Vietminh, Assistant Secretary of State Dean Acheson cautioned a special Department of State representative in Indochina that in future reporting he should "keep in mind Ho's clear record as agent international communism, absence evidence recantation Moscow's affiliations, confused political situation France and support Ho receiving French Communist Party".[37] Hardening Cold War attitudes gradually produced an intolerable tension in the Truman Administration's two-tier policy of pursuing the political independence of the Vietnamese people on the one hand and of guaranteeing its allies on the other hand. The increasing reliance on the French in Europe caused United States policymakers ultimately to sacrifice the once avowed interests of the Indochinese people. American analyses of the situation in Southeast Asia became decidedly one-dimensional and subordinated to anti-Soviet foreign policy considerations.

But there were always nagging doubts. In early February 1947, Secretary of State George C. Marshall observed that while the United States recognized French sovereignty in Indochina, "we cannot shut our eyes to the fact that there are two sides to this problem and that our reports indicate both a lack [of] French understanding of other side...and continued existence [of a] dangerously outdated colonial outlook and method in [the] area".[38]

Nonetheless, and indicative of the extent to which the nation's Vietnam policy remained a function of anti-Soviet communism in general, Marshall underscored the real danger in Vietnam. "We do not lose sight [of the] fact", he noted, "that Ho Chi Minh has direct Communist connections and it should be obvious that we are not interested in seeing colonial administrations supplanted by philosophy and political origin emanating [from] and controlled by [the] Kremlin". The peculiar realities of Vietnam became less and less important in and of themselves. "[The] fact does remain, however", observed Marshall, pointing out the broad implications for Vietnam, "that a situation does exist in Indo-China which can no longer be considered, if it ever was considered, to be of a local character". The problem remained of course in proving Ho's connection with Moscow, at that time a difficult proposition. As late as July 1948, Marshall wrote that the State Department had "no evidence of [a] direct link between Ho and Moscow but *assumes* it exists".[39]

Further doubts with respect to Ho's presumed Soviet source of support were reinforced in a survey of Communist influence in Southeast Asia conducted by the Department of State's Office of Intelligence Research in the fall of 1948. "If there is a Moscow-directed conspiracy in Southeast Asia", observed the report, "Indo-China is an anomaly so far".[40] The analysis of the possible reasons for this situation is revealing. Among the possibilities given were, first, "no rigid directives have been issued by Moscow"; second, "the Viet-Nam government considers that it has no rightist elements that must be purged"; third, "the Viet-Nam Communists are not subservient to foreign policies pursued by Moscow"; and, fourth and finally, "a special dispensation for the Viet-Nam government has been arranged in Moscow". Having said that, the report then concluded that of these possibilities the most likely were that Moscow had both not issued rigid directives and also had provided a special dispensation to Ho's government. The third possibility— i.e., that Ho was independent of the Kremlin—had apparently no support.

By the spring of 1949, and with the "loss" of China facing the Truman Administration squarely in the face, such differentiations had become academic. Or, as Acheson put it in May 1949: "Question whether Ho as much nationalist as Commie is irrelevant. All Stalinists in colonial areas are nationalists. With achievement nat[ionalist] aims (i.e. independence) their objective necessarily becomes subordination state to commie purposes and ruthless extermination not only opposition but all elements suspect even slightest deviation".[41]

Nonetheless, and despite Acheson's growing concern with communism in general and Vietnamese communism in particular, some American policymakers still realistically viewed the situation. Such State Department officials as Abbot Low Moffat, Chief of the Division of Southeast Asian Affairs, observed in early 1947 that the only alternative to an independent Vietnam was a "gigantic armed colonial camp".[42] The problem was, of course, that the name of Ho Chi Minh had become anathema. A State Department position paper, dated September 1948, frankly admitted that the Truman Administration's greatest difficulty lay in its "inability to suggest any particular solution to the Indo-China problem, as we are all too well aware of the unpleasant fact that Communist Ho Chi Minh is the strongest and perhaps the ablest figure in Indo-China and that any suggested solution which excludes him is an expedient of uncertain outcome".[43] Or, as Marshall himself conceded a year earlier, "Frankly we have no solution of [the] problem to suggest".[44] In any case, American planners found themselves caught on the horns of a dilemma. "We are naturally hesitant", continued the position paper, "to press the French too strongly or to become deeply involved so long as we are not in a position to suggest a solution or until we are prepared to accept the onus of intervention".[45] Equally important, and part of the recurring motif of the United States-Vietnamese-French triangle throughout the 1940s, was the recognition that

American considerations were "complicated by the fact that we have an immediate interest in maintaining in power a friendly French government, to assist in the furtherance of our aims in Europe"; further, "this immediate and vital interest has in consequence taken precedence over active steps looking toward the realization of our objective in Indo-China". Such considerations, although not always for the same reasons, survived well into the decade of the 1950s.

The triumph of Mao in China in 1949, together with other events perceived to be related of that and the previous year—the Communist purges in Czechoslovakia, the Berlin Blockade, and especially the Soviet detonation of an atomic device—irrevocably began to alter United States policy considerations in Southeast Asia. For it was at this time American planners resolved to draw the line from which the United States would no longer retreat. In a draft of a National Security Council position paper, dated 23 December 1949, United States policymakers contended that it was "now clear that southeast Asia is the target of a coordinated offensive directed by the Kremlin". Further, and much more ominously, the paper went on "the extension of communist authority in China represents a grievous political defeat for us; if southeast Asia is also swept by communism we shall have suffered a major political rout the repercussions of which will be felt throughout the world, especially in the Middle East and in a then critically exposed Australia".[46]

As a solution to this predicament, the study called for the "gradual reduction and eventual elimination of the preponderant power and influence of the USSR in Asia to such a degree that the Soviet Union will not be capable of threatening from that area the security of the United States or its friends". Among the study's recommendations, the most important was that "the United States should now...scrutinize more closely the development of threats from Communist aggression, direct or indirect, and be prepared to help within our means to meet such threats by providing political, economic, and military assistance and advice where clearly needed to supplement the resistance of the other governments in and out of the area which are more directly concerned".[47] At the Fiftieth Meeting of the National Security Council, held in late December 1949, the report's recommendation became the official policy of the Truman Administration.

Thus, in much the same manner as United States Vietnamese foreign policy had been subordinated to larger American considerations in the immediate postwar period, United States Vietnamese foreign policy was now subordinated to the American preoccupation with communist threats everywhere. Forced to employ the vulgarized language of containment concepts, which had been implied in the Truman Doctrine message of March 1947 and, rightly or wrongly, attributed to Kennan's "X" article of the following July, American planners overwhelmingly tended to think and formulate policy in those terms. In this way, America's Vietnamese policy, as well as its foreign policy in general, metamorphosed itself into a form that bore little or no resemblance either to Roosevelt or earlier Truman policy.

In early February 1950, after the French parliament had ratified agreements with Bao Dai and the other Associated States of Indochina, the United States officially recognized (South) Vietnam, Laos, and Cambodia. And, as a correlative, the Truman Administration considered what specific steps might be taken to prevent what was perceived to be externally fostered dissension in the region. At the same time, the State Department professed alarm at the Soviet recognition of the government of North Vietnam. For Soviet recognition at this point provided the Administration with conclusive, and, until then, elusive proof that Moscow was the source of Ho's strength. "The recognition by the Kremlin of Ho Chi Minh's Communist movement in Indo-China", wrote Secretary of State Acheson in a curious sentence, "comes as a surprise".[48] Having assumed for a number of years that Ho was under orders from Moscow, Acheson skilfully utilized Soviet recognition to confirm publicly something he had previously not the slightest doubt about: "The Soviet acknowledgement of this movement should remove any illusion as to the 'nationalist' nature of Ho Chi Minh's aims and reveals Ho in his true colours as the mortal enemy of native independence in Indo-China". Thus the last part of the Vietnamese paradigm that was to serve successive American Administrations during the 1950s and 1960s was fitted into place.

On 16 February 1950, the French government made an appeal to the Americans for direct military and economic aid for Indochina, asserting that previous efforts had been "such a drain on France that a long-term program of assistance was necessary and it was only from the United States that it could come".[49] Then, engaging in the diplomatic blackmail that had been going on since late 1945, Paris reluctantly suggested the alternative: "Otherwise...it was very likely that France might be forced to reconsider her entire policy with the possible view to cutting her losses and withdrawing from Indo-China". Up to that time, and in accordance with the spirit, if not always the letter, of its traditional anticolonialist policy, the United States had officially refused to supply military equipment directly to Indochina, although the State Department had had no great doubts that military shipments sent to French ultimately found their way to Indochina. For, according to one observer, "This policy has been limited in its effects as we have allowed the free export of arms to France, such exports thereby being available for reshipment to Indo-China or for releasing stocks from reserves to be forwarded to Indo-China".[50] Now, in response to the French request, the United States abandoned all efforts to disguise the shipment of arms directly to France in Vietnam. Or, as Acheson phrased it: "The United States Government, convinced that neither national independence nor democratic evaluation exist in any area dominated by Soviet imperialism, considers the situation to be such as to warrant its economic and military equipment to the Associated States of Indo-China and to France in order to assist these states to pursue their peaceful and democratic evolution."[51] From this position further plans evolved, contributing to the incremental involvement of the United States in the destiny of Southeast Asia.

Several weeks later, in a National Security Council study on Indochina, American planners theorized that "in the present state of affairs, it is doubtful that the combined native Indochinese and French troops can successfully contain Ho's forces should they be strengthened by either Chinese Communist troops...or Communist supplied arms and material in quantity from outside Indo-China".[52] To bolster the French and to prevent such a situation, the study further reasoned that it was "important to United States security interests that all practicable measures be taken to prevent further communist expansion in Southeast Asia". Moreover, the study went on, in a manner adumbrating the much-used domino image of the 1950s, "Indo-China is a key area of Southeast Asia and is under imminent threat. The neighbouring countries of Thailand and Burma could be expected to fall under Communist domination if Indo-China were controlled by a Communist-dominated government. The balance of Southeast Asia would then be in grave hazard". From this proposition, it was argued that "the Departments of State and Defense should prepare as a matter of priority a program of all practicable measures designed to protect United States security interests in Indo-China".

A similar analysis by the Joint Chiefs of Staff was equally emphatic arguing that for a number of reasons, including the protection of "major sources of certain strategic materials required for the completion of United States stockpile projects", the mainland states of Southeast Asia were of current critical importance.[53] The JCS scenario in the event of the fall of Indochina evoked what became a haunting melody in the American military establishment. "The fall of Indo-China", concluded the JCS in 1950, "would undoubtedly lead to the fall of the other mainland states of Southeast Asia." Furthermore, continued the report, the fall of southeast Asia would require, inter alia, "changing the Philippines and Indonesia from supporting positions in the Asian off-shore island chain to front-line bases for the defense of the Western Hemisphere". Additionally, it would "bring about almost immediately a dangerous condition with respect to the internal security of the Philippines, Malaya, and Indonesia, and would contribute to their probable eventual fall to the communists". In sum, predicted the JCS, "the fall of Southeast Asia would result in the virtually complete denial to the United States of the Pacific littoral of Asia".

In any case, when the North Koreans invaded South Korea on 25 June 1950, the Truman Administration simply assumed that the North Korean attack marked the opening of a preparatory, wide-scale attack on the whole of Southeast Asia. "The attack upon Korea", declared Truman on 27 June 1950, in a statement to the American people, "makes it plain beyond all doubt that communism has passed beyond the use of subversion to conquer independent nations and will now use armed invasion and war". Truman had no doubt that the Soviets and North Korea planned and executed the attack[54] Indicative of the Administration's linking of Southeast Asia with Soviet- and possibly Chinese-inspired aggression, the President in his initial Korean strategy both accelerated the supply of military assistance to the French and to the Associated States in Indochina and dispatched a military mission to the area to coordinate working relations. In effect, Ho Chi Minh's North Vietnamese government became identified with the North Korean aggression and, by implication, with the international communist conspiracy operated and managed by Moscow and Beijing.

The outbreak of the Korean War and the American reaction to it, more than any other single event, crystallized the Cold War mentality that had been more or less in a state of fluidity from 1945 to 1950. As part of this process, American understanding and appreciation of Indochinese realities and aspirations, which had briefly been embraced during and immediately after 1945, were transformed into an almost unrecognizable body of knowledge, which in turn was then processed through a Cold War prism. With the North Korean invasion across the 38th Parallel, Indochina came to be seen mainly as an aspect of the larger problem of coping with the Soviet and Chinese communist conquest of the Free World. Or, as Truman put it: "We were seeing a pattern in Indo-China timed to coincide with the attack in Korea as a challenge to the Western world…a challenge by the Communists alone, aimed at intensifying the smouldering and anti-foreign feeling among most Asian peoples".[55]

Accordingly the legacy of the Cold War paradigm that portrayed the Indochina conflict as but a functional aspect of worldwide Communist aggression was passed on intact to the Eisenhower administration. The Korean War, argued President Eisenhower unequivocally, was "clearly part of the same calculated assault that the aggressor is simultaneously pursuing in Indo-China".[56] And, conversely, the working out of a settlement of the Korean War would presumably have a lasting impact on Indochina as well as on other nations in the region. That John F. Kennedy thought and acted upon the same assumptions can hardly be open to question. For in his words: "Viet-Nam represents the cornerstone of the Free World in Southeast Asia, the Keystone of the arch, the finger in the dike. Burma, Thailand, India, Japan, the Philippines and, obviously, Laos and Cambodia are among those whose security would be threatened if the red tide of Communism overflowed into Viet-Nam…. Moreover, the independence of Free Viet-Nam is crucial to the free world in fields other than military. Her economy is essential to the economy of all of Southeast Asia; and her political liberty is an inspiration to those seeking to obtain or maintain their liberty in all parts of Asia—and indeed the world". For these reasons, then, added JFK, "the fundamental tenets of this nation's foreign policy, in short, depend in considerable measure upon a strong and free Vietnamese nation".[57]

President Lyndon B. Johnson, like his predecessor, could not escape the conclusion that Vietnam, by whatever justification, was the test case of American determination to hold the line against further Communist incursions, thus continuing the obstruction of a clearer view of Vietnamese realities. As Johnson noted in his memoirs relating to the period from late 1961 to 1965: "It became increasingly clear that Ho Chi Minh's military campaign against South Viet-Nam was part of a larger, much more ambitious strategy being conducted by the Communists".[58] The President's perception is revelatory. "What we saw taking shape rapidly", recalled Johnson, "was a Djakarta-Hanoi-Peking-Pyongyang axis, with Cambodia probably to be brought in as junior partner and Laos to be merely absorbed by the North Vietnamese and Chinese". Given the presumed correctness of these assumptions, the argument concluded: "the members of this new axis were undoubtedly counting on South Viet-Nam's collapse and an ignominious American withdrawal.... The entire region would have been ripe in the plucking".

Similarly, Richard M. Nixon's policy of detente with the Soviet Union and China failed appreciably to alter the image of Vietnam as a vital test case and an aspect of a larger problem. "An American defeat in Viet-Nam", declared Nixon on 8 May 1972, in a message to the American people explaining his decision to mine the entrances to North Vietnamese ports, "would encourage this kind of aggression all over the world...small nations, armed by their major allies, could be tempted to attack neighbouring nations at will, in the Mid-East, in Europe and other areas".

Finally, there would have been no reason to have expected a change in the attitude of Gerald Ford's Administration. For in his formal and foredoomed request to Congress in early 1975 for continued military aid to South Vietnam (and Cambodia), President Ford reminded his recent colleagues that "US unwillingness to provide adequate assistance to allies fighting for their lives would seriously affect our credibility as an ally". Saigon fell on 30 April. The collapse of South Vietnam together with the defeat of the pro-Western forces in Cambodia and subsequently in Laos marked the end of American influence in the area. For some, it came as no real surprise, for others, there were no words to explain it.[59]

## NOTES

1. The historiography of American involvement in Vietnam is vast and varied. The best place to begin is Gary R. Hess, "The Unending Debate: Historians and the Vietnam War," *Diplomatic History* 18 (Spring 1994): 239-64.

2. Statistics were compiled by US Department of Defense, US Agency for International Development, US Senate Subcommittee on Refugees and Escapees, quoted in *New York Times*, 1 Apr. 1973.

3. Edwin E. Moise, *Tonkin Gulf and the Escalation of the Vietnam War* (Chapel Hill, 1996).

4. These figures are from Lawrence M. Baskir and William A. Strauss, *Chance and Circumstance: The Draft, the War and the Vietnam Generation* (New York, 1986); and Myra McPherson, *Long Time Passing and the Haunted Generation* (New York, 1986). Also see A. Garfinkle, *Telltale Hearts: The Origins and Impact of the Vietnam Antiwar Movement* (New York, 1995); and J. Carroll, *An American Requiem: God, My Father and the War That Came Between Us* (Boston, 1996).

5. Eugene J. McCarthy, *The Limits of Power: America's Role in the World* (New York, 1967), p. 187.

6. For example, see Leonard C. Meeker, "The Legality of United States Participation in the Defense of Viet-Nam," *Department of State Bulletin* 54 (Mar. 28, 1966): 477-89; Quincy Wright, "Legal Aspects of the Viet-Nam Situation," *American Journal of International Law* 60 (1966): 750-69; John N. Moore, "The Lawfulness of Military Assistance to the Republic of Viet-Nam," ibid., p. 61 (1967): 1-34; and Wolfgang Friedman, "Law and Politics in the Vietnamese War: A Comment," ibid., pp. 776-85.

7. Louis J. Halle, "After Viet-Nam – Another Witchhunt?" *New York Times Magazine,* 6 June 1971, pp. 36ff.

8. George W. Ball, "The Lessons of Viet-Nam: Have We Learned or Only Failed?" ibid., 1 Apr. 1973, pp. 12ff.

9. J. William Fulbright, *The Arrogance of Power* (New York, 1966).

10. Specifically, refer to Noam Chomsky, *American Power and the New Mandarins* (New York, 1967), pp. 258, 313; Gabriel Kolko, *The Roots of American Foreign Policy: An Analysis of Power and Purpose* (Boston, 1969), pp. 84-85; and David Horowitz, *Empire and Revolution: A Radical Interpretation of Contemporary History (New York*, 1969), pp. 230-32.

11. *New York Times,* 6 June 1971. For McNamara's admission 30 years later that "we were wrong, terribly wrong," see Robert S. McNamara (with Brian Van DeMark), *In Retrospect: The Tragedy and Lessons of Vietnam* (New York, 1995), p. xvi.

12. For the origins of the *Pentagon Papers* see McNamara, *In Retrospect*, p. 256; for contemporary criticism see Leslie H. Gelb, "Today's Lessons from the Pentagon Papers," *Life* (17 Sept. 1971): 34. *The Pentagon Papers* should be read with: Anne Blair, *Lodge in Vietnam: A Patriot Abroad* (New Haven, 1995); H.R. McMaster, *Dereliction of Duty: Lyndon Johnson, Robert McNamara, the Joint Chiefs of Staff, and the Lies that Led to Vietnam* (New York, 1997); Robert Dallek, "Lyndon Johnson and Vietnam: The Making of a Tragedy," *Diplomatic History* 20 (Spring, 1996): 147-42; and Department of State, *Foreign Relations of the United States, 1964-1968*, vol. 2, *Vietnam, January to June 1965*, and vol. 3 *June to December 1965* (Washington, 1996). (Hereafter this source will be referred to as *FRUS*.)

13. Joseph M. Siracsua, "Lessons of Vietnam and the Future of American Foreign Policy," *Australian Outlook*, 30 (Aug. 1976): 227-37.

14. Gary R. Hess, "Franklin Roosevelt and Indochina," *Journal of American History* 49 (Sept. 1972): 354.

15. See also the exchange between Roosevelt and Churchill on March 17 and 22, 1945, in *The Messages between Franklin D. Roosevelt and Winston S. Churchill, 1939-1945* (Microfilm edition, reel 5), Franklin D. Roosevelt Library, Hyde Park, NY.

16. Cordell Hull, *The Memoirs of Cordell Hull*, 2 vols. (New York, 1948), 2: p. 1955.

17. Earl of Avon, *The Memoirs of Anthony Eden, Earl of Avon: The Reckoning* (Boston, 1965), p. 438. Also see David G. Marr, *Vietnam 1945: The Quest for Power* (Berkeley, 1995), p. 262.

18. An account of this exchange is found in *The Price of Vision: The Diary of Henry A. Wallace, 1942-1946*, ed. by John Morton Blum (Boston, 1973), pp. 307-308.

19. Hull, *Memoirs*, vol. 2: pp. 1596-97.

20. "Memorandum by President Roosevelt to the Under Secretary of State," 3 November 1944, *FRUS*, 1944 (Washington, 1965), 3: p. 780.

21. For FDR's personal views on Indochina on the eve of the presidential election of 1944, consult the Hopkins conversation in the Prime Minister's Confidential Files (PREMIER 4), File 27, Folder 7, pp. 476-77, Public Record Office, London.

22. "Memorandum by President Roosevelt for the Secretary of State," 1 Jan. 1945, *FRUS*, 1945, 6: p. 293.

23. "The Director of the Office of European Affairs (Dunn) to the Director of the Civil Affairs Division, War Department (Hildering)," 14 Mar. 1944, *FRUS: 1944*, 5: pp. 1205-1206.

24. Claire Lee Chennault, *Way of a Fighter: The Memoirs of Claire Chennault* (New York, 1949), p. 342.

25. "The Ambassador in France (Caffrey) to the Secretary of State," 13 Mar. 1945, *FRUS* 1945, 6: p. 300.

26. "The Ambassador in France (Caffrey) to the Secretary of State," 30 Jan. 1945, ibid., p. 668.

27. *Complete Presidential Press Conferences of Franklin D. Roosevelt*, 25 vols (New York, 1972), 24: pp. 70-71.

28. "Memorandum of Conversation by the Adviser on Caribbean Affairs (Tausig)," 15 Mar. 1945, *FRUS* 1945, 1: p. 124.

29. See particularly "The Acting Secretary of State (Grew) to the Ambassador in France (Caffery)," 9 May 1945, *FRUS* 1945, 6: p. 307; and "Acting Secretary of State (Acheson) to the Chargé in China (Robertson)," 5 Oct. 1945, ibid., p. 313.

30. Cable, Ambassador Patrick J. Hurley to President Truman, 29 May 1945, White House Map Room File (Incoming Messages), Top Secret File, 1945-April-May, Truman papers, Harry S. Truman Library, Independence, Mo. (Hereafter cited as White House Map Room File.)

31. Cable, Ambassador Patrick J. Hurley to Acting Secretary of State (Grew), White House Map Room File (Incoming Messages), Top Secret File, 1945-June. In two conversations, one a half-hour interview, in the first week of March, 1945, with Secretary of War Stimson, Hurley did not broach the subject of Indochina. Henry Lewis Stimson Diaries, vol. 50, pp. 156, 171 (Microfilm edition, reel 9), Manuscripts and Archives, Yale University Library, New Haven, Conn.

32. "Report by the Subcommittee on Rearmament to the State-War-Navy Coordinating Committee," 21 March 1946, *FRUS* 1946, 1: p. 1154.

33. "Policy Paper Prepared in the Department of State," 22 June 1945, *FRUS* 1945, 6: pp. 557-58, 567-68.

34. US Department of State, *United States-Viet-Nam Relations*, I, sec. I, C-4, C-60, C-62, C-96, C-97.

35. See Stanley Karnow, *Vietnam: A History* (New York, 1983), pp. 128-60; and Joseph Buttinger, *Vietnam: A Dragon Embattled* (New York, 1966), vol. 1, pp. 373-436. On American public opinion see Marr, *Vietnam 1945*, pp. 291-95.

36. Abbott Memorandum, 12 Sept. 1946, *United States-Viet-Nam Relations*, 1: sec. I, C-103.

37. Acheson Tel., 5 Dec. 1946, *United States-Viet-Nam Relations*, 8: p. 85.

38. "The Secretary of State to the Embassy in France," 3 Feb, 1947, *FRUS* 1947, 6: pp. 67-68 (hereafter cited as "Marshall Memo").

39. Marshall Tel., 2 July 1948, *United States-Viet-Nam Relations*, 8: p. 127 (italics mine).

40. Ibid., I, sec. I, A-50.

41. Acheson Tel., 20 May 1949, ibid., 8: pp. 196-97.

42 ."The Consul General at Singapore (Josselyn) to the Secretary of State," 7 Jan. 1947, *FRUS* 1947, 6: p. 55.

43. "Department of State Policy Statement of Indo-China," 27 Sept. 1948, *United States-Viet-Nam Relations*, 8: pp. 145, 148-49. (Hereafter referred to as "Indo-China Statement.")

44. "Marshall Memo". Also see Edward R. Drachman, *United States Policy Toward Vietnam, 1940-1945* (Cranbury, NJ, 1970); and William J. Duiker, *The Communist Road to Power in Vietnam* (Boulder, CO, 1981).

45. "Indo-China Statement."

46. "The Position of the United States with Respect to Asia," 23 Dec. 1949, ibid., p. 248.

47. "Report by the National Security Council on the Position of the United States with respect to Asia," 30 Dec.1949, ibid., pp. 266-67.

48. *Department of State Bulletin* 20 (13 Feb. 1950): 244.

49. Paris Tel., 22 Feb. 1950, cited in *United States Viet-Nam Relations*, 1: sec. IV A. pp. 2, 7, 22.

50. Ibid., 8: pp. 145-146.

51. *Department of State Bulletin* 20 (22 May 1950): 821.

52. "The Position of the United States with respect to Indo-China," 22 Feb. 1950, *United States-Viet-Nam Relations*, 8: p. 285.

53. "The Position of the United States with respect to Indo-China," 21 Dec. 1950 (Enclosure "B"), ibid., p. 411.

54. Harry S. Truman, *Memoirs: Years of Trial and Hope*, 2 vols. (Garden City, NY, 1956), 2: p. 380.

55. Ibid. For a different view see A.J.P. Taylor, *From the Boer War to the Cold War* (London, 1995), pp. 400-401.

56. *Presidential Papers: Dwight D. Eisenhower, 1953* (Washington, 1960), 1: p. 16. For another, ironically more "realistic" view, see John Foster Dulles, *War or Peace* (London, 1950), p. 231.

57. John F. Kennedy, "America's Stake in Vietnam," *A Symposium on America's Stake in Vietnam* (New York, 1956), p. 10; quoted in L. Cooper's *The Lost Crusade: America in Vietnam* (New York, 1970).

58. Lyndon Baines Johnson, *The Vantage Point* (London, 1971), pp. 135-136.

59. John Fairbank's comment, "Now we are out, and still ignorant, even of the depth of our ignorance," said it all. *New York Review of Books*, 12 June 1975, pp. 30-31.

# CHAPTER 5

# AMERICA, AUSTRALIA & THE ORIGINS OF THE COLD WAR

The Cold War saw Australia, naturally and even automatically, on the side of America. In this sense the traditional image of Australia as a safe ally of the United States is substantially correct. However, it implies a tendency to subservience on the side of the junior partner that generally has been conspicuously lacking. The two Pacific nations customarily have been as one on major ideological and strategic issues. Their relationship in other areas justly could be called turbulent, particularly during the tense and frustrating years of developing East-West confrontation immediately after the defeat of the Axis. The recurring collisions between Canberra and Washington in the early Cold War period did not reflect any real ideological difference between the Australian Labor government and the Truman administration. The main source of contention was paradoxically the bipartisan determination of Australian leaders to establish a binding security relationship between their country and the United States and the equally firm and bipartisan resolve of American policymakers not to embark upon anything of the kind in the existing circumstances. Australia wanted an alliance; the United States wanted cooperation; and neither got exactly what it wanted.

Strains in the relationship had been apparent even before the defeat of their common enemies. Australian Prime Minister John Curtin and Minister for External Affairs Herbert V. Evatt were appalled to discover early in 1942 that the Americans had originated the "Atlantic First" strategy, which assigned top priority to the defeat of Germany rather than to Japan.[1] This revelation engendered suspicions of American intentions in the Pacific that at times approximated paranoia.

Allied successes in the Pacific through 1943 gradually allayed Australian anxieties over the possibility of Japanese victory. From then on Australian fears were concentrated on the implications of

American victory. These appeared to derive some substance from statements by US Navy Secretary Frank Knox and Robert B. McCormick, editor of the *Chicago Tribune*, that after the war US security might require the control of bases in the island groups of the British Commonwealth as well as in former Japanese mandates in the Pacific.[2] Australian concern was not allayed in the least by the assurance of Undersecretary of State Sumner Welles that the United States had no intention of interfering with the sovereignty of the island peoples of the region.[3] Evatt next engineered with New Zealand a joint agreement affirming that there should be no change of sovereignty affecting any of the former colonial territories south of the equator without the sanction of Canberra and Wellington. Reactions in Washington were predictably unfavourable. Secretary of State Cordell Hull ridiculed the so-called ANZAC Pact as proposing "a Monroe Doctrine for the South Pacific", and told New Zealand Prime Minister Peter Fraser that it "seemed to be on all four, so far as the tone and method are concerned, with the Russian action toward Great Britain".[4] The New Zealander agreed, thus strengthening Hull's disposition to cast Evatt as the villain of the piece. Former US Ambassador to Japan Joseph C. Grew also referred to Evatt's "assertive leadership," and thought US policy toward territorial problems in the South Pacific should be "chiefly to prevent the somewhat expansionist tendencies which have their roots mainly in Australia rather than in New Zealand from unduly complicating the relations of the United States with the United Kingdom, France and the Netherlands".[5] Consequently, each government suspected the other's ambitions.

Part of the problem undoubtedly lay in Evatt's personality. No altruistic and unequivocally Western-aligned diplomat ever succeeded in making himself more detested by the people he was most anxious to placate. Sir Alexander Cadogan, the admittedly acerbic British Under-Secretary of State for Foreign Affairs, described him as "the most frightful man in the world", and he noted gleefully that "everyone by now hates Evatt so much that his stock has gone down a bit and he matters less".[6] State Department Legal Specialist Henry Reiff warned that Evatt's presence at the United Nations "bodes trouble" and that his arguments were only a facade to mask Australian ambitions in the region.[7] Even Hull was impressed by Evatt's bad manners. The US representative in Canberra, Nelson T. Johnson, found the Australian minister's "increasing megalomania" more deserving of comment.[8] It was not an auspicious beginning for a close and harmonious relationship.

It was also quite misleading. Evatt was anything but anti-American in either his public policy or his private statements. He was sincere when he told Secretary of State Jarnes F. Byrnes that "leadership by your country is the basis of the Pacific settlement". The basic difficulty was that the Truman Administration was not prepared to assume the particular leadership role that Evatt had in mind. There were two main reasons for this. First, Evatt clearly believed that Australian-American relations should be conceived in terms of a partnership of equals with full and effective consultations on all matters of common interest. The United States was not prepared to recognize Australia as an equal partner. American policy-makers were not prepared to accept the right of Australia to be consulted on issues in which no real Australian interest could be discerned. Second, and perhaps an even more serious concern was Evatt's conviction that the United States should underwrite a formal military alliance in the Pacific, which the Americans considered to be both politically unacceptable and strategically counterproductive. Empire by invitation seldom ran smoothly.[9]

Australian-American confrontation, therefore, was effectively guaranteed. Evatt was prepared to allow the US Navy to establish a base on the island of Manus in the Australian-mandated Admiralty Group, on the condition that reciprocal facilities were made available to the Royal Australian Navy in American ports. The Americans preferred to abandon the Manus project.[10] Evatt then demanded that the United States include in its peace treaty with Thailand a clause denying Thailand the right to enter into any international commodity arrangements unless Australia also were given the opportunity to join, and he told John R. Minter, US chargé in Canberra, that he regarded American interference in Thai affairs as an unfriendly act. Minter replied that Evatt's insistence on including the clause could be regarded as equally unfriendly".[11] The peace settlement went through as planned. Undersecretary of State Dean G. Acheson warned President Truman that Evatt's concept of a "US-Australia-New Zealand joint defense scheme analogous to the US-Canada joint defense scheme" should be resolutely opposed as being "premature, inadvisable and likely to encourage the USSR to advocate similar over-all arrangements elsewhere not to the advantage of the United Nations or the US".[12] To make sure that

Evatt's opportunities to push this particular barrow himself in Washington would be limited, Acting Chief of Protocol Stanley Woodward advised that requests by the Australian Minister for External Affairs for an audience with Truman should not be overly encouraged. "If an appointment is made", he wrote stiffly, "the Department hopes very much that it will be at the convenience of the President rather than at Mr Evatt's".[13]

On 8 July 1946, Acheson agreed that the two countries should establish full ambassadorial relations as "the natural consequence of the increasingly close and cordial relations between Australia and the United States".[14] However, the choice of appointees to the new positions served to illuminate the highly asymmetrical nature of the relationship. Richard G. Casey had been the first Australian Minister in Washington in 1941. One of the most experienced of Australian diplomats, Sir Frederic Eggleston, had held the post since 1945. The new ambassador, Norman J. Makin, was a former minister, a speaker of the House of Representatives, and the first President of the Security Council. By contrast, the first US ambassador to Australia, Robert Butler, was a businessman who had held his only previous official post thirty years before. He had then been deputy governor of Mindanao. Drew Pearson categorized him as "one of the most well-meaning but left-handed of American Ambassadors".[15] He certainly seemed incredibly unaware of what was expected of him on ceremonial occasions, opening an exhibition of paintings including works by the Duchess of Gloucester with the brief speech: "I like art; this is it".[16]

Butler nevertheless appears to have been popular in Australia. Not even the most adept ambassador could have done much to compensate for Evatt's unfailing skill in enraging his American colleagues. Another bitter wrangle soon developed over the decision of the Supreme Commander for the Allied Powers (SCAP) to authorize a Japanese whaling expedition to the Antarctic during the 1946-47 season. Evatt claimed that the decision had been taken unilaterally by SCAP, with no prior consultation with interested Allied governments such as Australia. George Atcheson, Jr., US political adviser in Japan, claimed that in fact there had been at least prior notification of the SCAP decision and that Evatt's statement was therefore dishonest in its implications. In any case Atcheson told Secretary of State George C. Marshall that,

Australian distorted pronouncements and unwarranted criticisms have been so violent and so widely publicized in the Far East that, US decisions having been made and announced, question has resolved itself into one of upholding prestige of US in Japan and throughout Far East.... It is the opinion here of those closely familiar with Australian political scene that Australian protesters flow from policy of endeavouring by loud assertion to bring Australia to place of effective predominance in the Far East...any appeasement of the Australians will without question seriously undermine American prestige in this part of the world.[17]

Australia and the United States once again appeared to be not so much partners in peace as rivals bitterly contending for the domination of the Pacific Basin. The contest obviously could not be a serious one. However, what was intensely serious in American eyes was the extent to which Australian intransigence was jeopardizing the effective implementation of Cold War grand strategy. On 8 May 1947, in a speech heralding the Marshall Plan, Acheson had linked Japan with Germany as "two of the greatest workshops of Europe and Asia, upon whose production Europe and Asia were to an important degree dependent before the war", but which "have hardly been able even to begin the process of reconstruction because of the lack of a peace settlement".[18]

The main impediment to the conclusion of a peace settlement with Japan was Evatt's commitment to a tough policy toward that country, ultimately involving the destruction of Japan's capacity to wage war, which logically would entail the substantial restriction and supervision of Japan's industrial recovery. The memory of the Japanese threat to the very existence of Australia was fresh. Evatt refused to accept an American invitation to attend a conference on 19 August 1947 to discuss the formulation of a draft peace settlement with Japan. He instead set up his own conference in Canberra for 26 August. An open breach appeared to have been deliberately programmed, but Evatt was consistent in his unpredictability. He visited General MacArthur in Tokyo in July and apparently was converted to the American position with respect to Japan, assuring the sceptical Atcheson on his departure that "his desire was that the British Commonwealth cooperate with the United States to the fullest in conjunction with Japan".[19] In the meantime back in Canberra, he told the bewildered Australian journalists that he and SCAP "found ourselves in agreement on the steps to be undertaken in negotiating the Japanese Peace Treaty, on the main principies which should be contained in it, and also on the possible lines of the supervisory machinery which should be established under the Treaty".[20] The Australian media could cope with this apparent reversal of attitude on Evatt's part only by suggesting that the Minister had discovered that General MacArthur all along had been following Australian policies.

There certainly could be no doubt, as State Department official Robert A. Lovett told Truman, that a serious gap between the two countries seemed to have been closed as a result of Evatt's visit to Tokyo, and that "he and General Macarthur got along famously".[21] Nor was there any possible doubt that Evatt had every desire to get along famously with President Truman. He assured the President that he was a devoted friend and admirer, lauded him for his "own innate strength which is stronger because of your humanity and your consideration at all times for the toilers and the underprivileged", claimed that "no sane man can doubt your complete devotion to the cause of peace and the betterment of all mankind", and concluded with the rather surprising news that Ambassador Butler "had won the confidence and friendship of all sections of this community".[22] Truman could have done no less under the circumstances than reply that he believed that it was "essential that Australia and the United States be on the friendliest terms," and that he hoped that Evatt would make it a point always to come and see him when he was in the United States,[23] a hope that his advisers obviously were determined should be fulfilled as seldom as possible. This almost conventional response to the President's evoked an even more effusive "personal message of good will and, if I may say, affectionate admiration" from Evatt presumably to inspire Truman in his impending contest with Governor Thomas E. Dewey.[24]

Evatt was sincere in his good wishes for Truman's victory at the polls. In one of his last ministerial speeches he stressed the need for "the maintenance of our special relationship with the United States of America", with which he considered Australia to be on terms of "close and cordial comradeship".[25] By contrast, the Americans could see nothing but trouble ahead so long as Evatt remained Minister for External Affairs. Lovett had warned Truman earlier about Evatt's "aggressive, egocentric manner and blunt address in debate and personal relations," and he felt that "it is not always clear whether he is motivated by true patriotism or simply by egotism".[26] A State Department policy paper noted grimly that "the Australian attitude towards the Indonesian decolonization conflict is not helpful to our efforts to obtain a satisfactory conclusion.... To the extent that this attitude on the part of Australia serves to weaken the democratic front, it has and will prove embarrassing to us".[27] Secretary of Defense James V. Forrestal recorded in similar terms that "Evatt, who is President of the General Assembly, is an active source of both irritation and uncertainty. The result of his activities...has been greatly to undermine the American position among the neutral nations".[28]

Even the CIA found the Australian Labor government to be soft on communism and noted for future reference that Evatt's brother had been the President of a Comrnunist front organization in New South Wales.[29] The US chargé in Canberra, Andrew B. Foster, believed that Evatt's "highly academic approach to international problems" would continue to lead to "an almost automatic opposition to United States proposals and policies in connection with the future of Japan" and that the Labor government as a whole was "extremely jealous of the independent position of Australia, suspicious of what it regards as American economic imperialism, and determined not to be pushed around", while at the same time continuing to share with the Australian people "the complacent assumption that when the next war comes, if it does, the United States will bail them out just as it did last time".[30] It appeared that Australia expected to enjoy all the advantages of being an ally without undertaking any of the responsibilities.

Relations scarcely were improved by still another inauspicious US ambassadorial appointment. Myron M. Cowen, lawyer and businessman, had devoted his stint in Canberra between July 1948 and March 1949 mainly to resolving problems of double taxation between Australia and the United States. This in itself would not have aroused much hostility on either side of the Atlantic, but Evatt's sensibilities were outraged when Cowen was transferred on his own request to the Philippines before completing his normal tour of duty in Australia. Evatt's attempts to block his transfer appear to have inspired Cowen to foster Philippine interests at the expense of Australia. Australian Immigration Minister Arthur A. Calwell was amazed to find himself being accused by Cowen in Manila of pursuing "a private feud with the Philippines".[31] Evatt might have been even more amazed as well as enraged to discover that Cowen had been, on his account, "entirely responsible" for moves to have him replaced as President of the General Assembly by Filipino Carlos P. Romulo.[32] He presumably would have been more upset had he known that Truman had decided to give the post in Canberra to defeated Alabama Congressman Pete Jarman who had applied for it simply because he needed the money. "Since I really need to go on the payroll", Jarman appealed, "I will very much appreciate your expediting my appointment in any way possible".[33] Some of Truman's supporters did not think that Jarman merited such a handout, although they agreed that Canberra was a suitable place of exile for him. "I see you have nominated former Rep. Pete Jarman, of Alabama, as Ambassador to Australia", the international trustee of the International Woodworkers of America wrote to Truman. "That I am sorry to hear. We worked hard here to defeat him, as he was no friend to your program or Labor's, but again it may be wise if you were able to nominate several of the Rep's from the South to posts in some faraway places".[34] Indeed, it might have seemed that Washington was not placing high priority on the improvement of its relations with the Australian Labor government.

The Truman Administration. however, actually was counting on the early departure of the Labor government, taking Evatt with it. Conciliation or even cooperation effectively had been abandoned, and Australian diplomats were confronted with the alarming spectacle of Acheson at his conciliatory worst. Ambassador Makin approached the Secretary in September 1949, apologetically presenting a typically "urgent" message from Evatt, expressing the Minister's disturbance at learning that discussions had taken place in Washington regarding Far Eastern matters without the participation of an Australian representative. Acheson was furious. The message was "most surprising…it would be quite impossible for the United States to undertake that it would discuss no matter affecting the Far East except in the presence of a representative from Australia". Evatt was "to be under no illusion about the matter but to understand that we would continue to proceed as we had".[35] Assistant Secretary of State for Far Eastern Affairs W. Walton Butterworth urged in similar terms that the United States "should not accede to any request from Australia at this time to provide a security guarantee", if Evatt were to renew his appeal for a Pacific pact as the price for Australian concurrence in American proposals for a peace settlement with Japan.[36] Dominion Affairs Officer J. Harold Shullaw suggested on the eve of the Australian federal elections that "a Conservative Government would be less inclined to be demagogic and would tend to be more reasonable and less unsympathetic to the United States point of view".[37] On election day Ambassador Jarman even wrote to Richard G. Casey, federal President of the Liberal party, congratulating him in advance on his party's defeat of Labor. It was an interesting return for all of Evatt's expressions of goodwill for the Democrats.

Evatt's absence only could make the course of Australian-American relations more harmonious. Washington, however, had not taken full account of what it might be confronted with in his stead. James Plimsoll, a member of the Australian delegation on the Far Eastern Commission, visited his old friend, John M. Allison, director of the Office of Northeast Asian Affairs, to warn him that while the new Australian government "would wish to go as far as possible in cooperating with the United States on Japanese matters", he was "certain that such cooperation could be made easier if some sort of definite defense arrangements could be concluded regarding the Pacific between the United States and Australia".[38] Evatt might have passed into the shadows of the Opposition, but his policies were still in the foreground.

In fact, they had acquired a new protagonist who was in many ways far more formidable than Evatt himself. Nobody ever suggested that the new Australian Minister for External Affairs, Sir Percy C. Spender, possessed Evatt's philosophical breadth and intellectual vision but no one denied that he possessed other qualities more appropriate to the diplomatic arena. Originally, he planned a career as a professional athlete, but he decided instead to practice law where his treatment of hostile witnesses earned him the admiring, if unaffectionate, sobriquet of "the butcher bird". His skills were exhibited in his first weeks as minister when he railroaded a series of proposals on economic cooperation through a Commonwealth foreign ministers' conference in Colombo, in January 1950. Opposition was put to flight by simply leaking to the Sydney press a story denouncing the "disposition in powerful quarters to let things go for the time being...a continuation of the wartime thinking of putting Europe first and letting Asia wait".[39]

One particular lesson that Spender learned at Colombo was that the Commonwealth in itself was not an appropriate basis on which to erect a structure of collective security. The question of a Pacific defense pact was, he claimed, "in this manner, deliberately raised, in order to be dismissed".[40] Accordingly, on 9 March 1950, he tuned his song to American ears in a speech that insisted on the need for urgent short-term measures to confront the "consolidation of Communism in China and the evident threat of its emergence as a growing force throughout South and South East Asia". Efforts to "stabilize governments and to create conditions of economic life and living standards under which the false ideological attractions which Communism excites will lose its [sic] force" would be "essentially long term measures". In the meantime. it would be necessary that "all governments who are directly interested in the preservation of peace throughout South and South East Asia, and in the advancement of human welfare under the democratic system should consider immediately whether some form of regional pact for common defense is a practical possibility".[41]

Circumstances played much more favourably into Spender's hands than into those of Evatt's. On 24 June the US ambassador in Seoul, John Muccio, reported "a heavy attack, different from patrol forays that had occurred in the past", amounting in his opinion to "an all-out offensive against the Republic of Korea".[42] Keith C. Shann, the Australian representative in the United Nations acting on Spender's instructions, asked immediately what we could do in the way of meeting force with force. He thought perhaps the Australians were in a position to help if the United Nations decided to take strong action.[43] Squadron 77 of the Royal Australian Air Force was already on stand-by in Japan, being under the operational control of the 5th US Air Force. On 29 June these aircraft, along with the destroyer *Bataan* and the frigate *Shoalhaven* were formally offered to Acheson. On the morning of 2 July, Mustangs of Squadron 77 were in action, strafing North Korean T-34s and occasionally South Korean forces heading in the same direction. The Australians were not exactly the first to make a positive offer of assistance, but they were the first actually to get into the fight.

Spender had another alternative. On 30 June, Truman decided to send US ground troops into action in Korea. The Joint Chiefs of Staff considered that "Australia is capable of furnishing three infantry battalions…and that such a contribution from Australia is highly desirable".[44] Australian Prime Minister Robert G. Menzies decided to visit London to consult with the British government before determining Australian policy. He was told that the British were in accord with his own decision not to commit troops. With Menzies halfway across the Atlantic, the British then decided to send their own force. Spender was apprised of British intentions by Australian diplomat Sir Alan Watt. The Minister immediately proceeded to bully Acting Prime Minister Sir Arthur Fadden into issuing, on his authority and without consulting either Menzies or other ministers, a statement written by Spender, to the effect that the Australian government had decided to provide ground troops for use in Korea in response to the appeal of the United Nations. Spender's timing was perfect. His highly unorthodox announcement actually was made simultaneously with that of the British government. Australia had finally made it to the head of the Commonwealth queue.[45]

Spender was now looking for a quid pro quo. Menzies, under British influence, was opposed totally to the idea of a Pacific pact, from which most other Commonwealth countries would be necessarily excluded. He told Fadden to warn Spender that the project was "not on the map" and referred to it himself as "a superstructure on a foundation of jelly".[46] This had no effect whatsoever on the butcher bird. Spender told the annual conference of the New South Wales Division of the Liberal party on 4 August that "consultation between Members of the British Commonwealth is not always satisfactory or effective". Accordingly, the Australian government maintained that

> since it came into office in December last [it had] placed special emphasis upon its desire for the closest relation with the United States.... What has taken place in Korea is indicative of the close association which we have endeavoured to create. It would be the purpose of the Australian Government to make those ties closer still, so that, on both sides of the Pacific, there will be two nations understanding each other, who will be able to work with the other democracies in the area for the purpose of bringing stability to this part of the world.[47]

He was even more specific in an address to the nation on the eve of his departure for London and Washington. He proclaimed that "Australia must seek to revive the close working association with our American friends which existed during the war. This relationship should, in due course, be given formal expression within the framework of a Pacific Pact".[48]

Spender still had to persuade the Americans, and he cleverly decided to try the candid approach when he met with President Truman. He explained that a Pacific pact would be meaningless unless the United States were a party to it, but that he had failed completely to make any headway at all in his discussions on this issue with other Commonwealth governments. Truman agreed to discuss it with Secretary Acheson, who did not immediately warm to Spender. The Secretary briefly told Spender that he could not conceive of Australia's being subject to hostile attack, or US failure to provide aid. Apart from that, Acheson merely delivered "generalities directed to the difficulties of any regional security arrangement...and the great differences which existed between the North Atlantic groups of nations and those of the western Pacific and Asia. This was becoming a familiar refrain".[49] Special Representative John Foster Dulles was even more uncompromising when Spender met with him at Flushing Meadows to discuss the Japanese peace treaty. Dulles began by confronting Spender, without any preliminaries, with the most extreme and uncompromising version of the American position, presenting him with a document that omitted any reference at all to limitations on Japanese freedom to rearm. Spender was having none of it. He told Dulles that Australia never would accept such a treaty, and he did not regard Dulles's proposal that the United States should retain troops in Japan as providing the slightest security for Australia; the only solution was a Pacific pact. Dulles stated that Spender's fears of Japan were exaggerated, to which Spender replied that Dulles's objections were illusory. Dulles nonetheless agreed that a compromise solution would have to be found.

The compromise agreed on in further discussions on 30 October among Spender, Dulles, and Dean Rusk amounted virtually to the acceptance in principle of the Australian proposal. Referring to a draft approved by Rusk, Spender told the federal parliament in Canberra that

> he had found in the United States that a most genuine friendship exists towards Australia and Australians...there is no doubt, at this moment, that this warm-hearted nation would immediately and effectively come to our aid in the event of an act of aggression against Australia. But it is not a one-way traffic in obligations with which Australia is concerned.... What we desire is a permanent regional basis of collective security, constructed in accordance with the United Nations Charter, which has as its pivotal point some obligation comparable to that set forth in Article 5 of the North Atlantic Treaty – namely, that an armed attack upon one shall be deemed an armed attack upon all. We desire to see formal

machinery set up to which, amongst others, the United States of America and ourselves are parties, which will enable us effectively to plan the use of our resources and military power.[50]

Spender's desires might have remained unrealized except that the United States was in urgent need of a reliable ally, as Chinese forces had entered the Korean War on 25 October. British Foreign Secretary Ernest Bevin flatly stated that he could not endorse the US suggestion that the Chinese intervention might necessitate the violation of the Manchurian border by UN forces".[51] By contrast, Spender urged that it should be made clear within the Security Council that it would be unreasonable and militarily disadvantageous for UN forces to continue indefinitely to observe restraint.[52] He warned Australians that the Soviets were using China to do their work for them in pursuit of a long-term plan to dominate the world. He stressed that under such circumstances "we must permit nothing to prevent the free peoples, in particular the British people, standing steadfast with the United States of America in the difficulties that confront us".[53] These protestations of support helped the Joint Chiefs of Staff to reach the decision that the State Department should explore at the earliest opportunity the possibilities of a Pacific pact with Australia. The Joint Chiefs, however, were not prepared to contemplate the prospect of having an Australian military mission arrive in Washington to discuss specifics with them. They strongly believed that,

> from the military point of view, any possible advantages to be gained as a result of inviting the Australian Government to send a high level military mission to Washington would be transitory and, in all probability, negligible; on the other hand, they perceive serious and far-reaching military disadvantages in having such a group in Washington, particularly in light of the present and projected status of the United States planning for a global war.[54]

However, it was becoming increasingly difficult to ignore Australian approaches. Spender was in full flight again. A US resolution in the Security Council on 20 January 1951, which denounced the Chinese for being engaged themselves in aggression in Korea, was drafted substantially by Shann on Spender's instructions despite the fact that Menzies himself was counselling caution on directions from London.[55] The Melbourne *Age*, noting Shann's frequent shifts of position depending on whether Menzies or Spender had gotten to him last, asked: "Is our new policy to be one of saying 'yes' to whatever emanates from Washington?"[56] As far as Spender was concerned, it was to be the policy until at least a Pacific pact had been signed; victory was in his hands. His influence had succeeded in producing, according to Sir Alan Watt, a degree of cordiality in Australian-American relations that had not been known since the days of the Pacific War.[57] Spender's efforts in this direction undoubtedly were made easier by the lack of effective parliamentary opposition, except indeed from his own Prime Minister. Bipartisanship in the true sense scarcely was to be looked for in the Australian political climate, but the Labor party was providing at least indirect support by denouncing, with perfect justice, the decidedly limited nature of Australian military support in Korea. Labor leader Joseph B. Chifley asserted that "it was not a matter of what sort of government operated in North or South Korea. The thing that mattered was that a country had been ruthlessly and wantonly attacked contrary to the principles of the Charter".

However, there was still a long road to travel. Menzies remained loathe to alienate the British. Dulles arrived in Canberra on 14 February for talks with the Australians and New Zealanders and was ready to pretend that the issue of a Pacific pact had never been raised in connection with that of a Japanese peace treaty. Spender informed him promptly that the Australian government never would accept a treaty such as Dulles was proposing without accompanying arrangements to ensure Australian security. Menzies himself urged Spender not to press too hard for a tripartite defense pact for fear of jeopardizing the chances of at least a Presidential guarantee of Australia and New Zealand. But the butcher bird knew with whom he was dealing. Dulles finally admitted that he had intended to discuss a Pacific pact all along. After three more days of vehement wrangling the three delegations agreed on a draft security treaty, which represented with marginal changes the text of the final ANZUS Pact.

Australian attitudes toward the United States had not changed fundamentally with the change of government in Canberra. Evatt had sought an alliance with the United States as earnestly as Percy Spender. The difference was simply that Evatt's attempts had failed and Spender's had succeeded. Also, circumstances had favoured Spender and not Evatt. Spender was unquestionably a more adept operator, but all the tactical skill in the world would have been unavailing against the ironbound intransigence of Acheson and Dulles had not the Chinese intervention in Korea made it urgently desirable for the United Slates to conclude a peace settlement with Japan without positively estranging its vociferous supporter in the South Pacific. In this sense, Mao Zedong was the real godfather of ANZUS; nevertheless, the bipartisan element in Australian policy can not be overstressed. Spender deliberately aligned himself with the United States wherever possible, while Evatt appeared, at least in Washington, to be doing exactly the opposite. However, Spender's chase had an end in view. The ANZUS Pact finally was pried out of Washington despite the misgivings of the State Department and the firm resolve of the Joint Chiefs to keep contacts with the Australians and New Zealanders on defense matters as superficial as possible.

In summary, ANZUS—or the Australian-New Zealand-US Security Treaty—was signed at San Francisco on 1 September 1951, ratified by President Truman on 15 April 1952, and entered into force two weeks later on 29 April. Conceived in close connection with the conclusion of a "soft" Japanese peace treaty, and contrary to historical charges of subservience on the side of the junior partner, the ANZUS alliance was negotiated only after much tough bargaining. The main source of contention was, paradoxically, the bipartisan determination of Australian leaders to establish a binding security relationship between their country and the United States and the equally firm and bipartisan resolve of American policymakers not to embark upon anything of the kind. Put simply, Canberra wanted strategic reassurance that America would come to Australia's aid in her next time of troubles; Washington wanted cooperation, an opportunity to take advantage of Australia's unique geographical position in the Western Pacific, as well as the overall political position in Southeast Asia. Neither got exactly what it wanted, Australia's future leaders, reserving the right to see the alliance a little differently form the way the United States saw it. In any case, "for the decision-makers in Canberra", recalled historian Coral Bell who was in the Department of External Affairs at the time, "the original interpretation…was that the rationale of the treaty should be seen as 90 per cent security blanket against revival of Japanese ambitions in the Pacific, and 10 per cent insurance policy against possible future Chinese expansionism". Asia would always be a dangerous place for Australia without America's strategic engagement.[58]

## NOTES

1. Glen St.J. Barclay, "Australia Looks to America: The Wartime Relationship, 1939-1942," *Pacific Historical Review* 46 (May 1977): 251-71.

2. External Affairs II, Commonwealth Record Series (CRS) A989 441735/260/4, *US Use of Postwar Installations,* Australian Archives: and high commissioner for Australia in New Zealand to Evatt, 20 Dec. 1943, External Affairs II, CRS A989, 44/735/321/8, *PWR Far East and the Pacific. Post War Security Bases,* Australian Archives.

3. CRS A989,44/735/260/4, *US Use of Postwar Installations.*

4. For full documentation, see US, Department of State, *Foreign Relarions of the United States 1944: The British Commonwealth and Europe,* 3 (Washington, 1965), pp. 16-209. Hereafter cited as *FRUS.* Robin L. Kay, ed., *The Australian-New Zealand Agreement 1944* (Wellington 1972); and Glen St.J. Barclay and Joseph M. Siracusa, eds., *Australian-American Relations Since 1945: A Documentary History* (Sydney, 1976).

5. Grew to Henry L. Stimson, 22 June 1945, *FRUS* 1945, 6: pp. 574-76.

6. D. Dilks, ed., *The Diaries of Sir Alexander Cadogan, 1938-1945* (London, 1971), p. 745.

7. Memorandum for President, 30 October 1945, "Australia and the ICJ", United Nations File, 1944-46, Papers of Henry Reiff, Harry S. Truman Library, Independence, Missouri.

8. Johnson to Hull, 1 Feb. 1944, 747.474/26. Decimal Files, Department of State, National Archives, Washington (herealter cited by file number, followed by DF, DSNA).

9. Memorandum of conversation, 27 Oct. 1945, 711.47/10-2745, DF, DS NA. See also P.G. Edwards, "Evatt and the Americans," *Historical Studies* 18 (Oct. 1979): 546-60.

10. Roger J. Bell "Australian-American Discord: Negotiations for Postwar Bases and Security Arrangements in the Pacific, 1944-46," *Australian Outlook* 27 (Apr. 1973): 12-33.

11. Miniter to Acheson, 12 Apr. 1946, *FRUS*, 1946, 8: pp. 963-64.

12. Acheson to Truman, 8 May 1946, PSF, Foreign Affairs-Australia, Truman Library.

13. Woodward to Matthew Connally, 4 June 1946, OF, 48-D, Australia, Truman Library.

14. Press release, 8 July 1946, ibid.

15. Butler to Connally, 26 Dec. 1947, PPF, file 1054, Truman Library.

16. Butler to Truman, 11 June 1947, ibid.

17. Atcheson to Marshall, 5 luly 1947, *FRUS* 1947, 7: pp. 248-51.

18. Dean G. Acheson, *Present at the Creation* (New York, 1970). p. 345.

19. Atcheson to Marshall, 1 Aug. 1947, *FRUS*, 1947, 6: pp. 268-69.

20. Australian Department of External Affairs, *Current Notes on International Affairs* vol. 18 (Aug. 1947), pp. 469-74 (hereafter cited as *CNIA*).

21. Lovett to Truman, 7 Oct. 1947, PSF, Foreign Affairs-Australia, Truman Library.

22. Evatt to Truman, 12 Feb. 1948, ibid.

23 Truman to Evatt, 8 Mar. 1948, ibid.

24. Makin to Truman, 10 Sept. 1948, PPF, Papers of Harry S. Truman, Truman Library (hereafter cited as Truman Papers).

25. *CNIA* 20 (Feb. 1949).

26. Lovett to Truman, 7 Oct. 1947, PSF, Foreign Affairs-Australia, Truman Library.

27. Policy Statement on Australia, 18 Aug. 1948, 711.47/8-1848. DF, DSNA.

28. W. Millis, ed. *The Forrestal Diaries: The Inner History of the Cold War* (London, 1952), p. 496.

29. CIA, ORE 9-49, "Communist Influence in Australia," 15 Apr. 1949, PSF, Foreign Affairs-Australia, Truman Library.

30. Foster to Acheson, 13 May 1949, *FRUS*, 1949. 7: pp. 744-46.

31. Calwell to Cowen, 18 July 1949, Miscellaneous Correspondence-Australia, Papers of Myron M. Cowen, Truman Library.

32. Cowen to Foster, 4 Aug. 1949, ibid.

33. Jarman to Donald Dawson, 25 May 1949, PPF, Truman Papers.

34. John L. Hawkins to Truman, ibid.

35. Memorandum of conversation, 21 Sept. 1949, Papers of Dean G. Acheson, Truman Library.

36. Butterworth to Acheson, 18 Nov. 1949, *FRUS*, 1949, 7: pp. 901-2.

37. Shullaw to Acheson, 9 December 1949, 747.U7M.51A, DF, DSNA.

38. Memorandum of conversation, 27 Dec. 1949, *FRUS*, 1949, 7: pp. 933-34.

39. Charles E. Buttrose to Spender, 11 Oct. 1957, Box 1, Papers of Percy C. Spender, National Library of Australia (hereafter cited as Spender Papers).

40. "Minutes of Colombo Conference," Jan. 1950, Box 8, Spender Papers.

41. *CNIA* 21 (Mar. 1950), pp. 153-72.

42. Transcript, John Muccio Oral History Interview with Robert A. McKenzie, 20, Truman Library.

43. Memorandum of conversation by Charles P. Noyes, Adviser on National Security Council Affalrs, 25 June l950, *FRUS*, 1950, 7: pp. 144-17

44. "Proposed Military Assistance in Korea from Certain UN Nations," JSPC to JCS, 10 Aug. 1950, DSNA.

45. Percy C. Spender, *Politics and a Man* (Sydney, 1972), pp. 280-85.

46. Percy C. Spender, *Exercises in Diplomacy* (Sydney, 1969), pp. 578-82.

47. *CNIA*, 21 (Aug. 1950), pp. 578-82.

48. Ibid., p. 582.

49. Spender, *Exercises in Diplomacy*, pp. 43-44.

50. Ibid, pp. 72-75.

51. Bevin to Sir Oliver Franks, 16 Nov. 1950, *FRUS*, 1950, 7: p. 1172.

52. Jarman to Acheson, 17 Nov. 1950, ibid., 7: p. 1171-72.

53. *CNIA* 21 (Dec. 1950), pp. 881-86.

54. Marshall to Acheson, 16 Jan. 1951, *FRUS*, 1951, 6: pp.141.

55. Shann to Spender, 25 Oct. 1957, Box 1, Spender Papers.

56. Melbourne *Age*, 30 Jan. 1951.

57. R. Rosecrance, *Australian Diplomacy and Japan, 1945-1951* (Melbourne, 1962), p. 184.

58., Coral Bell, *Australia's Alliance Options* (Canberra, 1991), pp. 38-39. Also see Joseph G. Starke, *The ANZUS Treaty Alliance* (Melbourne, 1965); H.C. Gelber, *The Australian American Alliance: Costs and Benefits* (Baltimore, 1968), Trevor R. Reese, *Australia, New Zealand and the United States: A Survey of International Relations, 1941-1968* (London, 1969); Coral Bell, *Dependent Ally: A Study in Australian Foreign Policy* (Canberra, 1984), 40-62; Henry S. Albinski, *ANZUS, the United States and Pacific Security* (Lanham, Maryland, 1987); Geoffrey

Bolton, ed., *The Oxford History of Australia* (Melbourne, 1990), vol. 5, *1942-1988: The Middle Way*, by G. Bolton, pp. 79, 149; Alan Burnett, *The ANZUS Triangle* (Canberra, 1988); and *The ANZUS Documents,* ed., Alan Burnett (Canberra, 1991).

# CHAPTER 6

# CONCLUSION

By the spring of 1945, Western forces had liberated France and pushed across the Rhine in a final drive into the heart of the German Third Reich. In a parallel development the Soviet Red Army began a last offensive within thirty miles of Berlin. Anticipating the political value that would accrue to the conqueror of the Nazi capital, the British, led by Prime Minister Winston Churchill, sought to launch a quick drive to reach Berlin first but were overruled on military grounds by General Dwight Eisenhower and the American government. Guided by the more calculating hand of Soviet leader Marshal Josef Stalin, the Red Army liberated all the ancient capitals of central Europe, including Prague, Vienna, and Budapest. The American decision to hold back was probably a mistake, the full implications of which became clear only after the war. In any case, by the second week of April, the Americans had reached the Elbe River just sixty-three miles from Berlin, while the Soviets prepared for the final assault.

The sudden death of President Franklin Roosevelt on 12 April 1945 came at this fateful moment in the war. The feeling of loss among the leaders and peoples of the United Nations was intense. The British *Economist* summed it up this way: "It would be difficult to find hyperbole strong enough to exaggerate the sense of loss felt all over the free world at the sudden news of President Roosevelt's death. Never before in a statesman of another country and rarely for one of our own leaders have the outward pomp of ceremonial mourning and also the inward and personal lamentation of the public been more universal and heartfelt". Much the same was said in the Soviet Union where, according to the Moscow correspondent of *The Times* of London, "President Roosevelt has been the personification of enlightened American liberalism". The "juggler", who took pride in not letting his right hand know what his left hand was doing, would be sorely missed.[1]

The mantle of American leadership fell upon the shoulders of Harry S. Truman, the seventh vice-president to succeed to the presidency upon the death of the chief executive. Not unlike many other leaders of the nation, Truman rose to his position from humble beginnings. Born in Lamar, Missouri, on 8 May 1884, the thirty-third President of the United States was educated in the public school system, operated the family farm near Independence, Missouri, and served in World War I, seeing action in France. Studying law at night for two years in the early 1920s, Truman became involved in county government through the backing of Kansas City political "Boss" Tom Pendergast.

Though elected to the United States Senate in 1934, it was not until America entered World War II that Truman distinguished himself, reaching national prominence as chairman of the Senate Committee to Investigate the National Defense Program. During his chairmanship of the Senate's war investigating committee, Truman was voted by Washington correspondents, according to the *New York Times*, "as the civilian who, next to President Roosevelt, 'knew most about the war'". From his Senate position and because of his record, Truman became the eventual compromise candidate for the vice-presidency at the Democratic convention in Chicago in 1944 in the bitter conflict between Harry A. Wallace, vice-president during FDR's third term and the undisputed choice of party radicals, and James F. Byrnes, director of war mobilization and reconversion, the almost undisputed choice of the conservatives.

In sharp contrast to the image of Truman held by his contemporaries as a man with a strong capacity for national leadership, scholars of all political persuasions have usually portrayed him as generally uninformed about his predecessor's foreign policies and forced to rely heavily on Roosevelt's political and military advisers. To some extent this was so. For example, FDR had failed to bring him into the larger picture of the internal workings of the Grand Alliance as well as to inform him of the atomic bomb project; but, then, Roosevelt had always acted as his own secretary of state in alliance matters. Still, for all his limitations, Truman was a man of his times, an avowed internationalist and an accomplished politician. Though acutely aware that, in his own words, "No man could possibly fill the tremendous void left by the passing of that noble soul [FDR]", the new occupant of the White House soon showed qualities of considerable executive ability, and was fully determined to be President in his own right, wholly responsible for the decisions that would have to be made. Like Roosevelt, Truman too would learn the art of managing the unmanageable, *Realpolitik*.

During the transition of power in Washington, Germany collapsed under Allied hammer blows. As Soviet shells fell into Berlin, Adolf Hitler committed suicide on 30 April 1945, his body cremated in the garden by loyal followers. Facing the inevitable, German armies surrendered unconditionally at Reims on 7-8 May. The Third Reich, which was supposed to last a thousand years, was finished.

President Truman initially adhered to Roosevelt's official policy of collaboration with the Soviet Union, though privately FDR was having second thoughts about how best to deal with Stalin. Truman, like his advisers, came to recognize that Moscow viewed conciliatory gestures as a sign of weakness. The composition of the government of the reemerging Polish state continued to remain the great stumbling block, symbolizing in Western eyes Stalin's determination to have his own way throughout eastern Europe and elsewhere.

By the time Vyacheslav Molotov, the People's Commissar for Foreign Affairs, arrived for talks in Washington in April 1945 en route to the founding conference of the United Nations to be held in San Francisco, Truman had served notice, to cite one account of the shift in mood, "that our agreements with the Soviet Union so far had been a one-way street and that could not continue: it was now or never". In their celebrated meeting of 23 April, the President rebuked Molotov for Soviet behaviour, all in the roughest Missouri language; the Soviet Foreign Minister, a dour, humourless man, defended his nation's interpretation of the Polish accord worked out at Yalta, in February, adding that he had never been spoken to in such terms. According to Truman's interpreter, Charles Bohlen, these were "probably the first sharp words uttered during the war by an American President to a high Soviet official", although it is hard to imagine this particular aide of Josef Stalin having escaped similar language at home.[2]

On 11 May 1945, following the Nazi collapse, Truman ordered a sharp cutback in lend-lease shipments, including those to Russia; unfortunately, subordinates enforced the directive even more narrowly than the President probably intended, recalling Russian-bound ships at sea. Lend-lease to the USSR had previously been on a special basis—no information requested, no conditions of any kind—and apparently the President meant to send a signal to the Kremlin indicating a change in attitude. Stalin professed to be deeply pained and offended by the order, though the episode was soon smoothed over.

The way was then cleared for the last of the wartime summit conferences—code-named "Terminal"—held at Potsdam, near Berlin, from 17 July to 2 August 1945. Churchill was replaced midway through the conference by Clement Atlee whose Labour party had won the recent general election. The Allies (excluding the USSR on Japanese matters) agreed upon a last warning to Tokyo to surrender and agreed to establish a Council of Foreign Ministers to prepare treaties for Italy and the lesser Axis states, i.e., Rumania, Hungary, Bulgaria, and Finland. Moreover, the Big Three reaffirmed the policy of a joint occupation of vanquished Germany with fixed, zoned boundaries. The vexing problem of reparations was also tentatively settled.

According to the compromise reached, each occupying force would obtain its share of reparations from its own zone, with the Soviet Union to be compensated for its greater losses by 25 per cent of the capital goods located within the western industrialized zones, a part of which in turn be exchanged for food shipments from the largely agricultural areas occupied by the Soviet element. Moreover, the occupying forces were to embark on an overall program designed to denazify, decentralize, disarm, and democratize Germany until such time as it was deemed fit to rejoin the family of nations. Finally, Stalin, who was still technically at peace with Tokyo, agreed to enter into the war against Japan on 15 August, making good a pledge given earlier that the Soviet Union would do so three months after the war in Europe had been concluded.

Potsdam, like the Yalta Conference before it, ended on a note of apparent friendship and continued cooperation. Truman's diary makes it clear that Stalin had impressed the President: "He [Stalin] is honest—but smart as hell". Still, Truman and the American planners were much less optimistic than their public remarks indicated. Soviet leaders had clearly revealed the unilateral nature of their concept of cooperation and their own plans for the future of eastern Europe. Many years later Truman recalled:

I hardly ever look back for the purpose of contemplating 'what might have been': Potsdam brings to mind 'what might have been'...Certainly...Russia had no program except to take over the free part of Europe, kill as many Germans as possible, and fool the Western Alliance. Britain only wanted to control the Eastern Mediterranean, keep India, oil in Persia, the Suez Canal, and whatever else was floating loose.

There was an innocent idealist at one corner of that Round Table who wanted free waterways, Danube-Rhine-Kiel Canal, Suez, Black Sea Straits, Panama all free, a restoration of Germany, France, Italy, Poland, Czechoslovakia, Rumania, and the Balkans, and a proper treatment of Latvia, Lithuania, Finland, free Philippines, Indonesia, Indo-China, a Chinese Republic, and a free Japan.

What a show that was! But a large number of agreements were reached in spite of the set up—only to be broken as soon as the unconscionable Russian Dictator returned to Moscow! And I liked the little son of a bitch...[3]

The shape of the Cold War loomed ahead by the closing days of World War II.

Long-range B-29 bombers from Guam and other island bases had begun to rain destruction upon Japan by the close of 1944, culminating the next year in the greatest air offensive in history. All in all, approximately 160,000 tons of bombs were dropped upon Japan toward the end of the war, including fire-bomb raids that destroyed the centre of Tokyo and other large Japanese cities. These raids alone killed 333,000 Japanese and wounded an additional 500,000 more. Air raids by July 1945 had, then, all but smashed the Japanese war economy.

Although elements within Japan long recognized they had lost the war and were prepared to sue for peace, the American government, still committed to a policy of unconditional surrender, was not inclined to bargain with them. Truman's warning to the Japanese issued at Potsdam to surrender or face total destruction stood. The Japanese government and the Emperor favoured making peace, but the militarists, led by the army, resisted. No less than one million American and Allied casualties—or so it was said at the time—were estimated by the Joint Chiefs of Staff to be the cost of invading the home islands.[4]

Faced with this prospect, Truman and his advisers determined to use the atomic bomb against Japan in order to end the war as quickly as possible, assuming, of course, the final product of the multibillion dollar Manhattan Project lived up to expectations. In any case, the Administration easily rejected or never considered alternatives to the bomb. On the morning of 6 August 1945, shortly after 8.15AM, a lone B-29 bomber six miles up dropped the first atomic bomb on Hiroshima (population 350,000), the second most important military centre in Japan, killing 140,000 people on the day of the attack and in the weeks immediately after it. The first uranium bomb to be used possessed the equivalent of only 12,000 tons of TNT—puny and primitive by current thermonuclear standards. Still, in that one terrible moment 60 per cent of Hiroshima, an area equal to one-eighth of Manhattan, was destroyed. Three days later a second, slightly larger, atomic bomb was dropped on the city of Nagasaki, an important industrial and shipping area with a population of 253,000 of whom 70,000 were ultimately killed. This plutonium bomb possessed more power than 20,000 tons of TNT, a destructive force equivalent to the collective load of 4,000 B-29 bombers, or more than 2,000 times the blast power of what previously had been the world's most devastating bomb, the British "Grand Slam", a logical technological improvement in the strategy of "city-busting" that the Allies had developed at Hamburg and Dresden. In any case, Truman made the choice, with insufficient forethought, based on his own war experience and information at hand.[5]

Meanwhile, reluctant to miss out on the kill, the Soviet Union declared war on Japan on 8 August, a week sooner than the deadline of the pledge Stalin gave Truman at Potsdam. Nine minutes after its declaration, the Soviet Union's Far Eastern Army and Air Force attacked Japanese troops along the eastern Soviet-Manchuria borderlands. Yielding to the reality of the situation, the Emperor, supported by civilian advisers, finally overcame the Japanese militarists and ordered a surrender on 14 August. For its part, the United States agreed to retain the institution of the Emperor system, stripped of pretension to divinity and subject to American occupation headed by General Douglas MacArthur. On 2 September, a great Allied fleet sailed into Tokyo Bay for the formal surrender ceremony which took place on board the USS *Missouri*. World War II was thus brought to a close.

The introduction of atomic weaponry into the American arsenal together with the implied peacetime use of the atom posed a number of serious problems for the Truman Administration. Fully recognizing the revolutionary character of harnessing atomic energy, though perhaps underestimating the relative ability of other nations to translate their theoretical knowledge into practical application—for some, a deadly illusion—President Truman approached his task from the domestic and the international level. At the domestic level he requested Congress in October 1945 to enact legislation aimed at the creation of an Atomc Energy Commission "for the control, use and development of atomic energy within the United States".

At the international level, Truman met in Washington in November with British Prime Minister Atlee and his Canadian counterpart, Mackenzie King, and agreed on the need for action under United Nations auspices to outlaw atomic weapons, to ensure the use of atomic energy for peaceful purposes only, and to provide for inspection safeguards. To facilitate such action the foreign ministers of the Big Three, meeting in Moscow in December, consented to co-sponsor a resolution in the United Nations General Assembly establishing a United Nations Atomic Energy Commission. This was done on 24 January 1946.

To prepare American strategy, Secretary of State James Byrnes appointed a special committee chaired by Under Secretary of State, Dean G. Acheson, aided by a board of consultants headed by David Lilienthal, the chairman of the Tennessee Valley Authority and later the first chairman of the United States Atomic Energy Commission. The result, the Acheson-Lilienthal Resport, made public on 28 March 1946, concluded that the only way to ensure that nuclear energy could not be used for weapons was to create an international authority that would hold a monopoly over nuclear research and development. To this end, the report proposed a supranational International Atomic Development Authority, to be entrusted with all phases of the development and use of atomic energy, having the power to manage, control, inspect, and license all related activities. What the proposed agency would not have was authority to apply sanctions against wrongdoers. Truman chose Bernard Baruch, a financier and longtime Democrat, to present the plan to the United Nations' Atomic Energy Commission in June.

The Baruch Plan, really an effort to extend the US monopoly, proposed the cessation of the manufacture of atomic bombs, the disposal of existing American bombs, and the creation of the international authority recommended in the Acheson-Lilienthal Report. More important, Baruch's plan provided for sanctions not subject to the veto of any permanent member of the United Nations Security Council and insisted that an adequate system of control and inspection be in effect *before* the United States handed over control of its nuclear facilities.

Moscow's response came five days later in an address delivered by the Soviet United Nations Representative, Andrei Gromyko. Already preparing its own weapons, the Soviet Union rejected the American proposal, calling simply for the prohibition of the production and use of nuclear weapons, and for the destruction of existing stockpiles while providing for no serious inspection scheme to monitor compliance. The Soviet counterproposal was, in turn, rejected by the United States. Moscow's principal motive in rebuffing the American proposal derived from fear that the Baruch Plan would subject the USSR to permanent strategic inferiority and its economy to outside interference, not to mention waiving the Soviet right to veto in the case of punishment. Furthermore, any effective inspection system would necessarily mean a breach of the Iron Curtain, and this Premier Stalin refused to tolerate. Both sides agreeing only to disagree, the proceedings were adjourned indefinitely on 30 March 1948.[6]

Upon his return from Potsdam, President Truman continued publicly to emphasize Allied unity. Like Roosevelt before him, Truman said he found it easy to get along with Stalin. Furthermore, declared the President to the American people in August 1945, "there was a fundamental accord and agreement upon the objectives ahead of us"—an assertion that hardly reflected the deep-seated Soviet-American differences over such matters as reparations and occupation policies in Germany and Austria. While relations between the Allies appeared tranquil enough on the surface, policymakers at the highest levels had moved well in the direction of locating and identifying the Soviet Union as the most serious threat to international peace.

On 5 October 1945, in a radio broadcast originating from Washington, Secretary of State Byrnes announced to the nation that the first session of the Council of Foreign Ministers, which had met in London in September, closed in stalemate. The tensions that had undermined Allied diplomacy in the closing stages of World War II threatened to surface. The London Conference broke up mainly over the unexpected Soviet refusal to allow China and France to participate in the drafting of peace treaties with Italy and the lesser

Axis nations, the objection being that only nations signatory to surrender documents had the right to speak on the subject at this time.

Other difficulties included the joint Anglo-American refusal to recognize the pro-Soviet governments of Bulgaria and Rumania. The Americans based their refusal squarely on the ground that freedom of speech and assembly were still being denied to the Bulgarian and Rumanian people, basic rights without which political self-determination could not be realized. Draft treaties for Italy, Rumania, Hungary, Bulgaria and Finland were finally arranged by the time a peace conference of twenty-one nations assembled in Paris in July 1946. They were signed and went into effect on 10 February 1947, but not before the Cold War rivalry that would animate Soviet-American relations for the next generation and beyond had taken root.

Despite late efforts to assuage Soviet fears, and in a manner that foreshadowed the Administration's hardening attitude toward Stalin in the wake of fruitless second meeting of the Council of Foreign Ministers, the United States State Department vigorously continued to object to the Soviet establishment of totalitarian political regimes and economic control over the countries of eastern and central Europe. In full conformity with the American position of self-determination and equality of commercial opportunity, State Department planners argued that America should use its influence to break the Soviet grip. The method chosen to resist the Soviets lay principally in the economic sphere—a natural choice, given the dominance of the American economy in the postwar period.

Specifically, through the granting of credits, the United States hoped to encourage more political independence for nations behind the Iron Curtain—countries east of the line from Stettin in the Baltic to Trieste in the Adriatic—to use Churchill's famous allusion. At the same time, the United States hoped to persuade the Kremlin to loosen its grip over the same countries. With the proverbial battle line drawn, the Truman Administration began to abandon hope of accommodating Stalin's fears and plans for expansion by early 1946. "I'm tired of babying the Soviets", President Truman was alleged to have told his Secretary of State.

For their part, Soviet leaders undertook the difficult task of preparing the Russian people for the struggle ahead, for the continued sacrifices they would have to make in the name of rebuilding their war-torn economy, and for the inevitable postponement of the production of consumer goods in favour of heavy industry. To achieve their goal the Communist party of the Soviet Union appealed to the heightened sense of Russian nationalism that accompanied the Red Army's victory over Nazi Germany and Japan and to the Marxist theme of capitalist antagonism to industrial socialism. The most significant appeal was that made by Stalin on 9 February 1946. In a speech regarded by some as the single most important Soviet pronouncement of the immediate postwar world, Stalin revived international class conflict in a way that suggested that the USSR was clearly a revolutionary power. In a characteristic reaction, H. Freeman Matthews, the State Department's Director of the Office of European Affairs, noted that Stalin's speech constituted, "the most important and authoritative guide to postwar Soviet policy".

In the so-called Long Telegram of 22 February 1946, a response to a State Department request for an interpretive analysis of the significance and meaning of Stalin's and other related pronouncements, the American chargé in Moscow, George F. Kennan, formulated an assessment of Soviet foreign policy that captured the mood of the Truman Administration's determination to resist the perceived threat of Stalinist Russia to world peace. Not only was Kennan able to explain the basis of Soviet foreign policy, he also had a remedy: containment. What "we have here", argued Kennan persuasively, is "a political force committed fanatically to the belief that with the [United States] there can be no permanent *modus vivendi*, that it is desirable and necessary that the international harmony of our society be disrupted, our traditional way of life be destroyed, the international authority of our state be broken, if Soviet power is to be secure".

What to do about it was compounded by the fact that Soviet leadership was "seemingly inaccessible to consideration of reality in its basic reaction", though not in the same sense that informed Hitler's reckless ambitions. "Impervious to logic of reason", concluded Kennan, "it [USSR] is highly sensitive to the logic of force. For this reason it can easily withdraw—and usually does— when strong resistance is encountered at any point". Kennan became permanently and unwittingly identified with this policy in his famous "X" article published in the influential journal, *Foreign Affairs*, in 1947.[7] At that time he refined what has since become the classic definition of containment: "Soviet pressure against the free institutions of the western world is something that can be contained by the adroit and vigilant application of counterforce at a series of constantly shifting geographical and political points, corresponding to the shifts and manoeuvres of Soviet policy, but which cannot be charmed out of existence". On 24 November 1948, the doctrine of containment was officially adopted by the Truman Administration.

Throughout 1946 Soviet actions tended to confirm the Administration's worst fears. While pursuing obstructionist policies in the occupation control councils in Germany and Austria, the Soviets continued to retain forces in Manchuria and northern Iran, in the latter area preventing government troops from intervening against communist-organized rebels in the province of Azerbaijan. In March 1946, Iran protested to the United Nations Security Council, demanding the evacuation of the Red army from the disputed territory. By early May Soviet troop withdrawal had been completed but not before the United Nations had showed its powerlessness in the face of the Kremlin's veto power. The Iranian crisis, together with Soviet threats against Turkey at the same time, prompted Washington to begin to plan for war with the Soviet Union, suggesting the extent to which early Cold War diplomats were prepared to play power politics.[8]

The United States learned the lesson that the USSR could only be checked by policies initiated by Washington. Accordingly, the Truman Administration was determined to resist what it regarded as Soviet aggression the next time it reared its head, although the actual form and timing of that resistance were much in doubt. The immediate background of the pronouncement of the Truman Doctrine was the official disclosure in February 1947 that the British government would shortly be terminating its military and economic support of the existing Greek and Turkish regimes. The President's response both to the plight of the British and to the deteriorating situation in Greece and Turkey was swift and unequivocal. Requesting urgent economic and financial assistance for the relief of these countries, Truman declared to a joint session of Congress on 12 March 1947: "I believe that it must be the policy of the United States to support free peoples who are resisting attempted subjugation by armed minorities or by outside pressures. I believe that we must assist free peoples to work out their own destinies in their own way". The exact meaning of these words, although

Truman specifically qualified them to mean "that our help should be primarily through economic and financial aid", has been the subject of much historical debate.[9]

Whatever the President meant, there can be little doubt that his speech was a major turning point in modern American foreign policy. Significantly, this was a policy that had the support of Republicans and Democrats alike, the former organized under the direction of Senator Arthur Vandenberg of Michigan, the leading Republican spokesman on foreign policy in the Senate and one of the earliest supporters of a bipartisan approach to postwar international relations. The only element left to argue about was tactics.

By late May 1947 it had become alarmingly apparent that the Administration had grossly underestimated the destruction of the European economy in the aftermath of World War II. "Europe is steadily deteriorating", observed Under Secretary of State William L. Clayton; furthermore, "the political position reflects the economic". As the fate and well-being of the United States were invariably bound up with the fate and well-being of Western Europe, it was only natural that Washington would seek to repair the fortunes of its natural allies.

During commencement exercises at Harvard University on 5 June 1947, the eminent soldier and Secretary of State George C. Marshall observed that in the name of enlightened self-interest, "It is logical that the United States should do whatever it is able to do to assist in the return of normal economic health in the world, without which there can be no political stability and no assured peace". Marshall called for the reconstruction of Europe by Europeans, and so was born the Marshall Plan or, more accurately, the European Recovery Program, signed into law by President Truman on 3 April 1948.[10] Two weeks later the sixteen Western European nations involved met in Paris to set up the necessary machinery for economic cooperation—the Organization for European Economic Cooperation. From that time until the Marshall Plan officially came to an end in December 1951, the United States pumped $13 billion into the economy of Western Europe.

The repeated failure of the Council of Foreign Ministers to reach agreement on Germany by late 1947 led to moves by the Western powers towards the creation of a unified and self-governing West Germany. The Anglo-American elements had already taken one large step in that direction by the economic merging of their three zones. Consultations in London in the spring of 1948 resulted in agreements, announced 7 June, proposing the creation of a West German government with some safeguards planned for the control of the Ruhr industries. The Germans of the Western zones would elect members of a constituent assembly, which in turn would draw up a constitution for a federal state that might eventually include the Eastern Zone.

Accordingly, the German Federal Republic was inaugurated at Bonn in September 1949. Military government terminated, although occupation forces remained. The Federal Republic was soon made eligible for Marshall Plan aid, and under its first chancellor, Konrad Adenauer, showed a spirit of willing cooperation with the West. For its part the Kremlin resolved to do everything possible to defeat the program of American "imperialism". Communist-inspired strikes in France and Italy sought in vain to deter these countries from accepting the Marshall Plan aid. Treaties of defensive alliance linking the Soviet Union with Finland, Bulgaria, Hungary and Rumania were added to treaties previously negotiated with Czechoslovakia, Poland, and Yugoslavia. And in February 1948 a communist coup overthrew the democratic government of Czechoslovakia and installed one firmly attached to the Kremlin. This blow to the West was partly compensated for later in the year when Yugoslavia, under Marshal Tito, broke with Moscow.

Complaining that the Western powers (including France) had destroyed the four-power control over Germany, the Soviets set out to eject their erstwhile allies from Berlin, which lay wholly within the Soviet zone. Berlin, with no guaranteed surface corridor of communications with the West, had restrictions upon the movement of persons to and from the city imposed in April 1948 (followed in June by the prohibition of all surface transportation between Berlin and the Western Zone). The Western powers were faced with the prospect of withdrawing their garrisons form Berlin in defeat or of supplying not only them, but also the two million inhabitants of West Berlin. Despite the initial impression in some quarters that the Western forces might consider leaving the former German capital if the suffering of the populace became too great, the Truman Administration decided to act.

Rejecting advice that he open the road by military force, the President, in consultation with the British, resorted to air transport, the only means for which the West had signed agreements with the Soviets. The "airlift" not thought possible by some observers on the scene commenced at once, and, by September, American and British planes were flying in four thousands tons of supplies daily. Soviet planes occasionally threatened but never ventured to attack. Allied persistence and patience finally paid dividends as the Soviets ended the blockade in May 1949.[11] Shortly afterward the Soviet-sponsored German Democratic Republic was called into existence. Like its competitor at Bonn, East Germany rested upon a constitution dedicated to the unification of all Germany, though it is clear Stalin never wanted a separate state. Unlike its competitor, it would not be allowed to deviate from the party line emanating from Moscow.[12]

The communist coup in Czechoslovakia and the Berlin "blockade" greatly alarmed the Western powers. There was, after all, no guarantee that the Soviets, with their preponderant number of armed forces, might not renew efforts to oust the Western allies from Berlin or to strangle the German Federal Republic in its infancy. "Containment" of Soviet Russia, till now dependent mainly upon economic and political means, appeared in need of more military backing. For if the USSR could be certain that an act of aggression against any one of the free nations of Western Europe would mean a conflict with the others and also with the United States, it might be deterred from such acts. Neither America's nuclear monopoly nor the United Nations Security Council, because of the Soviet veto, could supply such a deterrent. It was in this context that the West turned to Article 51 of the United Nations Charter, which legalized "collective self-defense" by groups within the United Nations. In the Americas, the Rio Pact of September 1947, had already invoked Article 51 in a hemispheric collective-security agreement; in Europe a beginning had been made in March 1948 when Great Britain, France, and the Benelux countries signed at Brussels a fifty-year treaty of economic, social, and cultural collaboration and collective self-defense.

Support for the treaty was promptly proposed by President Truman in address to Congress in March 1948. The President spoke frankly of the danger from Moscow, calling for the adoption of a universal military training program (which Congress defeated), and temporary reenactment of Selective Service legislation. The buildup of American armed forces strength, which had been allowed to disintegrate since 1945, began with the draft act of June 1948, requiring military service of men from nineteen to twenty-five years of age. With the aid of this, and under the stimulus of the Korean War, the combined strength of the American armed forces grew from 1,350,000 in 1948 to 3,630,000 in June 1952. The way for collective action was cleared when the Senate, in the Vandenberg Resolution of 17 June 1948, articulated the proposition that the United States should associate itself, "by constitutional processes, with such regional and other collective arrangements as are based on continuous and effective self-help and mutual aid, and as affect its national security".

The Vandenberg Resolution was the prelude to the North Atlantic Treaty (1949), a significant and profound venture in search of meaningful collective security. The treaty—a fundamental departure from the American principle of "no permanent alliances"— was signed by twelve nations of the northern Atlantic and western European areas, a number increased to fifteen in 1955 with the inclusion of West Germany. The parties agreed to settle all disputes peacefully among themselves and to develop their capacity to resist armed attack. But the heart of the treaty was Article 5 with its "Three Musketeers" pledge that an armed attack upon any one of the members in Europe or North America would be considered an attack upon all; furthermore, the treaty pledged each member to assist any attacked party "by such action as it deems necessary, including the use of armed forces". Thus originated the North Atlantic Treaty Organization, or NATO.

Two other events in 1949 greatly shaped the direction of the United States defense effort. The first was the revelation in September that the USSR had exploded its first atomic bomb; the second was the completion of the Communist conquest of all of mainland China, followed by the proclamation of the People's Republic of China at Beijing in October. The latter event was regarded as a major triumph in the Kremlin's program of world revolution; the former, a potential mortal danger to the continental United States itself. One top-secret document, Policy Paper Number 68 of the National Security Council (or NSC 68), approved by President Truman in September 1950, went so far as to estimate, in the "period of peril" motif so often employed in modern times, "that within the next four years the U.S.S.R. will attain the capability of seriously damaging vital centres of the United States, provided it strikes a first blow and provided further that the blow is opposed by no more effective opposition than we now have programmed". Though existing American retaliatory capability was adequate to deter the Soviets from launching a direct military attack, NSC 68 warned that the time was fast approaching when the power would not be sufficient.

Washington therefore concluded it had little choice but to increase both its atomic and (if feasible) its thermonuclear capabilities. The Soviet possession of atomic weapons, according to NSC 68, had the dual effect not only of putting a premium on a more violent and ruthless prosecution of the Kremlin's design for world conquest, but also of putting "a premium on piecemeal aggression against others, counting on our willingness to engage in atomic war unless we are directly attacked". To counter such an eventuality as well as to provide an argument for raising the Defense Department's budget of $13.5 billion, NSC 68 recommended a more rapid buildup of political, economic, and military strength than had been previously contemplated. Only such a program, concluded NSC 68, could "postpone and avert the disastrous situation which, in light of the Soviet Union's probable fission bomb capability and possible thermonuclear bomb capability, might arise in 1954 on a continuation of our present program". Accordingly, "by acting promptly and vigorously in such a way that this date is, so to speak, pushed into the future, we could permit time for the process of accommodation, withdrawal, and frustration to produce the necessary changes in the Soviet system".[13] The "selling" of NSC 68 to the American people came from unexpected quarters.

The North Koreans, on the morning 25 June 1950 (Korean time), launched a well-organized attack along the entire width of the 38th parallel, the postwar dividing line between the Soviet-supported Democratic People's Republic of Korea and the American-supported Republic of Korea, or South Korea. Within a few hours of receiving the news, President Truman requested a meeting of the UN Security Council, and on the afternoon of 25 June (New York time), that body adopted a resolution, introduced by the United States, declaring the North Korean action a "breach of peace", demanding that the aggressor withdraw beyond the 38th parallel, and calling upon all members of the UN "to render every assistance to the United Nations in the execution of their resolution and to refrain from giving assistance to the North Korean authorities". Owing to the absence of the Soviet delegate (who had boycotted the UN because of its refusal to seat the representative of Communist China in place of the member of the Taiwan regime), the resolution passed the Security Council by a vote of 9-0 (Yugoslavia not voting). On 27 June the Council recommended that UN members "furnish such resistance to the Republic of Korea as may be necessary to repel the armed attack and to restore international peace and security in the area". Two weeks later General Douglas MacArthur was named commander for all UN forces serving in Korea.

President Truman acted promptly and properly in throwing the weight of America into the balance. On 27 June he announced that he had ordered United States air and sea forces to provide Korean government troops with cover and support. Three days later in Tokyo, the President authorized the use of American ground troops in Korea, ordered a naval blockade of the Korean coast, and directed the air force to attack targets in North Korea "wherever militarily necessary". In his announcement Truman also revealed other action that constituted a distinct change of policy: "Communism had passed beyond the use of subversion to conquer independent nations and will now use armed invasion and war". Under the circumstances, the President felt justified in accelerating military assistance to French forces fighting Ho Chi Minh's independence movement in Indochina and to the Philippines, as well as stretching the nation's "defensive perimeter" to include Taiwan, the refuge of the defeated nationalist Chinese forces who had fled from the mainland.

Response to the Security Council's call to arms was less than universal. In addition to the United States and South Korea, fifteen other nations—from Australia to Great Britain—participated in the fighting. Overall troop contributions for the period of the war were: Republic of Korea, 500,000; America, 300,000; other, 40,000. Of the 411,000 killed, wounded, captured or missing in action, South Korea suffered 63 per cent of the losses; the United States, 33 per cent; and the others, 4 per cent.

Such was the initial superiority of the North Koreans in equipment and preparations that they were able to push back the South Koreans and the first UN troops to the extreme southeast corner of the Korean peninsula, an area that fortunately included the important port of Pusan. The tide of war turned abruptly on 15 September when General MacArthur undertook a risky manoeuvre by landing UN forces far behind North Korean lines at Inchon. Large elements of the North Korean army were either destroyed or captured, with the remainder driven beyond the 38th parallel. Supported by the authority of a UN General Assembly resolution reiterating the objective of a "unified, independent and democratic Korea", United Nation's forces crossed the 38th parallel on 7 October (Korean time), twelve hours before the UN resolution was passed, and pressed forward to the Yalu River, Korea's northern border. Truman backed the decision to cross the parallel—a calculated risk—because he reasoned that a reunified Korea would not only inflict a momentous defeat on the strategy of Soviet world revolution, but also guarantee for Koreans the right of national self-determination. Communist China had other plans;[14] it felt called upon to prevent the extinction of North Korea. After a skillful buildup whose significance eluded the American command, Chinese armies, launched a massive attack in late November. Within a few weeks Beijing had hurled the UN armies back below the 38th parallel and recaptured the South Korean capital of Seoul. By early 1951, however, the line had been stabilized, and the UN forces counterattacked, pushing the Chinese and North Koreans again beyond the parallel.

On 11 April 1951, President Truman relieved General MacArthur of his dual position as Commander of UN forces in Korea and of the occupation forces of the United States in Japan. Increasing friction between MacArthur and Truman had resulted from the General's impatience at the restraints placed upon his military activities and his irritating habit of publicly voicing his disagreements with Administration and UN policy. In particular, MacArthur had complained about the prohibition against bombing enemy sources of supply and communications in what he termed the "privileged sanctuary of Manchuria".

MacArthur's recall set off a violent political debate in the United States—a debate that continued in muted tones until well after the Korean War. The issue for many was whether to limit the war to Korea or to go all out for victory against Beijing at the risk of provoking the Soviet Union. For his part, Truman gave Europe first place and deferred to the opinion of allies in the UN, in sharp contrast to MacArthur and his supporters, who believed Asia to be the decisive theatre in the struggle with Communism, and who would have had the United States "go it alone if necessary". A long investigation by two Senate committees ended inconclusively, and the Administration adhered to its policy of limited war.

On 23 June 1951, in New York, the head of the Soviet delegation to the United Nations, Yakov A. Malik, responded to a secret inquiry from Washington by stating publicly that the Korean conflict could be settled if both parties so desired. The Soviet delegate's statement led to the opening of armistice negotiations on July 10 at Kaesong, just north of the 38th parallel. There, and later at Panmunjom, the negotiations proceeded with a number of interruptions until 27 July 1953. The questions that proved the most troublesome were the location of the cease-fire line, machinery for enforcing the armistice terms, and repatriation of prisoners. By the spring of 1952, agreement had been reached on all but the last point. The People's Republic of China demanded that all prisoners of war be repatriated, but the UN would not agree to compulsory repatriation of thousands of Chinese and North Korean prisoners who were simply unwilling to return to Communism. On this issue the negotiations stuck until after the 1952 presidential election.

In any case, the seedtime of the Cold War was over, while prospects of a "hot war" were increasing. In this sense, and in a manner that, in retrospect, should not be underestimated, the outspoken, mutual, and unrelieved hostility of the USSR toward the West coincided with the culmination of "the American diplomatic revolution". The Communist purges in Czechoslovakia, the Berlin blockade, the triumph of Mao in China, and the North Korean invasion of South Korea all confirmed basic American policy formulated in the period from late 1944 to 1950. In the words of historian Ernest R. May, "Truman and his associates did not just become antipathetic towards the Soviet Union; they adopted the position that communist Russia represented a threat which the United States had to resist, if necessary by war.[15]

On the other side, to complete the image of the Cold War emerging in Moscow, Soviet policymakers saw the American decision over Berlin, the creation of the North Atlantic Treaty Organization, and President Truman's swiftness in committing troops to Korea as confirmation of what they came to regard as a threat to their own Eastern European and Far Eastern empire. The Cold War was now fully engaged. The American diplomats and decisionmakers of this period laid the basis of the alliance diplomacy and conventional and nuclear deterrence that would ultimately win the Cold War with the Soviets in 1991, seventy-four years after Lenin's *coup d'etat*.

They also laid the basis of some grievous errors. The Korean invasion caused American leadership to be overly concerned about the "military" aspects of Stalin's possible future adventures. While Truman's advisors rightfully focused on Europe, subsequent Cold Warriors began looking around the globe for Communists to challenge. This caused Washington to intervene in civil wars, oppose all revolutionary forces and attempt to create "NATOs and Marshall Plans" around the world. Much of this US action/reaction stemmed from the fact that America had developed an increasingly rigid ideological view of the world—anti-communism, anti-socialism and anti-leftist—that came to rival that of Communism. This was reflected in the globalization of containment, the projection of the fantasies, myths and obsessions of a society—America's inner demons—and in McCarthyism at home, the collective delusion that transformed others into purveyors of evil.[16] The latter produced a garrison-state mentality which came to govern much of America's policymaking and led straight to Vietnam.

Still, the early cold war players should get high marks. For while they thought and talked in terms of moral principles they acted in terms of power, the language of the Kremlin and the Soviet system of government.

Who was to blame? And which side contributed most to the way in which the Cold War developed? Such questions and attempts to answer them have informed much of the Cold War literature during the past fifty years. Realists, who deplored what diplomat George Kennan called the "moralistic-legalistic" approach of the United States to international affairs, argued that had Washington conceded to the Soviets their own sphere of influence and recognized American limitations in controlling events outside the American sphere of influence, the worst episodes of the Cold War could have been avoided. More idealistic commentators in turn condemned the realists for presumably betraying the nation's traditional commitment to the equality of all states, as well as adherence to the right of national self-determination. Moderate revisionists attempted to place the postwar struggle between the two superpowers within the context of what English historian Herbert Butterfield called the "terrible human predicament", a situation in which even intelligent and reasonably well-intentioned policymakers move inexorably toward conflict and hostility[17] a situation best captured by Louis J. Halle's image of a scorpion and a tarantula in a battle, each impelled to fight the other to the death.[18] Whatever their differences, Realists and their early critics agreed that Moscow generally had only itself to blame for the intensity and duration of the struggle.

The New left diplomatic historiography that emerged in the 1960s and 1970s nearly reversed that picture, portraying the Soviets on the defensive and American "aggression" as responsible for the near-catastrophe and bitterness that marked the postwar era. Driven by the structural dynamics of America's inherently expansionist political economy and by an American idealism that casually transformed itself into a kind of missionary anticommunism, the United States after World War II, according to the New Left model, sought to create a freely trading open-door world conducive to providing markets for American surpluses on the one hand and importing vitally needed raw materials on the other. From such a world American policymakers believed democratic institutions and practices would flow, absorbing at once United States interests and ideals. The pursuit of such a world, however, ran counter to Soviet needs and desires, particularly their drive for security against a potential third German invasion in this century.

What the New Left diplomatic literature of the 1960s proved without question was the truly self-interested nature of American foreign policy—a fact the moral superiority of the Realists prevented them from admitting. Or as William Diebold Jr., put it: "The United States has not really been Santa Claus".[19] What could not be proved were the "unspoken assumptions" revisionist historians attributed to the motives of policymakers; and for this reason the bulk of the radical literature seemed unintelligible to those who did not speak their language or share their value system. In the process, the New Left, for a season, replaced the traditional historicizing question, *Wie eingentlich gewesen*? (How it actually was?) with the very different question, *Wie es dazu kommen konnte*? (How was it possible for it to come about?). And it is for this, one suspects, they will be most remembered.[20]

Postrevisionists led by John Lewis Gaddis,[21] whose aim was revise the revisionists not to refute them, and Melvyn P. Leffler[22] whose work drew on all schools of Cold War historiography, have in effect underscored the complex interaction of foreign and domestic developments inside both the United States and the Soviet Union, generally concluding that both sides share more or less responsibility for the onset of the Cold War. Both believe that early

Cold War diplomats were intelligent but not necessarily wise. Neither deals with the most intriguing question of all: What would the world look like today if they had done nothing? The answer to that is hard to imagine.

## NOTES

1. Warren F. Kimball, *The Juggler: Franklin Roosevelt as Wartime Statesman* (Princeton, NJ, 1991), p. 7.

2. See Joseph M. Siracusa, ed., *The American Diplomatic Revolution: A Documentary History of the Cold War, 1941-1947* (Sydney, 1976), pp. 78-97.

3. Quoted in Joseph M. Siracusa, *The Changing of America, 1945 to the Present* (Arlington Heights, IL, 1986), p. 5.

4. The orthodox position on the use of the atomic bomb is found in Henry L. Stimson, "The Decision to Use the Atomic Bomb," *Harper's* 197 (Feb. 1947): 97-107, and Harry S. Truman, *Memoirs: Year of Decisions* (Garden City, 1955). Also see John Ray Skates, *The Invasion of Japan: Alternative to the Bomb* (Columbia, SC, 1994).

5. Alonzo Hamby, *Man of the People: A Life of Harry S. Truman* (New York, 1995); and Robert H. Farrell, *Harry S. Truman and the Modern American Presidency* (Boston, 1983), p. 38. For the reintroduction to the "atomic diplomacy" debate, see Gar Alperovitz, *The Decision to use the Atomic Bomb and the Architecture of an American Myth* (New York, 1995), Michael J. Hogan, ed., *Hiroshima: In History and Memory* (New York, 1996), and Robert J. Maddox, *Weapons for Victory: The Hiroshima Decision Fifty Years Later* (Columbia, Mo, 1995).

6. Siracusa, *The American Diplomatic Revolution*, pp. 112-35.

7. "X", "The Sources of Soviet Conduct," *Foreign Affairs* 25 (July 1947): 566-82. Also see Kennan's comments in *International Herald-Tribune*, 14 Mar. 1994.

8. Eduard Mark, "The War Scare of 1946 and Its Consequences," *Diplomatic History* 21 (Summer 1997): 383-415.

9. Siracusa, *The American Diplomatic Revolution*, pp. 217-57.

10. Ibid. Also see Michael J. Hogan, *The Marshall Plan: America, Britain and the Reconstruction of Europe, 1947-1952* (New York, 1987).

11. John Lewis Gaddis, *We Now Know: Rethinking Cold War History* (New York, 1997), p. 48. Also see Avi Shalaim, *The United States and the Berlin Blockade, 1948-1949: A Study in Crisis Decisionmaking* (Berkeley, 1983) and Hannes Adomeit, *Soviet Risk-Taking and Crisis Behavior: A Theoretical and Empirical Analysis* (London, 1982), pp. 67-182.

12. Norman N. Naimark, *The Russians in Germany: A History of the Soviet Zone of Occupation, 1945-1949* (Cambridge, MA, 1995), pp. 266, 270-271, and Dietrich Staritz, "The SED, Stalin, and the German Question: Interests and Decision-Making in the Light of New Sources," *German History* 10 (Oct. 1992): 274-89.

13. See Robert H. Johnson, *Improbable Dangers: U.S. Conceptions of Threat in the Cold War and After* (New York, 1994).

14. For the view from the other side, based on new documentation, see Shuguang Zhang, "Threat Perception and Chinese Communist Foreign Policy," in Melvyn P. Leffler and David S. Painter, eds., *Origins of the Cold War: An International History* (London, 1994), pp. 276-92.

15. Ernest R. May, *"Lessons" of the Past: The Use and Misuse of History in American Foreign Policy* (New York, 1973), p. 31. Also see May's "National

Security in American History," in Graham Allison and Gregory F. Treverton, eds., *Rethinking America's Security: Beyond Cold War to New World Order* (New York, 1992).

16. See A.J. Dunning, *Extremes: Reflections on Human Behaviour* (London, 1993), p. 147.

17. Herbert Butterfield, *History and Human Relations* (London, 1951), pp. 9-36.

18. Louis J. Halle, *The Cold War As History* (New York, 1967), p. xiii.

19. William Diebold Jr., "The Economic System at Stake," *Foreign Affairs* (Oct. 1972): 171.

20. Joseph M. Siracusa, *New Left Diplomatic Histories and Historians: The American Revisionists* (2nd ed., Claremont, CA, 1993), p. vii.

21. John Lewis Gaddis, *The United States and the Origins of the Cold War, 1941-1947* (New York, 1972); and *We Now Know.*

22. Melvyn P. Leffler, *A Preponderance of Power: National Security, the Truman Administration, and the Cold War* (Stanford, 1992).

# APPENDIX 1

# THE TOLSTOY DOCUMENTS

## RECORD OF MEETING AT THE KREMLIN, MOSCOW, 9TH OCTOBER, 1944, AT 10 PM.

Present:

| | |
|---|---|
| The Prime Minister | Marshal Stalin |
| The Secretary of State | M. Molotov |
| Sir A. Clark Kerr | M. Pavlov |
| Mr A. Birse | |

THE PRIME MINISTER gave Marshal Stalin a signed photograph of himself in return for the one sent him some weeks ago by the Marshal.

THE PRIME MINISTER hoped they might clear away many questions about which they had been writing to each other for a long time. As time had passed many things had arisen, but were out of all proportion to the greatness of the common struggle. By talking to each other he and Stalin could avoid innumerable telegrams and letters—and they could give the Ambassador a holiday.

MARSHAL STALIN replied that he was ready to discuss anything.

THE PRIME MINISTER suggested beginning with the most tiresome question—Poland. He said that they should have a common policy in regard to Poland. At present each had a game cock in his hand.

MARSHAL STALIN said (with a laugh) that it was difficult to do without cocks. They gave the morning signal.

THE PRIME MINISTER remarked that the question of the frontier was settled as agreed. He would like presently to check up on the frontier with a map.

MARSHAL STALIN remarked that if the frontier was agreed on the Curzon Line it would help their discussion.

THE PRIME MINISTER said he wanted to explain what was in his and the Secretary of State's mind as they understood the situation. The time would come when they would meet at the armistice table, and that might also be the peace table. The Americans would find it easier to settle at an armistice table, because there the President could decide, whereas at a peace table the Senate would have to be consulted. At the armistice table the Prime Minister would support the frontier line as fixed at Tehran and he thought it likely that the United States would do the same. That decision had been endorsed by the British War Cabinet, and he felt it would be approved by his country. He would say it was right, fair and necessary for the safety and future of Russia. If some General Sosnkowski objected it would not matter, because Britain and United States thought it right and fair. He and Mr Eden had for months been trying to get Sosnkowski sacked. He had now been sacked and as for General Bor, the Germans were looking after him.

MARSHAL STALIN remarked that the Poles were now without a Commander-in-Chief.

THE PRIME MINISTER thought that some colourless man had been left. He could not remember his name. The Prime Minister went on to ask Marshal Stalin a question. Would he think it worth while to bring Mikolajezyk and Romer to Moscow? He had them tied up in an aircraft and it would only take 36 hours to Moscow.

MARSHAL STALIN asked whether they had authority to settle questions with the Polish Committee for National Liberation.

THE PRIME MINISTER was not sure, but he thought they would not be anxious to go to bed with the Committee. If, however, they were in Moscow they could, with British and Russian agreement, be forced to settle.

MARSHAL STALIN had no objection to making another attempt, but Mikolajezyk would have to make contact with the Committee. The latter now had an army at its disposal and represented a force.

THE PRIME MINISTER pointed out that the other side also thought they had an army, and part of which had held out in Warsaw. They also had a brave army corps in Italy, where they lost seven or eight thousand men. Then there was the armoured division, one brigade of which was in France. A Polish division which had gone to Switzerland when France fell was coming out in driblets. They were well equipped and they had many friends in England. They were good and brave men. The difficulty about the Poles was that they had unwise political leaders. Where there were two Poles there was one quarrel.

MARSHAL STALIN added that where there was one Pole he would begin to quarrel with himself through sheer boredom.

THE PRIME MINISTER thought that Marshal Stalin and he himself as well as M. Molotov and Mr Eden between them had more chance of bringing the Poles together. The British would bring pressure to bear on their Poles, while the Poles in the East were already in agreement with the Soviet Government.

MARSHAL STALIN agreed to try.

THE PRIME MINISTER asked if there was any objection to M. Grabski's coming to Moscow.

MARSHAL STALIN had no objection.

THE PRIME MINISTER then referred to the armistice terms for the satellites who had been coerced by Germany and had not distinguished themselves in the war. If Marshal Stalin agreed, the Prime Minister thought that M. Molotov or Mr Eden might discuss these terms. The terms for Hungary were important. He hoped the Russians would soon be in Budapest.

MARSHAL STALIN said it was possible.

THE PRIME MINISTER pointed out that there were two countries in which the British had particular interest, one was Greece. He was not worrying much about Roumania. That was very much a Russian affair and the treaty the Soviet Government had proposed was reasonable and showed much statecraft in the interests of general peace in the future. But in Greece it was different. Britain must be the leading Mediterranean Power and he hoped Marshal Stalin would let him have the first say about Greece in the same way as Marshal Stalin about Roumania. Of course, the British Government would keep in touch with the Soviet Government.

MARSHAL STALIN understood that Britain had suffered very much owing to her communications in the Mediterranean having been cut by the Germans. It was a serious matter for Britain when the Mediterranean route was not in her hands. In that respect Greece was very important. He agreed with the Prime minister that Britain should have the first say in Greece.

THE PRIME MINISTER said it was better to express these things in diplomatic terms and not to use the phrase "dividing into spheres", because the Americans might be shocked. But as long as he and Marshal understood each other he could explain matters to the President.

MARSHAL STALIN interrupted to say that he had received a message from President Roosevelt. The President wanted Mr Harriman to attend their talks as an observer and that the decisions reached between them should be of a preliminary nature.

THE PRIME MINISTER agreed. He had told the President—he and the President had no secrets—that he would welcome Mr Harriman to a good number of their talks but he did not want this to prevent intimate talk between Marshal Stalin and himself. He would keep the President informed. Mr Harriman might come in for any formal talks as an observer. Mr Harriman was not quite in the same position as they were.

MARSHAL STALIN said he had only sent a reply to the effect that he did not know what questions would be discussed, but as soon as he did know he would tell the President. He had noticed some signs of alarm in the President's message about their talks and on the whole did not like the message. It seemed to demand too many rights for the United States leaving too little for the Soviet Union and Great Britain, who, after all, had a treaty of common assistance.

MARSHAL STALIN went on to say that he had no objection to Mr Harriman's attending the formal talks.

THE PRIME MINISTER referred to the Conference at Dumbarton Oaks. The President had not wanted this to be discussed in Moscow but only when the three heads got together. The President had not said so, but he must have had in mind the coming election. The President would be more free to talk in about a month's time. It was fair to say that while at first His Majesty's Government had inclined to the American view they now saw a great deal of force in the other point of view. Supposing China asked Britain to give up Hong Kong, China and Britain would have to leave the room while Russia and the United States settled the question. Or, if the Argentine and the United States had a quarrel they would object if England, China and Russia had to settle it. The Prime Minister pointed out that all this was off the record. The wise thing was not to refer in Moscow to this question, but to wait until the meeting of the three heads, when it could be settled.

THE PRIME MINISTER then raised the question of the interests of the two Governments in the various Balkan countries and the need to work in harmony in each of them. After some discussion it was agreed that as regards Hungary and Yugoslavia each of the two Governments was equally interested, that Russia had a major interest in Roumania and that Britain was in the same position with regard to Greece. The Prime Minister suggested that where Bulgaria was concerned the British interest was greater than it was in Roumania. This led to some discussion about the crimes committed by Bulgaria.

MARSHAL STALIN recalled the Treaty of Brest-Litovsk, where the Bulgarians had been on the German side and three divisions had fought against the Russians in the last war.

THE PRIME MINISTER declared that Bulgaria owed more to Russia than to any other country. He said that in Roumania Britain had been a spectator. In Bulgaria she had to be a little more than a spectator.

M. MOLOTOV asked whether the Turkish question related to this matter.

THE PRIME MINISTER replied that he had not touched upon Turkey. He was only saying what was in his mind. He was glad to see how near it was to the Russian mind.

M. MOLOTOV remarked that the Convention of Montreux still remained.

THE PRIME MINISTER said that was a Turkish question and not a Bulgarian.

MARSHAL STALIN replied that Turkey was also a Balkan country. According to the Convention of Montreux Japan had as much right as Russia. Everything had been adjusted to the League of Nations and the League of Nations no longer existed. If Turkey were threatened she could close the Straits and Turkey herself had to decide when she was faced with a real threat. All the paragraphs in the Montreux Convention were controlled by Turkey. This was an anachronism. Marshal Stalin had put this question in Tehran and the Prime Minister had expressed his sympathy. Now that they were discussing the Balkan question and Turkey was a Balkan country, did the Prime Minister think it appropriate to discuss it?

THE PRIME MINISTER agreed.

MARSHAL STALIN pointed out that if Britain were interested in the Mediterranean then Russia was equally interested in the Black Sea.

THE PRIME MINISTER thought that Turkey had missed her chance after the Tehran conference. The reason she was frightened was because she had no modern weapons, she thought she had a good army, whereas nowadays an army was not everything. Turkey was not clever.

MARSHAL STALIN remarked that Turkey had 26 divisions in Thrace and asked against whom they were directed.

THE PRIME MINISTER replied they were directed against Bulgaria, because Bulgaria was armed with French weapons taken by the Germans. The Prime Minister went on to say that, taking a long view of the future of the world, it was no part of British policy to grudge Soviet Russia access to warm-water ports and to the great oceans and seas of the world. On the contrary, it was part of their friendship to help the Soviet Union. They no longer followed the policy of Disraeli or Lord Curzon. They were not going to stop Russia. They wished to help. What did Marshal Stalin think about the kind of changes required in the Montreux Convention?

MARSHAL STALIN could not say what point required amendment, but he felt the convention was unsuitable in present circumstances and the spearhead was directed against Russia. It should be dropped. If the Prime Minister agreed in principle with that point of view it might be possible to discuss the required changes. It was quite impossible for Russia to remain subject to Turkey, who could close the Straits and hamper Russian imports and exports and even her defences. What would Britain do if Spain or Egypt were given this right to close the Suez Canal, or what would the United States Government say if some South American Republic had the right to close the Panama Canal? Russia was in a worse situation. Marshal Stalin did not want to restrict Turkey's sovereignty. But at the same time he did not want Turkey to abuse her sovereignty and to grip Russian trade by the throat.

THE PRIME MINISTER replied that in principle he shared that point of view. He suggested that the Russians should let us know in due course what was required. Otherwise Turkey might be frightened that Istanbul was to be taken. When the three heads met later on there would not be the same difficulty. He was in favour of Russia's having free access to the Mediterranean for her merchant ships and ships of war. Britain hoped to work in a friendly way with the Soviet Union, but wanted to bring Turkey along by gentle steps, not to frighten her.

MARSHAL STALIN said he understood.

THE PRIME MINISTER said that, if they were sitting at the armistice table and Marshal Stalin asked him for free passage through the Straits for merchant ships and warships, he personally would say that Britain had no objection. Britain had no ties with Turkey except the Montreaux Convention, which was inadmissible to-day and obsolete.

MARSHAL STALIN said he did not want to hurry the Prime Minister, but only to point out that the question existed in their minds and he was anxious that it should be admitted that their claim was justified.

THE PRIME MINISTER thought Marshal Stalin should take the initiative and tell the United States what was in his mind. The Prime Minister thought Russia had a right and moral claim. Looking at the Balkans he thought they should do something to prevent the risk of civil war between the political ideologies in those countries. They could not allow a lot of little wars after the Great World War. They should be stopped by the authority of the three Great Powers.

MARSHAL STALIN agreed.

THE PRIME MINISTER said he wanted to talk about Kings. In no case would Britain try to force a King on Italy, Greece or Yugoslavia. At the same time the people ought to be left to decide matters by a free plebiscite in time of tranquillity. They could then say whether they wanted a republic or a monarchy. The people should have a fair chance of freedom of expression. Northern Italy was in the power of the Anglo-American armies. Britain did not care for the Italian King, but above all they did not want civil war after the troops had been withdrawn or before their withdrawal. Britain would like the Soviet Union to soft-pedal the Communists in Italy and not to stir them up. Pure democracy would settle what the people wanted, but he did not want to have disturbances in Turin or Milan and clashes between the troops and the people. The Italians were in a miserable condition. He did not think much of them as a people, but they had a good many votes in New York State. This was off the record.

The Prime Minister went on to say that he did not want to have trouble in Italy before the United States left it. The President was their best friend. They would never have such a good one. That was why he petted the Italians, though he did not like them much. He had not meant that the Soviet Union should influence the Communist vote in New York. He was referring to the Communists in Italy.

MARSHAL STALIN remarked that it was difficult to influence Italian Communists. The position of Communists differed in different countries. It depended upon their national situation. If Ercoli were in Moscow Marshal Stalin might influence him. But he was in Italy, where the circumstances were different. He could send Marshal Stalin to the devil. Ercoli could say he was an Italian and tell Marshal Stalin to mind his own business. When the Red Army entered Bulgaria, Bulgarian Communists proceeded to form Soviets. The Red Army stopped it. The Communists arrested the Bulgarian police and the Red Army freed the police. However, Ercoli was a wise man, not an extremist, and would not start an adventure in Italy.

THE PRIME MINISTER said he was only asking that they should not be stirred up.

MARSHAL STALIN expressed his fear that the Communists would send him to the devil. As regards the King, Ercoli had his own views. He had said he would collaborate with the King if the King stood by the people. Ercoli had referred to Germany, where there was no King, but where there was a man who was worse than the greatest despot.

THE PRIME MINISTER agreed. He then said that he had been talking the whole time and that it was now Marshal Stalin's turn.

MARSHAL STALIN reverted to the Balkans and suggested that our [Britain's] interest in Bulgaria was not, in fact, as great as the Prime Minister had claimed.

MR EDEN remarked that Britain wanted more in Bulgaria than in Roumania.

MARSHAL STALIN claimed that Bulgaria was a Black Sea country. Was Britain afraid of anything? Was she afraid of a Soviet campaign against Turkey? The Soviet Union had no such intention.

MR EDEN said Britain was not afraid of anything.

MARSHAL STALIN asked whether the Prime Minister thought Bulgaria was being punished less than she deserved. Bulgaria should be punished for her two wars on the side of Germany.

MR EDEN reminded Marshal Stalin that Britain had been at war with Bulgaria for three years and wanted a small share in the control of that country after Germany's defeat.

THE PRIME MINISTER suggested that M. Molotov and Mr Eden should go into details. This was agreed.

THE PRIME MINISTER suggested that in the presence of Mr Harriman they might have a talk about the future of Germany. He suggested that for about a month or so they should not say anything publicly because it would make the Germans fight harder. He had been shy of breathing fire and slaughter, but they might discuss it quietly among themselves.

MARSHAL STALIN agreed.

THE PRIME MINISTER said he was all for hard terms. Opinions were divided in the United States. The best thing would be to beat the Germans into unconditional surrender and then tell them what to do. He wanted to hear Marshal Stalin's opinion about the regime to be applied and how Germany was to be divided, what was to be done with Prussia, the Saar and the Ruhr, and with German weapons. Russian factories had been destroyed as well as Belgian and Dutch and the machines taken away would have to be replaced. Perhaps the Foreign Secretaries could discuss this matter with M. Molotov and Mr Harriman.

The President was for hard terms. Others were for soft. The problem was how to prevent Germany getting on her feet in the lifetime of our grand-children.

MARSHAL STALIN thought the Versailles peace was inadequate. It had not removed the possibility of revenge. Hard measures would stir a desire for revenge. The problem was to create such a peace that the possibility of revenge would be denied to Germany. Her heavy industry would have to be destroyed. The State would have to be split up. How that was to be done would have to be discussed. Her heavy industry would have to be reduced to a minimum.

THE PRIME MINISTER suggested it should apply to the electrical and chemical industries also.

MARSHAL STALIN agreed that it should apply to all industry producing war material. Germany should be deprived of the possibility of revenge. Otherwise every twenty-five or thirty years there would be a new world war which would exterminate the young generation. If approached from that angle the harshest measures would prove to be the most humane. Eight to ten million Germans had been lost after every war. Reprisals in Germany might not [sic] affect only one and a half million Germans. As regards concrete proposals, Mr Eden and M. Molotov should get together.

M. MOLOTOV asked what was the Prime Minister's opinion of the Morgenthau plan.

THE PRIME MINISTER said that the President and Mr Morgenthau were not very happy about its reception. The Prime Minister went on to say that as he had declared in Tehran, Britain would not agree to mass execution of Germans, because one day British public opinion would cry out. But it was necessary to kill as many as possible in the field. The others should be made to work to repair the damage done to other countries. They might use the Gestapo on such work and the Hitler Youth should be reeducated to learn that it was more difficult to build than to destroy.

MARSHAL STALIN thought that a long occupation of Germany would be necessary.

THE PRIME MINISTER did not think that the Americans would stay very long.

MARSHAL STALIN said France should provide some forces.

THE PRIME MINISTER agreed.

MARSHAL STALIN suggested the use of the small countries.

THE PRIME MINISTER thought United Poland could be employed.

MARSHAL STALIN said Silesia would go to the Poles and part of East Prussia. The Soviet Union would take Koenigsberg and the Poles would be very interested in the occupation of Germany.

THE PRIME MINISTER thought the population might be moved from Silesia and East Prussia to Germany. If seven million had been killed in the war there would be plenty of room for them. He suggested that M. Molotov and Mr Eden, with Mr Harriman, should talk this over and get a picture of the general proposals for Marshal Stalin and himself to think about, and thus when the end came they would not be without something unprobed. They should also decide what part the European Advisory Commission should play.

MARSHAL STALIN agreed.

THE PRIME MINISTER turned to the Anglo-American war against Japan. He pointed out that here again the utmost secrecy was required. He remarked how wonderfully well secrecy had been maintained considering the declaration made by Marshal Stalin at Tehran about Japan. The Prime Minister had asked the President to give a statement for use as an outline of the American plan for 1945 in the Pacific. Plans were moving quickly and the position was changing very much as island after island was taken, but the President had given Mr Harriman and General Deane an outline of the plan which he (the Prime Minister) was to be shown and it was to be discussed with the Soviet Generals. He suggested that conversations should begin with Mr Harriman and his General and that afterwards they might go away and talk separately, technically.

MARSHAL STALIN said that the Soviet military leaders had been informed of the existence of the President's plan and General Deane was to have had a talk with the Soviet High Command, but the latter were awaiting information from the Far East about Japanese strength. Marshal Stalin did not know details of the plan just as the Prime Minister did not know them, but he was prepared to acquaint himself with it. If they could all meet and examine the plan that would be better.

THE PRIME MINISTER said that he thought that Mr Harriman and General Deane had been authorised to tell Marshal Stalin in broad outline about the plan, but he thought it should be discussed with General Brooke, who was also a member of the Suvorov Order. General Brooke was going to take a ride in a tram as he was entitled to do, but he could not spare the time for a visit to the seaside. These were his privileges as a member of the Order of Suvorov. General Brooke was also ready to give an account of the operations in the West, in France and Italy and to tell how affairs stood. He would like Marshal Stalin to know that the British had as many divisions fighting against Germany in Italy and France as the United States and we had nearly as many as the United States fighting against Japan. Altogether 60 divisions of 40,000 men including a heavy backing of commissariat, artillery, & c.

RECORD OF MEETING AT THE KREMLIN, MOSCOW,
ON 10TH OCTOBER, 1944, AT 7 PM

Present:

| | |
|---|---|
| The Secretary of State | M. Molotov |
| Sir Archibald Clark Kerr | M. Vyshinski |
| Mr Oliver Harvey | M. Gusev |
| Mr A. Birse | M. Pavlov |

MR EDEN suggested they should talk about Bulgaria and the Balkans in general.

M. MOLOTOV suggested that they should first discuss Hungary in connexion [sic] with what Marshal Stalin had said to the Prime Minister. Marshal Stalin thought that after learning of the considerable losses sustained by the Red Army in Hungary, the army would not understand it if a principle of 50/50 were allotted. M. Molotov had been instructed by the Marshal to raise this question and to give his opinion.

MR EDEN said he would be glad to hear M. Molotov's opinion.

M. MOLOTOV began by saying that the 75/25 principle was what the Soviet Government proposed, for the reason that Hungary bordered on the Soviet Union and the Red Army was operating in that country and suffering losses. Hungary had been and always would be a bordering country. Russia's interest was therefore comprehensible. Russia did not want Hungary to be on the side of the aggressor in the future. At the same time, Russia had no territorial claims in Hungary.

MR EDEN remarked that His Majesty's Government would certainly consider the question of Hungary but he would prefer to have a chance of thinking it over.

MR EDEN went on to say that he would speak frankly. His Majesty's Government were unhappy over the whole situation in the Balkans. They were being presented with *"faits accomplis"*. Some months ago when Tito was in difficulties the British had given him refuge on the island of Vis under the protection of the Royal Navy and RAF, and it was only through British action that he was saved from complete extinction. The British had armed him and supported him and now, without a word or information from himself or from the Soviet Ally, he had left Vis and come to Moscow and was making an agreement about the Bulgarians in Yugoslavia which was quite unacceptable to the British. The Bulgarians treated the British as if Bulgaria had won the war and Britain had lost it. British officers in Northern Greece had, by order of the Bulgarian authorities, been confined to their houses. His Majesty's Government must ask the Soviet Union for support and for this to be brought to an end. Mr Eden was ready to discuss armistice terms for Bulgaria and he felt he was entitled to ask that instructions be sent through the Soviet Marshal in Sofia to the Bulgarians in Greece to treat British officers with proper respect pending the withdrawal of the Bulgarians from Greece.

M. MOLOTOV readily agreed that the matter should be put in order and that the Bulgarians must be made to feel they were not the victors. They had done enough damage to the Soviet Union and to the Allies and though Bulgaria had a new Government she should be held responsible for her past misdeeds. It was necessary to take practical measures to regulate these questions, and for Bulgaria to be taught to show respect to the Allies in Bulgaria. The Soviet Government appreciated the British claim.

MR EDEN did not know whether he had made himself clear. The trouble had occurred not where the Russians were stationed in Bulgaria but in Northern Greece. Orders had been given to British officers to keep to their houses and he would like Mr Molotov to telegraph to the Soviet Marshal in Sofia to tell the Bulgarians to instruct their authorities in Northern Greece to treat British representatives with proper respect. In that connexion [sic] His Majesty's Government were sending, in conjunction with the Greek Government, some further British officers to Northern Greece. He did not want them to be put in prison.

M. MOLOTOV pointed out that at the outset it had been agreed to make some preliminary conditions in the case of Bulgaria, for the withdrawal of her troops from Greece and Yugoslavia. So far the Soviet Government had not interfered in affairs beyond the borders of Bulgaria.

MR EDEN remarked that he understood and suggested, without asking for Soviet interference outside of Bulgaria, that British officers while in Greece should receive fair treatment and this the Bulgarians would do if they received instructions from the Soviet Government.

M. MOLOTOV thought they could reach an agreement on this point, but repeated that they had not interfered in affairs outside of Bulgaria and, in particular, in Greece. The question was how agreement could be reached. He would speak to Marshal Stalin.

MR EDEN said he would be ready to discuss the armistice terms but the above question would have to be settled. He thought that if the Soviet Government sent a telegram to their representative in Sofia to the effect that they understood some British officers in Northern Greece had been put under arrest by the Bulgarians and instructing the Soviet representative to request the Bulgarians immediately to put an end to this state of affairs, this would be enough to make the Bulgarians behave in Northern Greece until they withdrew. He hoped it would be soon.

M. MOLOTOV repeated that he would speak to Marshal Stalin.

MR EDEN then turned to the armistice terms. He suggested they should first discuss the difficult points. These would have to be finally settled and passed through the European Advisory Commission and agreed with their American friends. He thought that if they could agree on the general lines in Moscow they could telegraph to their representatives and then matters could be quickly arranged. The first question in dispute was where the negotiations were to be held.

M. MOLOTOV asked if this was important.

MR EDEN replied by asking the same question of M. Molotov.

M. MOLOTOV did not think it was important. They should take place where a speedy settlement could be made. That could be done in Moscow, where they had the experienced Moscow Commission.

MR EDEN said that the point was important. He was prepared to make concessions and he would suggest Moscow. The London

Commission would have to agree certain terms and then the Allied representatives would meet the Bulgarians. The question was: Where? M. Molotov had suggested Moscow and Mr Eden agreed.

M. MOLOTOV said they preferred Moscow, where they could have the help of Sir Archibald Clark Kerr.

MR EDEN said that the difficulty was the following, and he could not give way on it: His Majesty's Government insisted on some share in the Control Commission after the war with Germany was over. The Americans were also not prepared to give way on this point. He asked M. Molotov to understand that Britain had been at war with Bulgaria for three years and it simply would not be understood by the British people if Britain had no part in the Control Commission after the war with Germany was over. In other words, he would have to insist upon the amendment as proposed by the Americans about the future of the Control Commission.

M. MOLOTOV suggested that, before discussing that amendment, he would like to make one concession in return for Mr Eden's concession about the place for negotiations. It was about the signature. He did not know whether Mr Eden attached importance to the danger which lay in the wish to have two signatures, namely, Marshal Tolbukhin and General Wilson. Marshal Tolbukhin was not a naval man, but in so far as the Red Army had anything to do with the sea it was with the Black Sea. The signature of General Wilson meant that a general was signing who had something to do with Mediterranean affairs. If there was a Mediterranean General, and a Black Sea General, then Bulgaria might claim that she was not only a Black Sea Power but also a Mediterranean Power.

MR EDEN replied that there was no question of Bulgaria being a Mediterranean Power.

M. MOLOTOV said he understood and that Bulgaria should be punished for the help she had given to Germany. However, if this danger did not appear so great then the Soviet Government agreed to two signatures. This was a concession to British public opinion if they felt that they must have a greater share in Bulgarian affairs. The concession was greater than that made by Mr Eden.

MR EDEN said he was grateful for the gesture. It would have a good effect, and the Americans would also appreciate it. He could promise that the Royal Navy would keep the Bulgarians out of the Mediterranean.

M. MOLOTOV claimed that he could not understand the American amendment. In the case of the Control Commission in Italy and Roumania all was clear. It was clear who was responsible for the activities of the Control Commission. Experience had shown that the procedure was satisfactory. But what would happen if a new method were adopted for Bulgaria after the German surrender? Three people would be responsible for the activities of the Commission. There might be confusion which would lead to friction.

MR EDEN said that he did not mind so much about the machinery, but he was anxious to make plain that we had some share in the Control Commission. Roumania was quite different. The American proposal was possibly a way out because it was the same as in the case of Germany. However, he was ready to look at any proposal the Soviet Government might make provided the British and Americans were not observers as in Roumania but played a part in the Control Commission.

M. MOLOTOV pointed out that in Germany there would be three zones of occupation and the comparison with Germany was not clear. He had not heard of zones in Bulgaria. Marshal Stalin had said with regard to Bulgaria that it would be right for Russia to have 90 per cent interest in Bulgaria. If they could agree on a proportion of 90/10 then agreement could easily be reached on all the rest.

MR EDEN pointed out that this would put Britain in the same position as in Roumania.

M. MOLOTOV agreed it would be so as regards the principle, but as regards the form of procedure a way could be found. It might be possible to think out a way to meet American and British wishes. For instance the conditions might be discussed in London. The machinery of the Control Commission might be made more favourable for Britain.

MR EDEN said the American formula if accepted by the Soviet Government attracted him, but he was quite ready to consider anything the Russians proposed provided Britain had a little more in Bulgaria. It was necessary to act with speed. Delay was bad.

M. MOLOTOV agreed about the necessity for speed, but said he could not understand the American proposal. How would three representatives act in Bulgaria where there were no zones? Did the Americans and British contemplate stationing troops in Bulgaria. How could there be proper management in Bulgaria after the end of the war with Germany? It was obscure and might mean friction. He considered that 90/10 as proposed by Marshal Stalin was fair.

MR EDEN replied that there was no intention to station troops in Bulgaria. He suggested there might be a permanent Soviet chairman on the Control Commission.

M. MOLOTOV refused to consider this as the three representatives would decide affairs which would mean that the British and Americans would have 33 per cent each and the Soviet Union 1 per cent more than they because the President was a Soviet citizen. They would have 34 per cent instead of 90 per cent. He asked what was the object of the proposal.

MR EDEN pointed out that in Roumania the British and American officers were observers. For the period of hostilities with Germany they accepted that position also in Bulgaria. But after the surrender of Germany they would like to be more than observers and have active participation. He had no views as to how to express this. Britain's share was less than the Russian because Russia had troops and administration in Bulgaria.

M. MOLOTOV thought it would be a strange kind of management where no indication was given of who was responsible.

MR EDEN said the main responsibility would lie with the Soviet Union.

M. MOLOTOV declared that despite this responsibility the Soviet Union was asking for 90 per cent and not 100 per cent.

MR EDEN said he did not know much about these percentages. All he wanted was a greater share than we already had in Roumania. In Roumania we had 10 per cent which was almost nothing.

M. MOLOTOV pointed out that the idea of percentages arose from the meeting on the previous day, and it was worthy of consideration. Could they not agree on the following: Bulgaria, Hungary and Yugoslavia 75/25 per cent each?

MR EDEN said that would be worse than on the previous day.

M. MOLOTOV then suggested 90/10 for Bulgaria; 50/50 for Yugoslavia and Hungary subject to an amendment.

MR EDEN pointed out that they had not agreed about Bulgaria.

M. MOLOTOV remarked that he thought 90/10 was an ultimatum and meant the unconditional surrender of Moscow. However something would have to be done which would be acceptable to all three.

MR EDEN said he was ready to meet M. Molotov's wishes with regard to Hungary, but he asked for M. Molotov's help to get some participation in Bulgaria after the Germans had been beaten. Possibly some other formula would be accepted. For instance we and the Americans might each have an officer on the Control Commission who would not be as important as the Soviet representative.

M. MOLOTOV then suggested 75/25 for Hungary.

M. MOLOTOV continued that they had not finished with Bulgaria. If Hungary was 75/25, then Bulgaria should be 75/25 and Yugoslavia 60/40. This was the limit to which he could go.

MR EDEN said he could not make this suggestion to the Prime Minister who was greatly interested in Yugoslavia. He had been at pains to champion Tito and to furnish arms. Any change in Yugoslavian percentages would upset him. Mr Eden then suggested Hungary 75/25; Bulgaria 80/20; Yugoslavia 50/50.

M. MOLOTOV was ready to agree to 50/50 for Yugoslavia if Bulgaria were 90/10. If the figure for Bulgaria had to be amended then Yugoslavia would also have to be changed.

MR EDEN pointed out that with regard to Hungary we had made a concession.

M. MOLOTOV repeated that Hungary bordered on Russia and not on Britain. The Russians had suffered losses in Hungary. Marshal Stalin had mentioned this to the Prime Minister. What did 60/40 for Yugoslavia mean? It meant the coast where Russia would have less interest and would not interfere, but they were to have a greater influence in the centre.

MR EDEN repeated that Britain had been at war with Bulgaria for three years. The Bulgarians had treated us badly. They had beaten British and American prisoners. Russia had been at war with Bulgaria for 48 hours, and then Britain had been warned off Bulgaria who had received favourable treatment.

M. MOLOTOV did not agree. Russia had suffered more than Britain from the Bulgarians, to say nothing of the last war, but the Soviet Union did not want to increase its number of enemies. It had had the intention several times to declare war on Bulgaria. The harm done by Bulgaria to the Soviet Union was many times greater than that done to anyone else. Roumania and Bulgaria were Black Sea Powers. Neither of them had access to the Mediterranean so that Britain should have little interest in those countries. M. Molotov was not speaking of Greece. The Soviet Union was prepared to help Britain to be strong in the Mediterranean, but hoped that Britain would help the Soviet Union in the Black Sea. That was why they were interested in Bulgaria. Bulgaria was not Greece, Italy, Spain or even Yugoslavia.

MR EDEN said that they had little interest in Bulgaria and they were therefore asking for very little. But we [Britain] had been at war with her and the question should be looked at through British eyes. Tito happened to have been accessible and Britain had helped him with arms. He had now come to Moscow but Britain had been kept in ignorance. When the British public found this out there would be criticism and rightly so. He was making an arrangement for Bulgarian troops to stay in Yugoslavia, an arrangement between Bulgaria, Yugoslavia and Russia. A bad impression would be created and suspicion aroused as to Russian intentions.

M. MOLOTOV said he thought Marshal Stalin would agree to the following: 75/25 for Bulgaria, but 60/40 for Yugoslavia. He did not think that British sailors would call the Black Sea a "sea", but only a lake.

MR EDEN said it was the Soviet Union's lake.

M. MOLOTOV remarked that he had in mind the British point of view. The Black Sea was a lake. After such a war and the sacrifice of the Soviet Union anyone would understand that they had to make sure of their safety. As regards Marshal Tito, he had seen him for the first time in Moscow and Marshal Stalin had not seen him before. His impression was that Tito was an honest man and friendly to the Allies. There was no doubt of it. Mr Churchill's son had met him and would be able to speak of Tito's influence. He would confirm what M. Molotov had said about his honesty and friendliness. Tito had not told the British and Americans about his visit to Moscow. That was a double mistake and he was spoiling with the British and Americans to his own detriment. In the second place he was treating his meeting with Stalin as an advertisement to increase his prestige. In Italy he had met the Prime Minister. M. Molotov thought he was rather provincial.

He had spent too much time in the mountains. He liked mystery, but he had no ill will.

MR EDEN said he was sorry that His Majesty's Government had not been informed. For some time Tito could not be found. But he was not in the hills. He was on the island of Vis.

M. MOLOTOV thought he would soon be in Belgrade and his provincialism would fade away.

MR EDEN pointed out that meanwhile he was making an agreement with the Bulgarians.

MR MOLOTOV thought that if they told him what he was to do he could remedy his mistakes. He thought they could reach agreement on that point. As regards Bulgaria M. Molotov had proposed two alternatives. He would speak to Marshal Stalin. He asked Mr Eden which alternative he preferred.

MR EDEN said he did not care so much about the figures. He understood Russia's interest in Bulgaria and Britain accepted it. But Britain asked for something more there than in Roumania. If M. Molotov did not like the American formula, any other proposed by the Russians would be considered. For example, instead of calling it the Allied Control Commission it would be called the Soviet Control Commission, with an American and British representative.

M. MOLOTOV asked whether they could reach agreement in regard to Yugoslavia.

MR EDEN asked what they had to decide.

M. MOLOTOV claimed more weight for the Soviet Union. The Soviet Union had nothing to do with regard to affairs on the coast. They were ready to stay on their "lake".

MR EDEN preferred to have a common policy. There were various questions to decide. When Yugoslavia was free there was the question of the relations between Tito and the Government in London. Were they to come together? Was there to be joint administration? It was desirable that the Allies should pursue the same ideas.

M. MOLOTOV agreed that the question required attention. He asked Sir Archibald Clark Kerr for his advice how to proceed.

SIR ARCHIBALD CLARK KERR thought the best way was to bring Tito and Subasic together if the Soviet Government and His Majesty's Government used their influence in that direction and then they could decide what form of government they wanted—monarchy, or republic or anything else.

M. MOLOTOV said he would report to Marshal Stalin and thought they could find a way out. He thanked Sir Archibald for his help.

MR EDEN summing up, said the one question outstanding about Bulgaria was the Control Commission after the war with Germany was over. They had agreed that the discussions should take place in Moscow, and about the joint signature.

M. MOLOTOV claimed that this was bound up with Yugoslavia.

MR EDEN disagreed. He appealed for a settlement of the Bulgarian question within 24 hours as the delay was embarrassing in all reports.

M. MOLOTOV said that he would do his best for a settlement in 24 hours.

## RECORD OF MEETING AT THE KREMLIN, MOSCOW, ON THE 11TH OCTOBER, 1944, AT 3PM.

Present:

| | |
|---|---|
| The Secretary of State | M. Molotov |
| Sir Archibald Clark Kerr | M. Vyshinski |
| Mr O. Harvey | M. Gusev |
| Mr A. Birse | M. Pavlov |
| (Later) Mr Harriman | |
| Mr Page | |

M. MOLOTOV asked what questions they were to discuss?

MR EDEN replied he was in M. Molotov's hands.

M. MOLOTOV said he could reply to the previous day's questions. On the 10th October the General Staff of the Red Army had instructed Marshall Tolbukhin to instruct the Bulgarians that they were to treat British officers in Northern Greece in a proper manner. M. Molotov hoped the Bulgarians would take this to heart.

MR EDEN thanked M. Molotov and said the Prime Minister would also be glad.

M. MOLOTOV suggested dealing with the Hungarian question. Could it be agreed that if the Soviet Government accepted 80/20 for Hungary and Bulgaria and 50/50 for Yugoslavia, they could go on to the next questions. By mentioning 80/20 for Bulgaria, the Soviet Government accepted Mr Eden's proposal that after Germany's surrender there would be instead of an Allied Control Commission a Soviet Control Commission acting on the instructions of the Soviet High Command, with the participation of British and American representatives.

The text of this amendment was shown.

M. MOLOTOV went on to say that with regard to instructions of the Soviet High Command, this might be mentioned in the armistice terms. The terms contained provision for such instructions. M. Molotov then handed over the Russian text of the Bulgarian armistice terms.

M. MOLOTOV explained that during the first period, until Germany's surrender, the Allied Control Commission would be as in the case of Roumania. In the second period, after Germany's surrender, it would be as proposed by Mr Eden with the participation of Allied representatives. If acceptable, they could discuss how this should be worded.

M. VYSHINSKI then produced a formula for article 18. After some discussion this formula was accepted.

M. MOLOTOV said that the same principle might be applied to Hungary but in the case of Yugoslavia it would be 50/50.

MR EDEN said he would put it before the Prime Minister. For Yugoslavia he wanted the Soviet Government and Britain to have a common policy.

M. MOLOTOV said he agreed with Mr Eden.

MR EDEN suggested that he would telegraph at once to London and he asked the Russians to do the same to their representative saying agreement had been reached. It would be necessary to tell Mr Winant as he had been handling it in London. He would tell London that they had agreed about the place—Moscow—and about the double signature.

MR EDEN wanted to know what was the position about the withdrawal of Bulgarian troops from Yugoslavia and Greece.

M. MOLOTOV said that he would telegraph to Marshal Tolbukhin and it would be published as in the case of Finland. It would be published on the following day (?).

As regards the armistice terms he suggested that the wording should be checked by Sir Archibald Clark Kerr and Mr Harvey, and M. Vyshinski and M. Gusev.

MR EDEN turned to the Yugoslavian question. He had received a telegram informing him that Subasic had been invited by Tito to come to a meeting in Serbia in 10 days' time. This seemed good. Tito had said he was ready to discuss the formation of a single Government. This was also very good. The Prime Minister would be pleased to learn of it.

M. MOLOTOV expressed his pleasure ("OK").

MR EDEN suggested that both of them should send a message to Tito and to Subasic saying they were glad to hear of the coming meeting and that they looked to them to agree.

It was agreed that the text of the message should be prepared and agreed that night.

(At this point Mr Harriman was asked to come into the meeting.)

M. MOLOTOV said he wanted to give the two Ambassadors a letter on the Hungarian question.

M. PAVLOV read the letter.

M. MOLOTOV wished to add that he had seen the Hungarian Mission that morning and had received the text of their declaration. They had explained that the Hungarian Government accepted the preliminary conditions, but asked to be allowed to send some troops to Budapest to prevent a Jewish pogrom which the Germans had threatened. When the Mission left Budapest a fortnight ago there had been 4-5,000 Gestapo men in Budapest, two German divisions near the city and some "Volksdeutsche" in the town. They were preparing and talking about a pogrom. M. Molotov had told them that he was surprised that the Hungarian authorities could not prevent a pogrom, but had added that the Soviet Government wanted to prevent a massacre. The Soviet Government were willing to meet Hungarian wishes and were ready to instruct the Soviet Command to arrange with the Hungarian Command about the withdrawal of some troops from the front, during which the Red Army would interrupt its advance.

As regards the negotiations for an armistice, the Soviet Government proposed to begin these on the following day, if the Moscow Committee did not object. The draft terms would be submitted. They would be similar to the Roumanian terms. M. Molotov asked the Ambassadors to inform their Governments.

MR HARRIMAN said it was not clear to him what questions were asked in the letter.

M. MOLOTOV explained that there were two questions. First, Soviet troops were advancing. His letter suggested that the Soviet Command should arrange with the Hungarian Command that the advance should be stopped. The Soviet Government agreed to this plan. Did the British and American Governments agree? He had promised the Hungarians a reply that day. The second question was about the armistice terms: when were the negotiations to open? He suggested on the following day. They would have to decide about sending a mission to Hungary. It was not so much a question for the Governments, as for the Ambassadors.

MR EDEN pointed out that the question fundamentally concerned the Soviet Command. As regards the British, they agreed.

MR HARRIMAN thought his Government would also agree.

M. MOLOTOV said in that case the talks would open on the following day.

MR EDEN then discussed the change in the Bulgarian preliminary conditions, about sending a mission to Bulgaria.

A new text was agreed.

### MINUTES OF MEETING HELD AT THE KREMLIN ON 13TH OCTOBER, AT 4PM

Present:

| | |
|---|---|
| The Secretary of State | M. Molotov |
| Sir Archibald Clark Kerr | M. Dekanozov |
| Mr Harvey | M. Pavlov |
| Mr Ward | |
| Mr Harriman | |
| Mr Page | |

M. MOLOTOV said that he had called the meeting in order to hand over the draft of the Hungarian armistice terms.

MR HARRIMAN asked if it had any surprises.

M. MOLOTOV replied that it was like the Bulgarian text. The following were the differences. The preamble said that Hungary had accepted the preliminary condition and had been defeated in the war. Other essential points were reparations in Article 13 showing a total of American dollars 400 million dollars payable in five years in commodities. The clause about the Control Commission was as in the Bulgarian terms. M. Molotov hoped that they could discuss the draft after it had been discussed on the following day.

# APPENDIX 2

# THE KENNAN "LONG TELEGRAM"

**Moscow, February 22, 1946**

Answer to Dept's 284, Feb. 3, involves questions so intricate, so delicate, so strange to our form of thought, and so important to analysis of our international environment that I cannot compress answers into single brief message without yielding to what I feel would be dangerous degree of oversimplification. I hope, therefore, Dept will bear with me if I submit in answer to this question five parts, subjects of which will be roughly as follows:

(1) Basic features of postwar Soviet outlook

(2) Background of this outlook

(3) Its projection in practical policy on official level

(4) Its projection on unofficial level

(5) Practical deductions from standpoint of US policy

I apologize in advance for this burdening of telegraphic channel; but questions involved are of such urgent importance, particularly in view of recent events, that our answers to them, if they deserve attention at all, seem to me to deserve it at once. There follows:

**Part 1: Basic Features of Postwar Soviet Outlook, as Put Forward by Official Propaganda Machine, Are as Follows**

(a) USSR still lives in antagonistic "capitalist encirclement" with which in the long run there can be no permanent peaceful coexistence. As stated by Stalin in 1927 to a delegation of American workers: "In course of further development of international revolution there will emerge two centers of world significance: a socialist center, drawing to itself the countries which tend toward socialism, and a capitalist center, drawing to itself the countries that incline toward capitalism. Battle between these two centers for command of world economy will decide the fate of capitalism and of communism in entire world".

(b) Capitalist world is beset with internal conflicts, inherent in nature of capitalist society. These conflicts are insoluble by means of peaceful compromise. Greatest of them is that between England and US.

(c) Internal conflicts of capitalism inevitably generate wars. Wars thus generated may be of two kinds: intra-capitalist wars between two capitalist states and wars of intervention against socialist world. Smart capitalists, vainly seeking escape from inner conflicts of capitalism, incline toward latter.

(d) Intervention against USSR, while it would be disastrous to those who undertook it, would cause renewed delay in progress of Soviet socialism and must therefore be forestalled at all costs.

(e) Conflicts between capitalist states, though likewise fraught with danger for USSR, nevertheless hold out great possibilities for advancement of socialist cause, particularly if USSR remains militarily powerful, ideologically monolithic and faithful to its present brilliant leadership.

(f) It must be borne in mind that capitalist world is not all bad. In addition to hopelessly reactionary and bourgeois elements, it includes (1) certain wholly enlightened and positive elements united in acceptable communistic parties and (2) certain other elements (now described for tactical reasons as progressive or democratic) whose reactions, aspirations and activities happen to be "objectively" favorable to interests of USSR. These last must be encouraged and utilized for Soviet purposes.

(g) Among negative elements of bourgeois-capitalist society, most dangerous of all are those whom Lenin called false friends of the people, namely moderate-socialist or social-democratic leaders (in other words, non-Communist left-wing). These are more dangerous than out-and-out reactionaries, for latter at least march under their true colors, whereas moderate left-wing leaders confuse people by employing devices of socialism to serve interests of reactionary capital.

So much for premises. To what deductions do they lead from standpoint of Soviet policy? To following:

(a) Everything must be done to advance relative strength of USSR as factor in international society. Conversely, no opportunity must be missed to reduce strength and influence, collectively as well as individually, of capitalist powers.

(b) Soviet efforts, and those of Russia's friends abroad, must be directed toward deepening and exploiting of differences and conflicts between capitalist powers. If these eventually deepen into an "imperialist" war, this war must be turned into revolutionary upheavals within the various capitalist countries.

(c) "Democratic-progressive" elements abroad are to be utilized to maximum to bring pressure to bear on capitalist governments along lines agreeable to Soviet interests.

(d) Relentless battle must be waged against socialist and social-democratic leaders abroad.

## Part 2: Background of Outlook

Before examining ramifications of this party line in practice there are certain aspects of it to which I wish to draw attention.

First, it does not represent natural outlook of Russian people. Latter are, by and large, friendly to outside world, eager for experience of it, eager to measure against it talents they are conscious of possessing, eager above all to live in peace and enjoy fruits of their own labour. Party line only represents thesis which official propaganda machine puts forward with great skill and persistence to a public often remarkably resistant in the stronghold of its innermost thoughts. But party line is biding for outlook and conduct of people who make up apparatus of power—party, secret police and Government—and it is exclusively with these that we have to deal.

Secondly, please note that premises on which this party line is based are for most part simply not true. Experience has shown that peaceful and mutually profitable coexistence of capitalist and socialist states is entirely possible. Basic international conflicts in advanced countries are no longer primarily those arising out of capitalist ownership of means of production, but are ones arising from advanced urbanism and industrialism as much, which Russia has thus far been spared not by socialism but only by her own backwardness. Internal rivalries of capitalism do not always generate wars; and not all wars are attributable to this cause. To speak of possibility of intervention against USSR today, after elimination of Germany and Japan and after example of recent war, is sheerest nonsense. If not provoked by forces of intolerance and subversion, "capitalist" world of today is quite capable of living at peace with itself and with Russia. Finally, no sane person has reason to doubt sincerity of moderate socialist leaders in Western countries. Nor is it fair to deny success of their efforts to improve conditions for working population whenever, as in Scandinavia, they have been given chance to show what they could do.

Falseness of these premises, every one of which predates recent war, was amply demonstrated by that conflict itself. Anglo-American differences did not turn out to be major differences of Western world. Capitalist countries, other than those of Axis, showed no disposition to solve their differences by joining in crusade against USSR. Instead of imperialist war turning into civil wars and revolution, USSR found itself obliged to fight side by side with capitalist powers for an avowed community of aims.

Nevertheless, all these theses, however baseless and disproven, are being boldly put forward again today. What does this indicate? It indicates that Soviet party line is not based on any objective analysis of situation beyond Russia's borders; that it has, indeed, little do with conditions outside of Russia; that it arises mainly from basic inner-Russian necessities which existed before recent war and exist today.

At bottom of Kremlin's neurotic view of world affairs is traditional and instinctive Russian sense of insecurity. Originally, this was insecurity of a peaceful agricultural people trying to live on vast exposed plain in neighborhood of fierce nomadic peoples. To this was added, as Russia came into contact with economically advanced West, fear of more competent, more powerful, more highly organized societies in that area. But this latter type of insecurity was one which afflicted Russian rulers rather than Russian people; for Russian rulers have invariably sensed that their rule was relatively archaic in form, fragile and artificial in its psychological foundations, unable to stand comparison or contact with political systems of Western countries. For this reason they have always feared foreign penetration, feared direct contact between Western world and their own, feared what happen if Russians learned truth about world without or if foreigners learned truth about world within. And they have learned to seek security only in patient but deadly struggle for total destruction of rival power, never in compacts and compromises with it.

It was no coincidence that Marxism, which had smoldered ineffectively for half a century in Western Europe, caught hold and blazed for the first time in Russia. Only in this land which had never known a friendly neighbor or indeed any tolerant equilibrium of separate powers, either internal or international, could a doctrine thrive which viewed economic conflicts of society as insoluble by peaceful means. After establishment of Bolshevist regime, Marxist dogma, rendered even more truculent and intolerant by Lenin's interpretation, became a perfect vehicle for sense of insecurity with which Bolsheviks, even more than previous Russian rulers, were afflicted. In this dogma, with its basic altruism of purpose, they found justification for their instinctive fear of outside world, for the dictatorship without which they did not know how to rule, for cruelties they did not dare not to inflict, for sacrifices they felt bound to demand. In the name of Marxism they sacrificed every single ethical value in their methods and tactics. Today they cannot dispense with it. It is fig leaf of their moral and intellectual responsibility. Without it they would stand before history, at best, as only the last of that long succession of cruel and wasteful Russian rulers who have relentlessly forced country on to ever new heights of military power in order to guarantee external security of their internally weak regimes. This is why Soviet purposes must always be solemnly clothed in trappings of Marxism, and why no one should underrate importance of dogma in Soviet affairs. Thus Soviet leaders are driven [by] necessities of their own past and present position to put forward a dogma which [apparent omission] outside world as evil, hostile and menacing, but as bearing within itself germs of creeping disease and destined to be racked with growing internal convulsions until it is given final coup de grace by rising power of socialism and yields to new and better world. This thesis provides justification for that increase of military and police power of Russian state, for that isolation of Russian population from outside world, and for that fluid and constant pressure to extend limits of Russian police power which are together the nature and instinctive urges of Russian rulers. Basically this is only the steady advance of uneasy Russian nationalism, a centuries old movement in which conceptions of offense and defense are inextricably confused. But in new guise of international Marxism, with its honeyed promises to a desperate and war-torn outside world, it is more dangerous and insidious than ever before.

It should not be thought from above that Soviet party line is necessarily disingenuous and insincere on part of all those who put it forward. Many of them are too ignorant of outside world and mentally too dependent to question [apparent omission] self-hypnotism, and who have no difficulty making themselves believe what they find it comforting and convenient to believe. Finally we have the unsolved mystery as to who, if anyone, in this great land actually receives accurate and unbiased information about outside world. In the atmosphere of oriental secretiveness and conspiracy which pervades this Government, possibilities for distorting or poisoning sources and currents of information are infinite. The very disrespect of Russians for objective truth—indeed, their disbelief in its existence—leads them to view all stated facts as instruments for furtherance of one ulterior purpose or another. There is good reason to suspect that this Government is actually a conspiracy within a conspiracy; and I for one am reluctant to believe that Stalin himself receives anything like an objective picture of outside world. Here there is ample scope for the type of subtle intrigue at which Russians are past masters. Inability of foreign governments to place their case squarely before Russian policy makers—the extent to which they are delivered up in their relations with Russia to good graces of obscure and unknown advisers whom they never see and cannot influence—this to my mind is most disquieting feature of diplomacy in Moscow, and one which Western statesmen would do well to keep in mind if they would understand nature of difficulties encountered here.

## Part 3: Projection of Soviet Outlook in Practical Policy and Official Level

We have now seen nature and background of Soviet program. What may we expect by way of its practical implementation?

Soviet policy, as Department implies in its query under reference, is conducted on two planes: (1) official plane represented by actions undertaken officially in name of Soviet government; and (2) subterranean plane of actions undertaken by agencies for which Soviet Government does not admit responsibility.

Policy promulgated on both planes will be calculated to serve basic policies (a) to (d) outlined in part 1. Actions taken on different planes will differ considerably, but will dovetail into each other in purpose, timing and effect.

On official plane we must look for following:

(a) Internal policy devoted to increasing in every way strength and prestige of the Soviet state: intensive military-industrialization; maximum development of armed forces; great displays to impress outsiders; continued secretiveness about internal matters, designed to conceal weaknesses and to keep opponents in the dark.

(b) Wherever it is considered timely and promising, efforts will be made to advance official limits of Soviet power. For the moment, these efforts are restricted to certain neighboring points conceived of here as being of immediate strategic necessity, such as northern Iran, Turkey, possibly Bornholm. However, other points may at any time come into question, if and as concealed Soviet political power is extended to new areas. Thus a "friendly" Persian Government might be asked to grant Russia a port on Persian Gulf. Should Spain fall under Communist control, question of Soviet base at Gibraltar Strait might be activated. But such claims will appear on official level only when unofficial preparation is complete.

(c) Russians will participate officially in international organizations where they see opportunity of extending Soviet power or of inhibiting or diluting power of others. Moscow sees in UNO not the mechanism for a permanent and stable world society founded on mutual interest and aims of all nations, but an arena in which aims just mentioned can be favorably pursued. As long as UNO is considered here to serve this purpose, Soviet will remain with it. But if at any time they come to conclusion that it is serving to embarrass or frustrate their aims for power expansion and if they see better prospects for pursuit of these aims along other lines, they will not hesitate to abandon UNO. This would imply, however, that they felt themselves strong enough to split unity of other nations by their withdrawal, to render UNO ineffective as a threat to their aims or security, and to replace it with an international weapon more effective from their viewpoint. Thus Soviet attitude toward UNO will depend largely on loyalty of other nations to it, and on degree of vigor, decisiveness and cohesion with which these nations defend in UNO the peaceful and hopeful concept of international life, which that organization represents to our way of thinking. I reiterate, Moscow has no abstract devotion to UNO ideals. Its attitude to that organization will remain essentially pragmatic and tactical.

(d) Toward colonial areas and backward or dependent peoples, Soviet policy, even on official plane, will be directed toward weakening of power and influence and contacts of advanced Western nations, on theory that insofar as this policy is successful, there will be created a vacuum which will favor Communist-Soviet penetration. Soviet pressure for participation in trusteeship arrangements thus represents, in my opinion, a desire to be in a position to complicate and inhibit exertion of Western influence of Soviet power. Latter motive is not lacking, but for this Soviets prefer to rely on other channels than official trusteeship arrangements. Thus we may expect to find Soviets asking for admission everywhere thus acquired to weaken Western influence among such peoples.

(e) Russians will strive energetically to develop Soviet representation in, and official ties with, countries in which they sense strong possibilities of opposition to Western centers of power. This applies to such widely separated points as Germany, Argentina, Middle Eastern countries, etc.

(f) In international economic matters, Soviet policy will really be dominated by pursuit of autarchy for Soviet Union and Soviet-dominated adjacent areas taken together. That, however, will be underlying policy. As far as official line is concerned, position is not yet clear. Soviet Government has shown strange reticence since termination of hostilities on subject foreign trade. If large-scale long-term credits should be forthcoming, I believe Soviet Government may eventually again do lip service, as it did in 1930s, to desirability of building up international economic exchanges in general. Otherwise I think it possible Soviet foreign trade may be restricted largely to Soviet's own security sphere, including occupied areas in Germany, and that a cold official shoulder may be turned to principle of general economic collaboration among nations.

(g) With respect to cultural collaboration, lip service will likewise be rendered to desirability of deepening cultural contacts between peoples, but this will not in practice be interpreted in any way which could weaken security position of Soviet peoples. Actual manifestations of Soviet policy in this respect will be restricted to arid channels of closely shepherded official visits and functions, with superabundance of vodka and speeches and dearth of permanent effects.

(h) Beyond this, Soviet official relations will take what might be called "correct" course with individual foreign governments, with great stress being laid on prestige of Soviet Union and its representatives and with punctilious attention to protocol, as distinct from good manners.

**Part 4: Following May Be Said as to What We May Expect by Way of Implementation of Basic Soviet Policies on Unofficial, or Subterranean Plane, i.e., on Plane for Which Soviet Government Accepts No Responsibility**

Agencies utilized for promulgation of policies on this plane are following:

1. Inner central core of Communist parties in other countries. While many of persons who compose this category may also appear and act in unrelated public capacities, they are in reality working closely together as an underground operating directorate of world communism, a concealed Comintern tightly coordinated and directed by Moscow. It is important to remember that this inner core is actually working on underground lines, despite legality of parties with which it is associated.

2. Rank and file of Communist parties. Note distinction is drawn between these and persons defined in paragraph 1. This distinction has become much sharper in recent years. Whereas formerly foreign Communist parties represented a curious (and from Moscow's standpoint often inconvenient) mixture of conspiracy and legitimate

activity, now the conspiratorial element has been neatly concentrated in inner circle and ordered underground, while rank and file—no longer even taken into confidence about realities of movement—are thrust forward as bona fide internal partisans of certain political tendencies within their respective countries, genuinely innocent of conspiratorial connection with foreign states. Only in certain countries where communists are numerically strong do they now regularly appear and act as a body. As a rule they are used to penetrate, and to influence or dominate, as case may be, other organizations less likely to be suspected of being tools of Soviet Government, with a view to accomplishing their purposes through [apparent omission] organizations, rather than by direct action as a separate political party.

3. A wide variety of national associations or bodies which can be dominated or influenced by such penetration. These include: labor unions, youth leagues, women's organizations, racial societies, religious societies, social organizations, cultural groups, liberal magazines, publishing houses, etc.

4. International organizations which can be similarly penetrated through influence over various national components. Labor, youth and women's organizations are prominent among them. Particular, almost vital, importance is attached in this connection to international labor movement. In this, Moscow sees possibility of sidetracking Western governments in world affairs and building up international lobby capable of compelling governments to take actions favorable to Soviet interests in various countries and of paralyzing actions disagreeable to USSR.

5. Russian Orthodox Church, with its foreign branches, and through it the Eastern Orthodox Church in general.

6. Pan-Slav movement and other movements (Azerbaijan, Armenian, Turcoman, etc) based on racial groups within Soviet Union.

7. Governments or governing groups willing to lend themselves to Soviet purposes in one degree or another, such as present Bulgarian and Yugoslav governments, North Persian regime, Chinese Communists, etc. Not only propaganda machines but actual policies of these regimes can be placed extensively at disposal of USSR.

It may be expected that component parts of this far-flung apparatus will be utilized, in accordance with their individual suitability as follows:

(a) To undermine general political and strategic potential of major Western Powers. Efforts will be made in such countries to disrupt national self-confidence, to hamstring measures of national defense, to increase social and industrial unrest, to stimulate all forms of disunity. All persons with grievances, whether economic or racial, will be urged to seek redress not in mediation and compromise, but in defiant, violent struggle for destruction of other elements of society. Here poor will be set against rich, black against white, young against old, newcomers against established residents, etc.

(b) On unofficial plane particularly violent efforts will be made to weaken power and influence of Western Powers [on] colonial, backward, or dependent peoples. On this level, no holds will be barred. Mistakes and weaknesses of Western colonial administration will be mercilessly exposed and exploited. Liberal opinion in Western countries will be mobilized to weaken colonial policies. Resentment among dependent peoples will be stimulated. And while latter are being encouraged to seek independence [from] Western Powers, Soviet dominated puppet political machines will be undergoing preparation to take over domestic power in respective colonial areas when independence is achieved.

(c) Where individual governments stand in path of Soviet purposes pressure will be brought for their removal from office. This can happen where governments directly oppose Soviet foreign policy aims (Turkey, Iran), where they seal their territories off against Communist penetration (Switzerland, Portugal), or where they compete too strongly (like Labour Government in England) for moral domination among elements which it is important for Communists to dominate. (Sometimes, two of these elements are present in a single case. Then Communist opposition becomes particularly shrill and savage.)

(d) In foreign countries Communists will, as a rule, work toward destruction of all forms of personal independence—economic, political or moral. Their system can handle only individuals who have been brought into complete dependence on higher power. Thus, persons who are financially independent—such as individual businessmen, estate owners, successful farmers, artisans—and all those who exercise local leadership or have local prestige—such as popular local clergymen or political figures—are anathema. It is not by chance that even in USSR local officials are kept constantly on move from on job to another, to prevent their taking root.

(e) Everything possible will be done to set major Western Powers against each other. Anti-British talk will be plugged among Americans, anti-American talk among British. Continentals, including Germans, will be taught to abhor both Anglo-Saxon powers. Where suspicions exist, they will be fanned; where not, ignited. No effort will be spared to discredit and combat all efforts which threaten to lead to any sort of unity or cohesion among other [apparent omission] from which Russia might be excluded. Thus, all forms of international organization not amenable to Communist penetration and control, whether it be the Catholic [apparent omission] international economic concerns, or the international fraternity of royalty and aristocracy, must expect to find themselves under fire from many, and often [apparent omission].

(f) In general, all Soviet efforts on unofficial international plane will be negative and destructive in character, designed to tear down sources of strength beyond reach of Soviet control. This is only in line with basic Soviet instinct that there can be no compromise with rival power and that constructive work can start only when Communist power is dominant. But behind all this will be applied insistent, unceasing pressure for penetration and command of key positions in administration and especially in police power. This should never be lost sight of in gauging Soviet motives.

## Part 5: [Practical Deductions from Standpoint of US Policy]

In summary, we have here a political force committed fanatically to the belief that with US there can be no permanent modus vivendi, that it is desirable and necessary that the internal harmony of our society be disrupted, our traditional way of life be destroyed, the international authority of our state be broken, if Soviet power is to be secure. This political force has complete power of disposition over energies of one of world's greatest peoples and resources of world's richest national territory, and is borne along by deep and powerful currents of Russian nationalism. In addition, it has an elaborate and far-flung apparatus for exertion of its influence in other countries, an apparatus of amazing flexibility and versatility, managed by people whose experience and skill in underground methods are presumably without parallel in history. Finally, it is seemingly inaccessible to considerations of reality in its basic reactions. For it, the vast fund of objective fact about human society is not, as with us, the measure against which outlook is constantly being tested and re-formed, but a grab bag from which individual items are selected arbitrarily and tendentiously to bolster an outlook already preconceived. This is admittedly not a pleasant picture. Problem of how to cope with this force [is] undoubtedly greatest task our diplomacy has ever faced and probably greatest it will ever have to face. It should be point of departure from which our political general staff work at present juncture should proceed. It should be approached with same thoroughness and care as solution of major strategic problem in war and, if necessary, with no smaller outlay in planning effort. I cannot attempt to suggest all answers here. But I would like to record my conviction that problem is within our power to solve—and that without recourse to any general military conflict. And in support of this conviction there are certain observations of a more encouraging nature I should like to make:

(1) Soviet power, unlike that of Hitlerite Germany, is neither schematic nor adventuristic. It does not work by fixed plans. It does not take unnecessary risks. Impervious to logic of reason, and it is highly sensitive to logic of force. For this reason it can easily withdraw—and usually does—when strong resistance is encountered at any point. Thus, if the adversary has sufficient force and makes clear his readiness to use it, he rarely has to do so. If situations are properly handled there need be no prestige-engaging showdowns.

(2) Gauged against Western world as a whole, Soviets are still by far the weaker force. Thus, their success will really depend on degree of cohesion, firmness and vigor which Western world can muster. And this is a factor which it is within our power to influence.

(3) Success of Soviet system, as form of internal power, is not yet finally proven. It has yet to be demonstrated that it can survive supreme test of successive transfer of power from one individual or group to another. Lenin's death was first such transfer, and its effects racked Soviet state for 15 years. After Stalin's death or retirement will be second. But even this will not be final test. Soviet internal system will now be subjected, by virtue of recent territorial expansions, to series of additional strains which once proved severe tax on Tsardom. We here are convinced that never since termination of civil war have mass of Russian people been emotionally farther removed from doctrines of Communist Party than they are today. In Russia, party has now become a great and—for the moment—highly successful apparatus of dictatorial administration, but it has ceased to be a source of emotional inspiration. Thus, internal soundness and permanence of movement need not yet be regarded as assured.

(4) All Soviet propaganda beyond Soviet security sphere is basically negative and destructive. It should therefore be relatively easy to combat it by any intelligent and really constructive program.

For these reasons I think we may approach calmly and with good heart the problem of how to deal with Russia. As to how this approach should be made, I only wish to advance, by way of conclusion, following comments:

(1) Our first step must be to apprehend, and recognize for what it is, the nature of the movement with which we are dealing. We must study it with the same courage, detachment, objectivity, and same the determination not to be emotionally provoked or unseated by it, with which a doctor studies unruly and unreasonable individual.

(2) We must see that our public is educated to realities of Russian situation. I cannot overemphasize importance of this. Press cannot do this alone. It must be done mainly by Government, which is necessarily more experienced and better informed on practical problems involved. In this we need not be deterred by [ugliness?] of picture. I am convinced that there would be far less hysterical anti-Sovietism in our country today if realities of this situation were better understood by our people. There is nothing as dangerous or as terrifying as the unknown. It may also be argued that to reveal more information on our difficulties with Russia would reflect unfavorably on Russian-American relations. I feel that if there is any real risk here involved, it is one which we should have courage to face, and sooner the better. But I cannot see what we would be risking. Our stake in this country, even coming on heels of tremendous demonstrations of our friendship for Russian people, is remarkably small. We have here no investments to guard, no actual trade to lose, virtually no citizens to protect, few cultural contacts to preserve. Our only stake lies in what we hope rather than what we have; and I am convinced we have better chance of realizing those hopes if our public is enlightened and if our dealings with Russians are placed entirely on realistic and matter-of-fact basis.

(3) Much depends on health and vigor of our own society. World communism is like malignant parasite which feeds only on diseased tissue. This is point at which domestic and foreign policies meet. Every courageous and incisive measure to solve internal problems of our own society, to improve self-confidence, discipline, morale and community spirit of our own people, is a diplomatic victory over Moscow worth a thousand diplomatic notes and joint communiqués. If we cannot abandon fatalism and indifference in face of deficiencies of our own society, Moscow will profit—Moscow cannot help profiting by them in its foreign policies.

(4) We must formulate and put forward for other nations a much more positive and constructive picture of sort of world we would like to see than we have put forward in past. It is not enough to urge people to develop political processes similar to our own. Many foreign peoples, in Europe at lest, are tired and frightened by experiences of past, and are less interested in abstract freedom than in security. They are seeking guidance rather than responsibilities. We should be better able than Russians to give them this. And, unless we do, Russians certainly will.

(5) Finally we must have courage and self-confidence to cling to our own methods and conceptions of human society. After all, the greatest danger that can befall us in coping with this problem of Soviet communism is that we shall allow ourselves to become like those with whom we are coping.

# APPENDIX 3

## THE ROBERTS DESPATCHES

### Moscow, March 17, 1946
### Despatch 189

I undertook in my despatch No. 181 to endeavour to assess the main factors bearing upon Soviet policy and to estimate their effect upon Anglo-Soviet relations in the postwar world. I am only too well aware of the magnitude of the problem and of the difficulties of treating it thoroughly and objectively. I feel, however, that it must now be faced, although I submit the following review with the greatest diffidence and in full consciousness of its inadequacies and shortcomings.

2. There is one fundamental factor affecting Soviet policy dating back to the small beginnings of the Muscovite State. This is the constant striving for security of a State with no natural frontiers and surrounded by enemies. In this all-important respect the rulers and people of Russia are united by a common fear, deeply rooted in Russian history. National security is, in fact, at the bottom of Soviet, as of Imperial Russian, policy, and explains much of the high-handed behaviour of the Kremlin and many of the suspicions genuinely held there concerning the outside world. Russia has always been a more backward State than her neighbours. Even today the Soviet Union, despite its prestige in the world, is more backward than not only Britain or the United States, but than most other European countries. She has grown around a small principality in Moscow, with no natural frontiers and always surrounded by unfriendly neighbours—Tartars, Poles, Turks, Teutonic Knights and Swedes. At the very birth of the new Soviet State the whole world again seemed united against her, and the fears aroused by foreign intervention after 1917 cannot yet have been eradicated from the minds of the rulers of Russia, any more than the fear of communism has been eradicated from that of Western leaders, who nevertheless cooperated with the Soviet Union during the war. The frontiers of Russia have never been fixed and have gone backwards and forwards with defeats or victories in war. But even after her greatest victories in the past Russia has somehow found herself deprived of many of the fruits of those victories, and has never achieved the security which she thought her due reward. Despite this, over the centuries Russia has expanded, as much by peaceful colonisation (e.g., in Siberia) and by agreement with local leaders (e.g., in Georgia) as by actual conquest.

3. Russia's relations with Britain, which opened on a friendly footing in the mid-sixteenth century, grew steadily in scope and political importance from Peter the Great's reign onwards as Russia expanded towards areas in which Britain herself was closely interested. But wherever British and Russian political interests touched they seemed inevitably to come into conflict, if only because Russia was usually to be found upsetting a state of affairs which Britain regarded as tolerably satisfactory. The result was that Russia and Britain found themselves on opposite sides in the Baltic, in the Near East (where they struggled over the weakening Turkish Empire and over the passages from the Black Sea to the Mediterranean), in Persia and later in the Far East. But in the greatest crises of modern history Britain and Russia have had to turn to each other for support and have found themselves in the same camp. Ivan the Terrible, painfully building up the Russian State against strong foreign and internal enemies, made the first Russian treaty with Britain in order that British ships could bring in supplies by sea. Peter the Great also looked to Britain and Holland for help in building up the Russian navy and Russian economy. In the great crisis of the Napoleonic wars, despite many misunderstandings and clashes of interest between the two countries, Britain and Russia were again together, and between them they saved Europe from French domination. After the Treaty of Vienna and throughout the 19th century relations were strained. The Tsarist system was regarded with the same ideological aversion as the present Communist tyranny, and Alexander I and Nicholas I were feared as Stalin is today. On the other side the Russians distrusted Britain as the home of dangerous liberal ideas which, if they spread abroad, would lead to revolution and disorder. There were constant and serious clashes of interest throughout the Middle East and in South-Eastern Europe, which often threatened war but only once actually led to it. Towards the end of the century there was a fear of Russian strength and of Russian designs on India and the empire which was quite as strong and deep-seated as the anxieties concerning Russian intentions which are now spreading in the Western world. But despite all this, British and Russian interests were reconciled in the 1907 agreement (although this was reached when Russia was weak after her defeat by Japan and when she was a prey to internal troubles) and once again we found ourselves fighting together against Germany in 1914. Despite all the bitterness left on both sides by the Revolution and foreign intervention, Hitler brought us together again in 1941 and the alliance of 1942 led to our joint victory with the United States in 1945.

4. But until 1945 Britain and Russia were never left face to face. Their relations were conditioned by the coexistence of a strong France, of Prussia and later a powerful German Empire, of Austria-Hungary and even of the Turkish Empire. And, as I have already suggested, in all the greatest European crises since the French Revolution, Britain and Russia were brought together to fight against the domination of Europe by another Great Power, whether France or

Germany. Now all that has changed. France is no longer a Great Power. Germany is at all events for the time being of no account. Austria-Hungary and the Turkish Empire no longer exist. The only other world Power is the United States, and there is clearly no reason why Britain and Russia should be brought to combine against her as a menace to their interests or to the peace of the world. Therefore Britain and Russia are now in immediate contact as never before, with no other Power to unite them in self-defence or act as a buffer between them. And between them there is now a greater ideological gulf than even in the 19th century. Instead of the old balance of forces there now exist the UNO and the Big Three, which are in the Soviet view at least closely interconnected. The Soviet Government has always seen the UNO as a body which can only work so long as the Big Three are in agreement or can harmonise their interests behind the scenes. The course of events at the UNO meeting in London, which may well be repeated in New York, has shown that when Big Three cooperation breaks down the UNO itself is at once in danger and that the Soviet Union may then only regard it as a convenient forum in which to embarrass us and to appeal for the support of some among the smaller nations. As after the treaties of Vienna and Versailles, Anglo-Russian relations, with no common enemy to draw us together, are proving fragile and are not contributing to the promotion of closer international organisation.

5. In this new situation, what is the Soviet attitude towards the outside world in general and Britain in particular? This is shown in the ideological line laid down for the Soviet public by the Communist party, since this not only conditions the thinking of the Soviet public but also guides the activities of the Communist parties throughout the world. This party teaching is not encouraging for the future of Anglo-Soviet cooperation. The tone of party propaganda, and more particularly in the more thoughtful and authoritative publications such as *Bolshevik, World Economy and Peace and Party Organisation*, is not only critical of but hostile to the outside world. The great bulk of the information allowed to reach the Soviet public about Britain or the United States is critical or contemptuous. News items are weighted and selected in order to convey the desired impression of a civilisation inferior to that of the Soviet Union and containing within itself the seeds of its own destruction. The United States is painted as a land torn with strikes, with an acute Negro problem, and with the working classes exploited by selfish capitalists. Britain is shown as weakened by the war; the necessary reforms are not being put in hand with enough resolution; the Labour Government is disappointing its supporters and acting as a tool of sinister influences, while fascists are allowed full freedom to conduct their notorious activities. The picture is, of course, even blacker throughout the colonial empire, and in India and the Middle East, where we are found guilty of the sins not only of exploitation but of inefficient leadership.

6. But the Western democracies, weak and disunited though they may be, are shown as the main dangers in a continued capitalist encirclement of the Soviet Union. In this respect, Soviet propaganda and official pronouncements have harked back to the old Soviet attitude of the twenties and early thirties, and now that the German and Japanese menace has been removed, the former allies of the Soviet Union are represented as potential, if not actual, enemies. The capitalist world is, however, shown as profoundly divided both between States and within individual States. In fact, in the orthodox Marxist view, these capitalist States are bound to quarrel amongst themselves, more particularly over control of dwindling raw materials and over colonial territories still existing in the world. The Soviet Union would not be interested in such quarrels within a decaying civilisation were it not for the fact that even the Soviet Union is a member of world society and may be affected by such death struggles within the capitalist world. Above all there is the danger that some leaders of capitalist society might unite their countries in an attack upon the Soviet Union, if only to distract attention from their own internal problems. The Soviet Union must therefore be constantly on her guard, surrounded as she is by enemies. She must build up her industrial potential to the greatest possible extent and maintain a strong military establishment, even in time of peace. She must improve such backward arms as her air force and navy, and, above all, catch up with the Western democracies over the harnessing of atomic energy.

7. The picture might be less black and the prospects less gloomy if the Soviet Union were prepared to isolate herself completely from the infectious outside world. But this is not likely because, in the hostile capitalist world, there are many good elements such as the Communist party, fellow travellers and liberal elements, who may gain power and who in any case naturally sympathise with the Soviet Union and form a fifth column within individual States, prepared, as the Canadian spy case has shown, to put the interests of the Soviet Union above those of its own country. The Soviet Union cannot resist making use of such persons, fishing in troubled waters, and even appealing to them over the heads of the governments of States with whom it is in friendly relations and with whom it may even have alliances.

8. The above view of the outside world is sedulously propagated, despite much objective evidence that the picture is false. Recent history has shown that the Western democracies, far from uniting against the Soviet Union, contributed all the aid in their power in the common struggle against fascism. Far from wishing to encircle the Soviet Union, Britain and America have made, and are still making, every effort to increase intercourse between their countries and peoples and those of the Soviet Union, and to bring the Soviet Union fully into the world community. They have made concession after concession to encourage such cooperation, but so far with little response.

9. This brings us to the very important questions: Who are the real rulers of Russia propagating the above views, and how do their processes of thought really run in regard to the outside world? Ultimate power resides in the small circle of the Politburo, who have complete control of the military machine and of the ubiquitous and immensely powerful system of State security. The natural assumption is that Stalin is, in fact, a dictator as absolute as Hitler in Germany. There is little doubt that the last word rests with him; but we have so often found that views expressed by him in private conversation are belied by subsequent events, that it would seem either that he is exceptionally crafty in dealing with foreign statesmen or that he is himself dependent upon the collective decisions of his colleagues in the Politburo. The explanation may even lie deeper, in the information or lack of information which reaches him about the outside world. Many foreign observers in Moscow consider that, although Molotov is publicly recognised as the second personality in the Soviet State, in fact greater power is wielded behind the scenes by Malenkov, who largely controls the Communist party machine, and by Beriya, until recently the head of the State security system and now promoted to a general supervision of the machinery of government. Some well-informed students of the Soviet Union have speculated that there may be a growing circle of ambitious Red Army men and industrial executives who, knowing nothing of the outside world, are ready to risk a trial of strength with their former allies in pursuing an adventurous foreign policy. But this is mere speculation, and it would be safer to assume that control is firmly in the hands of Stalin, as advised by his fellow members of the Politburo and more particularly by Molotov, Malenkov and Beriya.

10. It is hard to say whether these men share the view of the outside world sedulously propagated in Communist party propaganda. But it would, I think, be safer to assume that, brought up in the pure Marxist doctrine from earliest manhood and for the most part ignorant of the outside world, and having no real contacts even with leaders of other nations, they do, in fact, believe their own dogma. All their training—first as underground revolutionaries and then as the rulers of a State working against the greatest internal difficulties and facing the hostility of the world—must make them suspicious and, insofar as they are themselves with no friendly feelings towards the Western democracies and with no scruples whatsoever in dealing with them, they no doubt attribute similar motives to their opposite numbers in London and Washington, more particularly when they see in London representatives of social democracy and of the Second International, with whom they have fought a long and bitter struggle, inside and outside the Soviet Union.

11. In determining Soviet policy Stalin and his colleagues have certain advantages over their opposite numbers elsewhere. They are less burdened with day-to-day problems. They do not have to justify themselves before Parliament and public opinion. And they have an

opportunity of planning a long-term policy which is often denied to democratic parliamentary governments. It would now appear that Stalin, in fact, passed his vacation at Sachi last autumn in planning the Soviet foreign and democratic policy which is causing us anxiety today. In his projects for building up the military and economic strength of the Soviet Union, as announced in his February election speech and developed in the first of three new Five-Year Plans put before the Supreme Soviet on the 15th of March, he is planning ahead in terms of ten, fifteen and even twenty years in a way which would be difficult in another country.

12. But the Soviet rulers would seem to have one great disadvantage in dealing with the outside world. They seem to [be] genuinely ill- or mis-informed about what goes on elsewhere. Their sources of information are (a) an ill-experienced, frightened and overworked diplomatic service, whose members probably do not dare to say anything which might cause offence to the Kremlin even if they are themselves able to form an objective view of the countries in which they are posted; and (b) a fifth column of Communists, fellow travellers and misguided idealists, who must convey to their Soviet friends a very strange and often excessively rose-coloured picture of the position in their respective countries. Although it may seem odd, it is indeed probable that such persons as Mr Harry Pollitt, the Dean of Canterbury and Mr Priestley are relied upon in Moscow for an objective picture of political developments in Britain. And even this defective information is filtered carefully through to Stalin by innumerable party and government authorities culminating in Malenkov, Beriya and Molotov, all of whom, no doubt, twist and censor it to suit their own interests and preconceived ideas. When finally we consider that all Communists, from the top to the bottom, have a conception of the outside world based upon what they have learnt in the works of Marx, Lenin and Stalin, and subconsciously fit all developments into this ideological pattern, it will be realised that the chances of the Soviet rulers being well informed upon the world situation are extremely slender, more particularly in view of their limited contacts with their opposite numbers in other countries. It is, indeed, possible that in any given crisis in international relations—as for example the recent Canadian spy case—a small group of high Communists or NKVD [People's Commissariat of Internal Affairs] officials might cover up their own clumsiness by convincing Stalin that what appeared like Soviet espionage was, in fact, only a further example of the determination of the outside capitalist world to stage a major anti-Soviet demonstration.

13. But however well- or ill-informed the Kremlin may be on the situation in the outside world it is certainly incapable, in conducting international relations, of the give-and-take which is normal and, indeed, essential between other States. When British delegates negotiate an agreement with delegates from any country other than the Soviet Union, there is usually an honest endeavour on both sides to

understand the point of view of the other and to arrive at an agreement which must to some extent represent a compromise between the interests of both. Once this compromise has been achieved there is a certain finality about the agreement reached which is intended to cover relations between the two countries on this particular issue for some time to come, at least until the time when new negotiations are required. This, in its turn, implies a reasonable fidelity to the spirit as well as to the letter of international contracts and treaty obligations. Without this minimum of goodwill and good faith international relations, even on their present relatively low plane of morality, would be impossible in our sense of the term. The Soviet Union, however, does not conceive international relations in this sense at all. She approaches a partner, whom she regards as potentially hostile, endeavours to exact the maximum advantage for the Soviet Union, if possible without any return, and, having obtained what she wants, reopens this issue or raises another at the earliest possible moment in order to achieve the next item on her programme. There is, therefore, no degree of finality about any agreement reached with the Soviet Union, despite her much vaunted fidelity to her international obligations—the true value of which has recently been shown in Persia. All nations are, of course, guided by self-interest, but most other great nations approach problems of common interest, *e.g.*, the provision of food for starving countries in Europe and the Far East, with a greater or a lesser desire to make their contribution and not only to exact the maximum advantage for themselves. There is among the other nations of the world a certain sense of world community, which is certainly not shown by the Soviet Union despite her new position in world affairs, which she has not only won for herself but been willingly accorded by her Allies. Instead of encouraging increased contact between nations and dealing with them primarily as potential partners and not as ultimate enemies, the Soviet Union has since the war increased, if that were possible, the isolation of her people from outside influence, and her appearance on the international scene are publicly admitted here to be designed mainly to further the Soviet interests. In short, the Soviet Union is ideologically and economically a closed community, controlled by a small handful of men, themselves cut off from the outside world, whose system of government is based upon an all-pervasive police system and the most wide-spread propaganda machinery. Lest this may appear little more than an idle generalisation, I attach annexes dealing very summarily with Soviet behaviour on certain specific problems affecting her relations with the outside world.

14. In the light of these facts and our recent experiences, one is driven to conclude not only that the rulers of the Soviet Union do not believe in the same things which Western democracies believe in, but that they are incapable of doing so. Reared as they have been in revolutionary traditions and impregnated with Marxist doctrine, they genuinely despise liberal ideas, tolerance, and the conceptions of right

and justice which are the basis of Western thinking, however inadequately they may be interpreted in practice. The small group ruling Russia believe that the end justifies the means, and that they are at the head of a chosen people, or rather a chosen group of peoples, with a chosen system destined to spread throughout the world. In their view relations with the outside world, and even alliances, are short-term arrangements for definite objectives, and can be modified or rejected as soon as they not longer suit the purpose of the Soviet Union. From Marxist-Leninist doctrine springs absolute confidence in the future of the Soviet State and system, deep suspicion and distrust of the outside world and complete disregard for all personal considerations and normal human relationships between individuals and States alike.

15. It is no use disguising the fact that the above situation is alarming. But there are, fortunately, other factors to be taken into account. Apart from a certain feeling of xenophobia based upon the conviction that they have not hitherto had their fair share of the good things of the world, the peoples of the Soviet Union, and above all the dominant Russian people, are not naturally hostile to the outside world, nor eager to dominate other peoples. The intelligentsia are friendly, cultivated and clever, and only too anxious to meet similar persons from other countries and to measure their wits against them. The masses are, for the most part, friendly, capable of sudden bursts of fury in which no excuse can be found for their behaviour but, as all foreigners in the Soviet Union can testify, fundamentally eager for good relations with the outside world and ready to be influenced by foreign ideas and foreign contacts. This is therefore a people very different from the Germans, who regarded themselves as a master race, destined to dominate the world, and who fully sympathised with the ruthless and ambitious policies of their leaders. In addition, there is a fundamental streak of laziness, indiscipline and inefficiency running through the Russian people, who must be constantly kept up to the mark if they are to preserve their position in the world. Granted these national characteristics, it is essential that the Soviet people should be ruled with the greatest firmness and, at the same time, deceived about the outside world. A foreign bogey and the fear of foreign aggression must be held before them to stimulate their efforts for the new Five-Year Plan, and to persuade them that a large proportion of these efforts must be devoted, not to improving the lot of the Soviet people, but to preparing either for the defence of the Soviet Union or for future expansion.

16. Another important, although somewhat speculative, consideration is how far the Revolution has stabilised itself in the Soviet Union. There is no doubt that the present Soviet regime is fully accepted by the overwhelming majority of the Soviet peoples. Large sections of the population now have a stake in the regime and all those under 40 know of nothing else. In fact, Soviet Russia has reached a similar stage in development as revolutionary France when the First Empire had become solidly established. Although Soviet Russia

intends to spread her influence by all possible means, world revolution is no longer part of her programme and there is nothing in internal conditions within the Union which might encourage a return to the old revolutionary traditions.

17. Any comparison between the German menace before the war and a Soviet menace today must also allow for the following fundamental differences:

(a) In the first place, the Soviet Union, unlike Germany, is a vast territory containing all the primary products necessary for a modern State and with more than enough scope for all the energies of its peoples in developing these vast resources. There is plenty of room for a population far larger than the present 190 million, and the greater part of the Soviet Union is backward and undeveloped. Although, therefore, Soviet energies are as dynamic as those of Germany, there is not the same motive force compelling the Soviet Union to burst out beyond its frontiers and carve out for itself its due place in the world.

(b) Moreover, the rulers of Russia are infinitely more flexible than those of Germany. However much they may be wedded to Marxist doctrine, this allows them considerable latitude in regard to tactics and timing. Whereas the Germans set themselves a definite goal to be achieved within a given time regardless of opposition and changes in the international situation, the Russians are capable of readjusting their projects if faced by opposition or unexpected difficulties. They do not charge into brick walls, even when they have the necessary strength to break them down, but prefer to wait and find some means of either getting round or climbing over the wall. There is, therefore, infinitely less danger of sudden catastrophe with the Russians than with the Germans.

(c) Furthermore, the rulers of Russia have not got the same sense of urgency as Hitler, who knew that if Germany was to dominate Europe and the world she must act quickly. The Kremlin, on the other hand, is confident that time is on its side and there is, therefore, no need to prejudice certain future progress by pressing ahead too sharply or rapidly with any particular project.

(d) Soviet Russia is also largely free from any sense of racial superiority or of a mission to dominate the world, though there is certain Messianic strain in the Russian outlook. Her methods are much more subtle and they aim at the ultimate creation of a communist or socialist society throughout the world in close communion of spirit with the Soviet Union. They do not call for open conquest and least of all for the launching of a war of aggression, except possibly for limited aims.

(e) Finally, the internal position inside the Soviet Union, and in particular the economic structure, is at present much weaker than might be imagined if one listened only to Soviet propaganda. The internal problems facing the Soviet Union are quite as serious as those facing the Western democracies and they are on an even larger scale, while there is infinitely more leeway to make up in assuring even a modest standard of life to the now expectant Soviet people. The advent of the atomic bomb has shown that the Soviet military machine is by no means invincible, and the rulers of Russia know very well the inadequacy of the Red navy and air forces. They also know that there are strong forces throughout the world—American capitalism, British social democracy and the Catholic Church among them—which would form strong centres of opposition to any attempt by the Soviet Union in the immediate future to dominate the world. In fact, the Soviet Union, although confident in its ultimate strength, is nothing like so strong at present as the Western democratic world, and knows it.

18. On the morrow of the greatest Russian victories in history, the rulers of the Soviet Union have seen their opportunity to achieve their ambitions, unless they are thwarted by the capitalist world uniting against them again and trumping what seemed the Red Army ace with the even better card of the atomic bomb. Basically, the Kremlin is now pursuing a Russian national policy which does not differ except in degree from that pursued in the past by Ivan the Terrible, Peter the Great or Catherine the Great. But what would, in other lands, be naked imperialism or power politics is covered by the more attractive garb of Marxist-Leninist ideology, which, in its turn, moulds the approach to world problems of statesmen whose belief in their own ideology is as profound as that of the Jesuits in their own faith during the Counter Reformation. This long-term policy would appear to fall under six main heads:

(a) In the first place every effort is being made to develop the Soviet Union into the most powerful State in the world, if necessary by its own unaided efforts, and meanwhile to provide for Soviet security. This means that at a time when other countries are busy demobilising and reducing their armed forces, the Soviet Union is maintaining a very large military establishment, modernising its equipment and industrial base, and hesitating even to reduce its garrison forces abroad, which probably number at least three million men. The search for security is a constantly expanding process. The establishment of the Soviet frontier on the Curzon Line has meant that a puppet Polish State must have its frontiers on the Oder and the Neisse. This, in its time, leads to Soviet control of the eastern zone of Germany through a faithful Communist party, and to encouragement of Communist influence in the rest of Germany and even in France. To take another example, the domination of Persian Azerbaijan to protect the oil in Baku leads on naturally to the domination of Persia as a whole, to encouragement of a puppet Kurdish republic, to the isolation of Turkey and eventually to infiltration into the whole Arab world. A legitimate demand for a large say in the control of the Dardanelles is at once followed by demands for bases in the Dodecanese and Tripolitania. In fact, Soviet security has become hard to distinguish from Soviet imperialism and it is becoming uncertain whether there is, in fact, any limit to Soviet expansion.

(b) The second and connected objective is to weaken capitalist or social-democratic countries in every way. So far as Britain is concerned, this means the encouragement of "national liberation movements" in India, throughout the colonial world, and in the Middle East. It also means constant intrigue against and undermining of our established position in Scandinavia, Western Europe, the Iberian Peninsula and Greece. Any tendency on the part of Western European countries to draw closer together will be bitterly opposed. In Britain itself the Communist party and fellow travellers will be used as a spearhead to undermine the mistrusted forces of social democracy now dominant with the Labour Government. Any discomfiture we may suffer anywhere in the world will be seized upon and exploited.

(c) Everything possible will be done to keep the Americans and ourselves apart.

(d) Although the Communist International no longer exists, Communist parties everywhere will be supported and used to further Soviet interests, and ultimately to take over the government. Nongovernmental international organisations such as the World Federation of Trade Unions and international youth and women's organisations will also be encouraged and used for Soviet political ends.

(e) Social democracy and all moderate progressive forces will everywhere be attacked bitterly and ruthlessly as the main dangers to communism and so to the Soviet Union. These forces are regarded not so much as an ultimate alternative to communism but rather as an opiate for the workers, who, after they have received certain limited benefits which social democracy can offer, will no longer have the necessary incentive to carry through the revolution within their own countries. In this sense, therefore, social democracy will always be regarded as a tool for capitalism and reaction.

(f) Finally, and perhaps most important at the moment, the full weight of Soviet propaganda, and where possible active support, will be brought to bear in favour of the so-called oppressed colonial peoples and against imperialist domination. This is in line with orthodox Marxist teaching, as well as with Soviet national interests, and there is little doubt that the Soviet peoples, from Stalin downwards, are embarking upon such a campaign with the zeal of crusaders and with a sincere belief that they are thereby contributing to the progress of the world.

19. In the heat of the current controversies and so soon after the end of the war it is difficult to determine with certainty how far these policies represent mainly a tactical short-term campaign designed (a) to get the maximum advantages for the Soviet Union in the present fluid state of international society, and (b) to intimidate us into renewed cooperation with the Soviet Union, but on their own terms, and how far it is a long-term strategy. With a regime whose ultimate ambitions, although not its immediate aims, are unlimited and which views the world as a whole *sub specie aeternitatis*, much as the Catholic

Church might do, policy is probably not so clear-cut and the contrast between short-term tactics and long-term strategy may be unreal. At all events we should be wise to frame our own policy on the assumptions

(i) That the Soviet regime is dynamic and that the Soviet Union is still expanding, although admittedly not as yet beyond areas where Russian interests existed before the Revolution;

(ii) That her long-term ambitions are dangerous to vital British interests as we now see them;

(iii) That security is the first consideration with the Soviet Union and that she will not endanger the realisation of her long-term projects by pressing immediate issues to the point of serious conflict, except as the result of a miscalculation of forces;

(iv) That it is therefore possible, though difficult, to reconcile British and Soviet interests in any problem with which we are likely to be faced, granted the right mixture of strength and patience and the avoidance of sabre-rattling or the raising of prestige issues; but

(v) That, except in the now unlikely event of Germany or some other Power again becoming a deadly menace to British and Russian survival, there is no longer in the new international situation any certainty of Britain and Russia being automatically drawn together in major international crises, as we were in 1812, 1914 and 1941.

I am sending a copy of this despatch to His Majesty's Ambassador at Washington.

I have, &c.

F.K. ROBERTS

## Appendix I
### Attitude to the United Nations Organisation

It must at once be admitted that the Soviet Government, whose basic attitude to the United Nations Organisation is mentioned in paragraph 4 of the covering despatch, have worked hard and made valuable contributions to the establishment of the United Nations Organisation. But from the very beginning, and more particularly in regard to the veto, they have insisted that the United Nations Organisation could never be used against Soviet interests. They have constantly pressed for representation in the United Nations Organisation for outside bodies in which Soviet influence is very strong, e.g., the World Federation of Trade Unions and the international youth and women's movements. These claims, if granted, would make it easier for the Soviet Union to appeal to other peoples over the heads of their governments and authorised representatives at the United Nations Organisation. Already at the San Francisco Conference last April Molotov, when pledging Soviet support for the new organisation, gave a clear warning that while the Soviet Union wanted it to succeed, she had other strings to her bow and was quite prepared to turn to other methods for retaining and spreading Soviet influence in the world if the United Nations Organisation did not come up to Soviet expectations. The recent London meeting of the General Assembly and Security Council provided an excellent example of the Soviet attitude to the United Nations Organisation. It is evidently to be used as a forum in which Soviet representatives can cover up high-handed Soviet actions and embarrass other countries by irresponsible charges designed to curry favour with the so-called oppressed peoples. Even in procedural and nonpolitical questions the Soviet representatives were constantly finding themselves supporting (to us) untenable theses and were heavily out-voted. In fact, the Soviet conception of international negotiations, whether in the United Nations Organisation, the Council of Foreign Ministers or between the Big Three, consists not so much of arriving at agreement as in reaching agreement exclusively on Soviet terms. Insofar as the Soviet people and possibly even the small circle of the rulers sincerely believe that they are the sole repositories of justice and right-thinking in the world, their representatives have no doubt returned from London with a sense of grievance and isolation which is not encouraging for the future of world cooperation.

## Appendix II
### *Intellectual Exchanges and Personal Contacts*

Never since the Revolution has the Soviet Union been so cut off from the outside world as today. Apart from a handful of American engineers installing oil refineries, and for a larger number of Communists and fellow travellers whose natural centre is Moscow, the only foreigners in the Soviet Union today are the diplomatic corps in Moscow, a dwindling body of foreign correspondents, and Axis prisoners of war who have not yet been released. The diplomatic corps and the correspondents are more carefully shepherded and more strictly segregated from all normal contacts with Russians than at any previous period, despite Stalin's repeated statements to British representatives that he does not desire such segregation. Constant endeavours by His Majesty's Government in London and through this embassy to encourage an exchange of visits between the two countries, to exchange teachers and students in order to promote real knowledge of each country by the other, have all been fruitless, if not actively discouraged. Cultural contacts are canalised through VOKS [Soviet Union Society for Cultural Relations with Foreign Countries], an institution whose purpose is to restrict rather than to encourage exchanges of knowledge and the promotion of real friendship. Meanwhile, specially selected visitors, usually fellow travellers like the Dean of Canterbury or Mr Priestley, are brought to this country, lavishly entertained and sent back to do Soviet propaganda in Britain. When by rare chance representative, honest and friendly visitors, such as the British Iron and Steel delegation, reach the Soviet Union and afterwards make some frank but friendly criticisms imbued with a genuine admiration for many aspects of Soviet life, they are branded as tools of reactionaries, if not as plain fascist beasts. Conversely, the only Russians allowed out of the Soviet Union are persons carefully vetted by the regime who can be relied upon not to form an objective impression of the countries they visit, but to do Soviet propaganda there and to return to Russia with enough adverse material to inspire unfavourable press comment in Moscow. Although private individuals and government spokesmen alike in Britain and the United States plead for the doors to be opened, these appeals pass unheeded on the Soviet side, and I know of no single step which they have taken parallel to the innumerable efforts from our side to encourage free, frank and friendly intercourse between Soviet citizens and their counterparts in the Western democracies. The experiences of our prisoners of war repatriated through the Soviet Union and of our troops wherever they have met the Red Army face to face in Europe have more than borne out the experience of foreign residents in Moscow.

### Appendix III
*Trade Policy*

The Soviet attitude to international trade is to obtain certain essential products, if possible on credit, but to rely mainly upon her own resources for the reconstruction and development of the Soviet Union. She has no general interest in increasing commercial exchanges between nations. She certainly does not regard international trade as a means of bringing the nations together and of increasing prosperity throughout the world. What she intends to do is to build up the economic strength of the Soviet Union and to indulge only in the limited degree of foreign trade necessary for that purpose. Her attitude to Bretton Woods and to the American proposals for an international trade and tariff conference has therefore been purely negative. Although she would like an American and even a British loan, or credit, she has not so far shown herself ready to lift a finger to encourage either the Americans or ourselves to make such a loan or credit and is certainly not ready to accept any awkward conditions for it. Throughout the whole of Eastern Europe the Soviet Union is carrying out a sort of Schacht plan in reverse, under which the countries within the Soviet orbit will find their economies increasingly geared to Soviet needs and to the Soviet five-Year Plan. Foreign interests meanwhile are being frozen out and discouraged in every way from playing a part in the economic life of Eastern Europe, except, of course, when it comes to giving charity through UNRRA [United Nations Relief and Rehabilitation Administration] with no countervailing advantages to the benefactor countries. On the other hand, the Soviet Union has no designs at present to compete on any scale in the world export markets and, once normal conditions return, a limited and mutually profitable Anglo-Soviet trade in goods essential to both parties can no doubt be resumed.

## Appendix IV

*Press Censorship and Presentation of News*

In no country, not even in Nazi Germany, has there been such a dishonest presentation of world news and such a dangerous censorship of foreign correspondents as there is today in the Soviet Union. World news reproduced in the Soviet press is carefully selected to fit into whatever happens to be the propaganda pattern of the day. The most important declarations of policy and developments are, if necessary, completely ignored or, alternatively, presented to the Soviet public in such a twisted form as to give an entirely misleading impression. On the other hand, minor items of no possible importance or interest are played up. I need not quote instances of this, as the Foreign Office files are already full of them. Meanwhile, the press censorship of Moscow works in such a way that only items favourable to the Soviet Union can be telegraphed out of the country; while more recently the Soviet censorship has taken to deciding itself not merely what is not to be said, but what is to be said, without even informing correspondents of what is going out over their signatures. The Soviet public is therefore constantly and systematically misled about the world situation, persuaded either that friends are enemies or that criticism is really applause. Similarly, the general public outside the Soviet Union receives an incomplete and misleading picture of developments here. At any given moment Soviet action and policy can be presented in the most favour light, while those of the Western democracies are traduced and misrepresented.

## Moscow, March 18, 1946, Section 3
## Despatch 190

It remains to consider the most important question of all: what British policy should be towards the Soviet Union if the assessment of Soviet policy attempted in my despatch No. 189 is approximately correct.

2. We have tried many methods in the recent past. After a brief attempt at the beginning of the Revolution to work with the new regime in order to keep Russia in the war, we tried armed intervention and the support of separatist movements throughout the Russian Empire in order to break down the Soviet regime and ensure its replacement by some government more akin to other European governments. This failed lamentably, and not even the most stubborn and shortsighted reactionaries would advocate another attempt at foreign intervention today. There then followed a period of isolation, during which there were no diplomatic relations between the Soviet Union and the greater part of the outside world. From the other side of a *cordon sanitaire* we watched with little sympathy the painful efforts of the Soviet Government to restore some sort of order and a passable standard of living within the shattered Russian Empire. On her side, the Soviet Union still propagated world revolution through

the Comintern. As it became clear that the Soviet regime had come to stay, diplomatic relations were opened, but it was not until the thirties, when the common German danger brought the Soviet Union into the League of Nations in the pursuit of collective security, that anything approaching normality existed between London and Moscow. The failure of the attempt to achieve collective security, the bitter memories of the Spanish civil war and of Munich (regarded by the Soviet Union as a betrayal by the West), and finally the Soviet counter-betrayal in the Soviet-German pact of 1939 brought to nothing what had seemed a promising experiment. Then came the German attack upon the Soviet Union, the Anglo-Soviet Alliance of 1942, the growth of Big Three cooperation, and finally the victory over Germany and Japan and the creation of the United Nations Organisation. During this last period Anglo-Soviet cooperation and relative confidence was built up slowly and painfully, with many setbacks, and by last summer a solid foundation appeared to have been achieved and there seemed reason to hope that the Soviet Union might settle down into a more or less normal member of international society, and that Anglo-Soviet relations could become progressively more intimate and more trusting. But unfortunately this last period was in no sense typical. Apart from the fact that we were both fighting for our lives and were therefore compelled to cooperate, all the concessions, approaches and even gestures came from our side, and the Kremlin must have found the course of Anglo-Soviet relations a very pleasant and convenient arrangement under which they received big gains, though it must be remembered that in Russian eyes at least the Soviet Union had borne the main burden of the war. They probably hoped and expected that this would continue after the war, and the present crisis in our relations is largely due to a realisation on both sides that the time for one-sided appeasement and concession is past.

3. It is easier to draw the conclusion that none of the methods adopted over the past thirty years should be repeated than to put forward any very positive or inspiring substitute for them. I would, however, suggest that the first essential is to treat the problem of Anglo-Soviet relations in the same way as major military problems were treated during the war. It calls for the closest coordination of political strategy, for a very thorough staff study embracing every aspect of Soviet policy—not forgetting the ubiquitous activities of the Communist parties directed, if not controlled in detail, from Moscow.

4. Of no other country is it harder to know the true position or to form an unbiased judgement. Hence the necessity not only for full factual information but for a readiness to face the facts and all their implications, however unpleasant they may appear at first sight.

5. Parallel with those should go a campaign to educate the British public with whom all decisions of policy ultimately rest. In the case of other important countries, the British public, or at least influential sections of it, have real knowledge on which to base their judgements. In the cases of the Soviet Union alone they are dependent upon either

Soviet propaganda or anti-Soviet prejudices, which are equally dangerous counsellors. Insofar as normal contacts do not exist between the Soviet and British publics and are unlikely to be permitted by the Soviet government, and as even press correspondents in Moscow can only send out news censored by the Soviet authorities (and already coloured by their own fears lest frankness might forfeit them a subsequent visa for the Soviet Union), the responsibility for educating the British public must rest with His Majesty's Government and the editors in London to an extent which would be altogether abnormal in dealing with other countries.

6. The most essential factor in our long-term strategy is, however, to ensure that our own country, the Commonwealth, the Colonial Empire and those countries—particularly in Western Europe and the Near and Middle East—whose fortunes are so closely bound up with ours should be healthy political and economic organisms, pursuing progressive policies, raising the standard of living of their peoples, and removing the causes of social strife. At the same time we can offer civil and personal liberties which are unknown in the Soviet Union and would be the envy of its inhabitants. In fact, we should act as the champions of a dynamic and progressive faith and way of life with an appeal to the world at least as great as that of the Communist system of the Kremlin. The Soviet Union would not, I fear, in the long run resist the temptation to infiltrate into and encroach upon a weak British Empire which was on the defensive and a prey to internal troubles and dissensions. Moreover, the Communist system propagated from Moscow thrives best in unhealthy organisms. But as long as we can offer our peoples and the world at large economic, social and political benefits which are still far from being realised in the Soviet Union itself, we can reasonably hope for the maintenance of Anglo-Soviet relations on a basis of mutual respect and regard for each other's interests.

7. Turning from strategy to tactics, it is essential to realise that there is no shortcut to good Anglo-Soviet relations. From time to time personal contacts may be necessary—either in the United Nations Organisation, between the Big Five or the Big Three, or between Britain and the Soviet Union alone. But although these personal contacts may solve some immediate problem, they can never be relied upon to influence Soviet policy in the future, least of all to provide a solid basis for relations. The day has also long gone when we might hope by unilateral gestures or concessions on our side gradually to influence Soviet policy and so to inspire similar gesture and concessions from the Soviet side. In dealing with the Soviet Union, as indeed with the old Russian Empire, we should base ourselves firmly on the principle of reciprocity and give nothing unless we receive a counter-advantage in return. This in turn implies great firmness in dealing with big matters and small alike, coupled, however with a friendly approach, with perfect politeness and with a formal correctness, which we may no longer consider necessary in our

dealings with other countries in this democratic age. In these respects the old should be mixed with the new diplomacy in the conduct of our relations with the Soviet Union, both in regard to secrecy and also to outward forms. When there are deadlocks, as there will often be, we should cultivate the same patience as is shown by our Soviet allies, and cease to feel that it is always our task to make an early gesture to break the deadlock. Such gestures are interpreted here as a sign of weakness and do harm rather than good to our relations. However unpromising the prospects may be, we should, however, continue to take the initiative in fostering closer contacts between the two peoples, e.g. cultural and other exchanges and visits by representative persons and delegations. Visitors to the Soviet Union should, however, be carefully chosen and this implies a certain degree of control, such as is exercised by the Soviet Union over visitors to Britain, in order to ensure that it is not only Communists and fellow travellers selected by the Russians who bring as false an impression of Britain to the Soviet people as the picture of the Soviet Union which they take back with them. As a part of this campaign and mutual education, we should continue to support our one regular means of propaganda in the Soviet Union—the *British Ally*—and foster with the greatest care the BBC programme in Russian which are about to begin. Finally, we should in our mutual interest restore at the earliest possible moment normal trade between the two countries. But this should be done on a basis of mutual needs and not of one-sided loans or other concessions, and we should clearly realise that Anglo-Soviet trade is unlikely to become a major factor in our relations, or in the international commercial balance as a whole.

8. In all our dealings with the Soviet Union we should constantly bear in mind the absolute need for earning and maintaining respect. This means that we must be strong and look strong. But this strength should never be paraded unnecessarily and it should always take account of Soviet susceptibilities and prestige. Above all, we should never rattle the sabre and make it difficult for the Russians to climb down without loss of face. It is significant that Soviet propaganda has reacted very sharply to Mr Churchill's frank statement at Fulton on the Soviet respect for strength. But, as some highly placed Russians told a diplomatic colleague, they do not object to the ideas expressed by Mr Churchill, even when he advocated the closest relations between Britain and America. They felt, however, that it was unnecessary and undesirable to state these obvious facts in public in a way which appeared to many Russians as provocative.

9. If we are to be strong, this, of course, implies cherishing our special relationship with the Dominions and also with America, fostering the natural community of interests between ourselves and the democracies of Western Europe, and supporting and strengthening our friends and allies in the Middle East. I cannot lay too much emphasis upon maintaining our special relationship with America in a form consistent with friendship with the Soviet Union. Whatever

private differences may arise between us, America and the British Commonwealth must remain firm friends in the eyes of the Soviet Union, otherwise she may succumb to dangerous temptations. The Soviet Union cannot legitimately object to such developments, which have no aggressive tendencies against her, although she will no doubt use her influence to retard them. Indeed, if we were thinking simply in terms of Anglo-Soviet relations, these could probably be most solidly established on the basis of zones of influence in which we each left the other party free from interference or criticism within specified areas.

10. I have not touched upon the problem of the United Nations Organisation in this context since I assume that we shall in any case continue to do all in our power to strengthen it, and this is, in any case, a problem much wider than that of Anglo-Soviet relations. If, however, we wish the United Nations Organisation to succeed, we must allow for the Soviet view that it can only do so on a basis of prior agreement on all important issues between the Big Three. Soviet behaviour may make this unattainable, in which event it might be wiser to accept the position and no longer to place what might prove a dangerous faith in the United Nations Organisation as a substitute for Big Three cooperation and for a reconciliation of British and Soviet interests.

11. I realise that the above may not seem a very inspiring policy and will indeed be a sad disappointment to those who had set their hopes of postwar Anglo-Soviet relations very high. But British relations with Russia were for three centuries maintained not unsuccessfully on such a basis of distant realism between governments. If we do not aim too high, we shall at least avoid constant irritations and disappointments. The many important interests we have in common, and most of all our joint determination that no other one Power shall ever become a menace to us both, should remain a solid bond, despite the deep gulf between our social systems.

I am sending a copy of this despatch to His Majesty's Ambassador at Washington.

I have, &c

F.K. ROBERTS

# Appendix 4

# NSC 68: United States Objectives and Programs for National Security
## (April 14, 1950)

**A Report to the President
Pursuant to the President's Directive
of January 31, 1950**

TOP SECRET
[Washington] April 7, 1950

## Contents

## TERMS OF REFERENCE

The following report is submitted in response to the President's directive January 31 which reads:

That the President direct the Secretary of State and the Secretary of Defense to undertake a reexamination of our objectives in peace and war and of the effect of these objectives on our strategic plans, in the light of the probable fission bomb capability and possible thermonuclear bomb capability of the Soviet Union.

The document which recommended that such a directive be issued reads in part:

It must be considered whether a decision to proceed with a program directed toward determining feasibility prejudges the more fundamental decisions (a) as to whether, in the event that a test of a thermonuclear weapon proves successful, such weapons should be stockpiled, or (b) if stockpiled, the conditions under which they might be used in war. If a test of a thermonuclear weapon proves successful, the pressures to produce and stockpile such weapons to be held for the same purposes for which fission bombs are then being held will be greatly increased. The question of use policy can be adequately assessed only as a part of a general reexamination of this country's strategic plans and its objectives m peace and war. Such reexamination would need to consider national policy not only with respect to possible thermonuclear weapons, but also with respect to fission weapons—viewed in the light of the probable fission bomb capability and the possible thermonuclear bomb capability of the Soviet Union. The moral, psychological, and political questions involved in this problem would need to be taken into account and be given due weight. The outcome of this reexamination would have a crucial bearing on the further question as to whether there should be a revision in the nature of the agreements, including the international control of atomic energy, which we have been seeking to reach with the USSR.

## ANALYSIS

### I. Background of the Present Crisis

Within the past thirty-five years the world has experienced two global wars of tremendous violence. It has witnessed two revolutions—the Russian and the Chinese—of extreme scope and intensity. It has also seen the collapse of five empires—the Ottoman, the Austro-Hungarian, German, Italian, and Japanese—and the drastic decline of two major imperial systems, the British and the French. During the span of one generation, the international distribution of power has been fundamentally altered. For several centuries it had proved impossible for any one nation to gain such preponderant strength that a coalition of other nations could not in time face it with greater strength. The international scene was marked by recurring periods of violence and war, but a system of sovereign and independent states was maintained over which no state was able to achieve hegemony.

Two complex sets of factors have now basically altered this historical distribution of power. First, the defeat of Germany and Japan and the decline of the British and French Empires have interacted with the development of the United States and the Soviet Union in such a way that power has increasingly gravitated to these two centers. Second, the Soviet Union, unlike previous aspirants to hegemony, is animated by a new fanatic faith, antithetical to our own, and seeks to impose its absolute authority over the rest of the world. Conflict has, therefore, become endemic and is waged, on the part of the Soviet Union, by violent or non-violent methods in accordance with the dictates of expediency. With the development of increasingly terrifying weapons of mass destruction, every individual faces the ever-present possibility of annihilation should the conflict enter the phase of total war.

On the one hand, the people of the world yearn for relief from the anxiety arising from the risk of atomic war. On the other hand, any substantial further extension of the area under the domination of the Kremlin would raise the possibility that no coalition adequate to confront the Kremlin with greater strength could be assembled. It is in this context that this Republic and its citizens in the ascendancy of their strength stand in their deepest peril.

The issues that face us are momentous, involving the fulfillment or destruction not only of this Republic but of civilization itself. They are issues which will not await our deliberations. With conscience and resolution this Government and the people it represents must now take new and fateful decisions.

## II. Fundamental Purpose of the United States

The fundamental purpose of the United States is laid down in the Preamble to the Constitution: "...to form a more perfect Union, establish Justice, insure domestic Tranquillity, provide for the common defense, promote the general Welfare, and secure the Blessings of Liberty to ourselves and our Posterity". In essence, the fundamental purpose is to assure the integrity and vitality of our free society, which is founded upon the dignity and worth of the individual.

Three realities emerge as a consequence of this purpose: Our determination to maintain the essential elements of individual freedom, as set forth in the Constitution and Bill of Rights; our determination to create conditions under which our free and democratic system can live and prosper; and our determination to fight if necessary to defend our way of life, for which as in the Declaration of Independence, "with a firm reliance on the protection of Divine Providence, we mutually pledge to each other our lives, our Fortunes, and our sacred Honor".

### III.  Fundamental Design of the Kremlin

The fundamental design of those who control the Soviet Union and the international communist movement is to retain and solidify their absolute power, first in the Soviet Union and second in the areas now under their control. In the minds of the Soviet leaders, however, achievement of this design requires the dynamic extension of their authority and the ultimate elimination of any effective opposition to their authority.

The design, therefore, calls for the complete subversion or forcible destruction of the machinery of government and structure of society in the countries of the non-Soviet world and their replacement by an apparatus and structure subservient to and controlled from the Kremlin. To that end Soviet efforts are now directed toward the domination of the Eurasian land mass. The United States, as the principal center of power in the non-Soviet world and the bulwark of opposition to Soviet expansion, is the principal enemy whose integrity and vitality must be subverted or destroyed by one means or another if the Kremlin is to achieve its fundamental design.

### IV.  The Underlying Conflict in the Realm of Ideas and Values between the US Purpose and the Kremlin Design

#### A.  NATURE OF CONFLICT

The Kremlin regards the United States as the only major threat to the achievement of its fundamental design. There is a basic conflict between the idea of freedom under a government of laws, and the idea of slavery under the grim oligarchy of the Kremlin, which has come to a crisis with the polarization of power described in Section I, and the exclusive possession of atomic weapons by the two protagonists. The idea of freedom, moreover, is peculiarly and intolerably subversive of the idea of slavery. But the converse is not true. The implacable purpose of the slave state to eliminate the challenge of freedom has placed the two great powers at opposite poles. It is this fact which gives the present polarization of power the quality of crisis.

The free society values the individual as an end in himself, requiring of him only that measure of self-discipline and self-restraint which make the rights of each individual compatible with the rights of every other individual. The freedom of the individual has as its counterpart, therefore, the negative responsibility of the individual not to exercise his freedom in ways inconsistent with the freedom of other individuals and the positive responsibility to make constructive use of his freedom in the building of a just society.

From this idea of freedom with responsibility derives the marvelous diversity, the deep tolerance, the lawfulness of the free society. This is the explanation of the strength of free men. It constitutes the integrity and the vitality of a free and democratic system. The free society attempts to create and maintain an environment in which every individual has the opportunity to realize his creative powers. It also explains why the free society tolerates those within it who would use their freedom to destroy it. By the same token, in relations between nations, the prime reliance of the free society is on the strength and appeal of its idea, and it feels no compulsion sooner or later to bring all societies into conformity with it.

For the free society does not fear, it welcomes, diversity. It derives its strength from its hospitality even to antipathetic ideas. It is a market for free trade in ideas, secure in its faith that free men will take the best wares, and grow to a fuller and better realization of their powers in exercising their choice.

The idea of freedom is the most contagious idea in history, more contagious than the idea of submission to authority. For the breadth of freedom cannot be tolerated in a society which has come under the domination of an individual or group of individuals with a will to absolute power. Where the despot holds absolute power—the absolute power of the absolutely powerful will—all other wills must be subjugated in an act of willing submission, a degradation willed by the individual upon himself under the compulsion of a perverted faith. It is the first article of this faith that he finds and can only find the meaning of his existence in serving the ends of the system. The system becomes God, and submission to the will of God becomes submission to the will of the system. It is not enough to yield outwardly to the system—even Gandhian non-violence is not acceptable—for the spirit of resistance and the devotion to a higher authority might then remain, and the individual would not be wholly submissive.

The same compulsion which demands total power over all men within the Soviet state without a single exception, demands total power over all Communist Parties and all states under Soviet domination. Thus Stalin has said that the theory and tactics of Leninism as expounded by the Bolshevik party are mandatory for the proletarian parties of all countries. A true internationalist is defined as one who unhesitatingly upholds the position of the Soviet Union and in the satellite states true patriotism is love of the Soviet Union. By the same token the "peace policy" of the Soviet Union, described at a Party Congress as "a more advantageous form of fighting capitalism," is a device to divide and immobilize the non-Communist world, and the peace the Soviet Union seeks is the peace of total conformity to Soviet policy.

The antipathy of slavery to freedom explains the iron curtain, the isolation, the autarchy of the society whose end is absolute power. The existence and persistence of the idea of freedom is a permanent and continuous threat to the foundation of the slave society; and it therefore regards as intolerable the long continued existence of freedom in the world. What is new, what makes the continuing crisis, is the polarization of power which now inescapably confronts the slave society with the free.

The assault on free institutions is world-wide now, and in the context of the present polarization of power a defeat of free institutions anywhere is a defeat everywhere. The shock we sustained in the destruction of Czechoslovakia was not in the measure of Czechoslovakia's material importance to us. In a material sense, her capabilities were already at Soviet disposal. But when the integrity of Czechoslovak institutions was destroyed, it was in the intangible scale of values that we registered a loss more damaging than the material loss we had already suffered.

Thus unwillingly our free society finds itself mortally challenged by the Soviet system. No other value system is so wholly irreconcilable with ours, so implacable in its purpose to destroy ours, so capable of turning to its own uses the most dangerous and divisive trends in our own society, no other so skillfully and powerfully evokes the elements of irrationality in human nature everywhere, and no other has the support of a great and growing center of military power.

## B. OBJECTIVES

The objectives of a free society are determined by its fundamental values and by the necessity for maintaining the material environment in which they flourish. Logically and in fact, therefore, the Kremlin's challenge to the United States is directed not only to our values but to our physical capacity to protect their environment. It is a challenge which encompasses both peace and war and our objectives in peace and war must take account of it.

1. Thus we must make ourselves strong, both in the way in which we affirm our values in the conduct of our national life, and in the development of our military and economic strength.

2. We must lead in building a successfully functioning political and economic system in the free world. It is only by practical affirmation, abroad as well as at home, of our essential values, that we can preserve our own integrity, in which lies the real frustration of the Kremlin design.

3. But beyond thus affirming our values our policy and actions must be such as to foster a fundamental change in the nature of the Soviet system, a change toward which the frustration of the design is the first and perhaps the most important step. Clearly it will not only be less costly but more effective if this change occurs to a maximum extent as a result of internal forces in Soviet society.

In a shrinking world, which now faces the threat of atomic warfare, it is not an adequate objective merely to seek to check the Kremlin design, for the absence of order among nations is becoming less and less tolerable. This fact imposes on us, in our own interests, the responsibility of world leadership. It demands that we make the attempt, and accept the risks inherent in it, to bring about order and justice by means consistent with the principles of freedom and democracy. We should limit our requirement of the Soviet Union to its participation with other nations on the basis of equality and respect for the rights of others. Subject to this requirement, we must with our allies and the former subject peoples seek to create a world society based on the principle of consent. Its framework cannot be inflexible.

It will consist of many national communities of great and varying abilities and resources, and hence of war potential. The seeds of conflicts will inevitably exist or will come into being. To acknowledge this is only to acknowledge the impossibility of a final solution. Not to acknowledge it can be fatally dangerous in a world in which there are no final solutions.

All these objectives of a free society are equally valid and necessary in peace and war. But every consideration of devotion to our fundamental values and to our national security demands that we seek to achieve them by the strategy of the cold war. It is only by developing the moral and material strength of the free world that the Soviet regime will become convinced of the falsity of its assumptions and that the pre-conditions for workable agreements can be created. By practically demonstrating the integrity and vitality of our system the free world widens the area of possible agreement and thus can hope gradually to bring about a Soviet acknowledgment of realities which in sum will eventually constitute a frustration of the Soviet design. Short of this, however, it might be possible to create a situation which will induce the Soviet Union to accommodate itself, with or without the conscious abandonment of its design, to coexistence on tolerable terms with the non-Soviet world. Such a development would be a triumph for the idea of freedom and democracy. It must be an immediate objective of United States policy.

There is no reason, in the event of war, for us to alter our overall objectives. They do not include unconditional surrender, the subjugation of the Russian peoples or a Russia shorn of its economic potential. Such a course would irrevocably unite the Russian people behind the regime which enslaves them. Rather these objectives contemplate Soviet acceptance of the specific and limited conditions requisite to an international environment in which free institutions can flourish, and in which the Russian peoples will have a new chance to work out their own destiny. If we can make the Russian people our allies in the enterprise we will obviously have made our task easier and victory more certain.

The objectives outlined in NSC 20/4 (November 23, 1948)...are fully consistent with the objectives stated in this paper, and they remain valid. The growing intensity of the conflict which has been imposed upon us, however, requires the changes of emphasis and the additions that are apparent. Coupled with the probable fission bomb capability and possible thermonuclear bomb capability of the Soviet Union, the intensifying struggle requires us to face the fact that we can expect no lasting abatement of the crisis unless and until a change occurs in the nature of the Soviet system.

## C. MEANS

The free society is limited in its choice of means to achieve its ends.

Compulsion is the negation of freedom, except when it is used to enforce the rights common to all. The resort to force, internally or externally, is therefore a last resort for a free society. The act is permissible only when one individual or groups of individuals within it threaten the basic rights of other individuals or when another society seeks to impose its will upon it. The free society cherishes and protects as fundamental the rights of the minority against the will of a majority, because these rights are the inalienable rights of each and every individual.

The resort to force, to compulsion, to the imposition of its will is therefore a difficult and dangerous act for a free society, which is warranted only in the face of even greater dangers. The necessity of the act must be clear and compelling; the act must commend itself to the overwhelming majority as an inescapable exception to the basic idea of freedom; or the regenerative capacity of free men after the act has been performed will be endangered.

The Kremlin is able to select whatever means are expedient in seeking to carry out its fundamental design. Thus it can make the best of several possible worlds, conducting the struggle on those levels where it considers it profitable and enjoying the benefits of a pseudo-peace on those levels where it is not ready for a contest. At the ideological or psychological level, in the struggle for men's minds, the conflict is worldwide. At the political and economic level, within states and in the relations between states, the struggle for power is being intensified. And at the military level, the Kremlin has thus far been careful not to commit a technical breach of the peace, although using its vast forces to intimidate its neighbors, and to support an aggressive foreign policy, and not hesitating through its agents to resort to arms in favorable circumstances. The attempt to carry out its fundamental design is being pressed, therefore, with all means which are believed expedient in the present situation, and the Kremlin has inextricably engaged us in the conflict between its design and our purpose.

We have no such freedom of choice, and least of all in the use of force. Resort to war is not only a last resort for a free society, but it is also an act which cannot definitively end the fundamental conflict in the realm of ideas. The idea of slavery can only be overcome by the timely and persistent demonstration of the superiority of the idea of freedom. Military victory alone would only partially and perhaps only temporarily affect the fundamental conflict, for although the ability of the Kremlin to threaten our security might be for a time destroyed, the resurgence of totalitarian forces and the re-establishment of the Soviet system or its equivalent would not be long delayed unless great progress were made in the fundamental conflict.

Practical and ideological considerations therefore both impel us to the conclusion that we have no choice but to demonstrate the superiority of the idea of freedom by its constructive application, and to attempt to change the world situation by means short of war in such a way as to frustrate the Kremlin design and hasten the decay of the Soviet system.

For us the role of military power is to serve the national purpose by deterring an attack upon us while we seek by other means to create an environment in which our free society can flourish, and by fighting, if necessary, to defend the integrity and vitality of our free society and to defeat any aggressor. The Kremlin uses Soviet military power to back up and serve the Kremlin design. It does not hesitate to use military force aggressively if that course is expedient in the achievement of its design. The differences between our fundamental purpose and the Kremlin design, therefore, are reflected in our respective attitudes toward and use of military force.

Our free society, confronted by a threat to its basic values, naturally will take such action, including the use of military force, as may be required to protect those values. The integrity of our system will not be jeopardized by any measures, covert or overt, violent or non-violent, which serve the purposes of frustrating the Kremlin design, nor does the necessity for conducting ourselves so as to affirm our values in actions as well as words forbid such measures, provided only they are appropriately calculated to that end and are not so excessive or misdirected as to make us enemies of the people instead of the evil men who have enslaved them.

But if war comes, what is the role of force? Unless we so use it that the Russian people can perceive that our effort is directed against the regime and its power for aggression, and not against their own interests, we will unite the regime and the people in the kind of last ditch fight in which no underlying problems are solved, new ones are created, and where our basic principles are obscured and compromised. If we do not in the application of force demonstrate the nature of our objectives we will, in fact, have compromised from the outset our fundamental purpose. In the words of the Federalist (No. 28) "[T]he means to be employed must be proportioned to the extent of the mischief". The mischief may be a global war or it may be a Soviet campaign for limited objectives. In either case we should take no avoidable initiative which would cause it to become a war of annihilation, and if we have the forces to defeat a Soviet drive for limited objectives it may well be to our interest not to let it become a global war. Our aim in applying force must be to compel the acceptance of terms consistent with our objectives, and our capabilities for the application of force should, therefore, within the limits of what we can sustain over the long pull, be congruent to the range of tasks which we may encounter.

## V. Soviet Intentions and Capabilities
### A. POLITICAL AND PSYCHOLOGICAL

The Kremlin's design for world domination begins at home. The first concern of a despotic oligarchy is that the local base of its power and authority be secure. The massive fact of the iron curtain isolating the Soviet peoples from the outside world, the repeated political purges within the USSR and the institutionalized crimes of the MVD [the Soviet Ministry of Internal Affairs] are evidence that the Kremlin does not feel secure at home and that "the entire coercive force of the socialist state" is more than ever one of seeking to impose its absolute authority over "the economy, manner of life, and consciousness of people" (Vyshinski, *The Law of the Soviet State*, p. 74). Similar evidence in the satellite states of Eastern Europe leads to the conclusion that this same policy, in less advanced phases, is being applied to the Kremlin's colonial areas.

Being a totalitarian dictatorship, the Kremlin's objectives in these policies is the total subjective submission of the peoples now under its control. The concentration camp is the prototype of the society which these policies are designed to achieve, a society in which the personality of the individual is so broken and perverted that he participates affirmatively in his own degradation.

The Kremlin's policy toward areas not under its control is the elimination of resistance to its will and the extension of its influence and control. It is driven to follow this policy because it cannot, for the reasons set forth in Chapter IV, tolerate the existence of free societies; to the Kremlin the most mild and inoffensive free society is an affront, a challenge and a subversive influence. Given the nature of the Kremlin, and the evidence at hand, it seems clear that the ends toward which this policy is directed are the same as those where its control has already been established.

The means employed by the Kremlin in pursuit of this policy are limited only by considerations of expediency. Doctrine is not a limiting factor; rather it dictates the employment of violence, subversion, and deceit, and rejects moral considerations. In any event, the Kremlin's conviction of its own infallibility has made its devotion to theory so subjective that past or present pronouncements as to doctrine offer no reliable guide to future actions. The only apparent restraints on resort to war are, therefore, calculations of practicality.

With particular reference to the United States, the Kremlin's strategic and tactical policy is affected by its estimate that we are not only the greatest immediate obstacle which stands between it and world domination, we are also the only power which could release forces in the free and Soviet worlds which could destroy it. The Kremlin's policy toward us is consequently animated by a peculiarly virulent blend of hatred and fear. Its strategy has been one of attempting to undermine the complex of forces, in this country and in the rest of the free world, on which our power is based. In this it has both adhered to doctrine and followed the sound principle of seeking maximum results with minimum risks and commitments. The present application of this strategy is a new form of expression for traditional Russian caution. However, there is no justification in Soviet theory or practice for predicting that, should the Kremlin become convinced that it could cause our downfall by one conclusive blow, it would not seek that solution.

In considering the capabilities of the Soviet world, it is of prime importance to remember that, in contrast to ours, they are being drawn upon close to the maximum possible extent. Also in contrast to us, the Soviet world can do more with less—it has a lower standard of living, its economy requires less to keep it functioning, and its military machine operates effectively with less elaborate equipment and organization.

The capabilities of the Soviet world are being exploited to the full because the Kremlin is inescapably militant. It is inescapably militant because it possesses and is possessed by a world-wide revolutionary movement, because it is the inheritor of Russian imperialism, and because it is a totalitarian dictatorship. Persistent crisis, conflict, and expansion are the essence of the Kremlin's militancy. This dynamism serves to intensify all Soviet capabilities.

Two enormous organizations, the Communist Party and the secret police, are an outstanding source of strength to the Kremlin. In the Party, it has an apparatus designed to impose at home an ideological uniformity among its people and to act abroad as an instrument of propaganda, subversion and espionage. In its police apparatus, it has a domestic repressive instrument guaranteeing under present circumstances the continued security of the Kremlin. The demonstrated capabilities of these two basic organizations, operating openly or in disguise, in mass or through single agents, is unparalleled in history. The party, the police and the conspicuous might of the Soviet military machine together tend to create an overall impression of irresistible Soviet power among many peoples of the free world.

The ideological pretensions of the Kremlin are another great source of strength. Its identification of the Soviet system with communism, its peace campaigns and its championing of colonial peoples may be viewed with apathy, if not cynicism, by the oppressed totalitariat of the Soviet world, but in the free world these ideas find favorable responses in vulnerable segments of society. They have found a particularly receptive audience in Asia, especially as the Asiatics have been impressed by what has been plausibly portrayed to them as the rapid advance of the USSR from a backward society to a position of great world power. Thus, in its pretensions to being (a) the source of a new universal faith and (b) the model "scientific" society, the Kremlin cynically identifies itself with the genuine aspirations of large numbers of people, and places itself at the head of an international crusade with all of the benefits which derive there from.

Finally, there is a category of capabilities, strictly speaking neither institutional nor ideological, which should be taken into consideration. The extraordinary flexibility of Soviet tactics is certainly a strength. It derives from the utterly amoral and opportunistic conduct of Soviet policy. Combining this quality with the elements of secrecy, the Kremlin possesses a formidable capacity to act with the widest tactical latitude, with stealth, and with speed.

The greatest vulnerability of the Kremlin lies in the basic nature of its relations with the Soviet people.

That relationship is characterized by universal suspicion, fear, and denunciation. It is a relationship in which the Kremlin relies, not only for its power but its very survival, on intricately devised mechanisms of coercion. The Soviet monolith is held together by the iron curtain around it and the iron bars within it, not by any force of natural cohesion. These artificial mechanisms of unity have never been intelligently challenged by a strong outside force. The full measure of their vulnerability is therefore not yet evident.

The Kremlin's relations with its satellites and their peoples is likewise a vulnerability. Nationalism still remains the most potent emotional-political force. The well-known ills of colonialism are compounded, however, by the excessive demands of the Kremlin that its satellites accept not only the imperial authority of Moscow but that they believe in and proclaim the ideological primacy and infallibility of the Kremlin. These excessive requirements can be made good only through extreme coercion. The result is that if a satellite feels able to effect its independence of the Kremlin, as Tito was able to do, it is likely to break away.

In short, Soviet ideas and practices run counter to the best and potentially the strongest instincts of men, and deny their most fundamental aspirations. Against an adversary which effectively affirmed the constructive and hopeful instincts of men and was capable of fulfilling their fundamental aspirations, the Soviet system might prove to be fatally weak.

The problem of succession to Stalin is also a Kremlin vulnerability. In a system where supreme power is acquired and held through violence and intimidation, the transfer of that power may well produce a period of instability.

In a very real sense, the Kremlin is a victim of its own dynamism. This dynamism can become a weakness if it is frustrated, if in its forward thrusts it encounters a superior force which halts the expansion and exerts a superior counterpressure. Yet the Kremlin cannot relax the condition of crisis and mobilization, for to do so would be to lose its dynamism, whereas the seeds of decay within the Soviet system would begin to flourish and fructify.

The Kremlin is, of course, aware of these weaknesses. It must know that in the present world situation they are of secondary significance. So long as the Kremlin retains the initiative, so long as it can keep on the offensive unchallenged by clearly superior counter-force— spiritual as well as material—its vulnerabilities are largely inoperative and even concealed by its successes. The Kremlin has not yet been given real reason to fear and be diverted by the rot within its system.

## B. ECONOMIC

The Kremlin has no economic intentions unrelated to its overall policies. Economics in the Soviet world is not an end in itself. The Kremlin's policy, in so far as it has to do with economics, is to utilize economic processes to contribute to the overall strength, particularly the war-making capacity of the Soviet system. The material welfare of the totalitariat is severely subordinated to the interest of the system.

As for capabilities, even granting optimistic Soviet reports of production, the total economic strength of the USSR compares with that of the US as roughly one to four. This is reflected not only in gross national product (1949: USSR $65 billion; US $250 billion), but in production of key commodities in 1949:

| | US | USSR Combined | USSR and European Orbit |
|---|---|---|---|
| Ingot Steel (million met. tons | 80.4 | 21.5 | 28.0 |
| Primary aluminum (thousands met. tons) | 617.6 | 13-135 | 140-145 |
| Electric power (billion kwh) | 410 | 72 | 112 |
| Crude oil (million met. tons | 276.5 | 33.0 | 38.9 |

Assuming the maintenance of present policies, while a large US advantage is likely to remain, the Soviet Union will be steadily reducing the discrepancy between its overall economic strength and that of the US by continuing to devote proportionately more to capital investment than the US.

But a full-scale effort by the US would be capable of precipitately altering this trend. The USSR today is on a near maximum production basis. No matter what efforts Moscow might make, only a relatively slight change in the rate of increase in overall production could be brought about. In the US, on the other hand, a very rapid absolute expansion could be realized. The fact remains, however, that so long as the Soviet Union is virtually mobilized, and the United States has scarcely begun to summon up its forces, the greater capabilities of the US are to that extent inoperative in the struggle for power. Moreover, as the Soviet attainment of an atomic capability has demonstrated, the totalitarian state, at least in time of peace, can focus its efforts on any given project far more readily than the democratic state.

In other fields—general technological competence, skilled labor resources, productivity of labor force, etc.—the gap between the USSR and the US roughly corresponds to the gap in production. In the field of scientific research, however, the margin of United States superiority is unclear, especially if the Kremlin can utilize European talents.

## C. MILITARY

The Soviet Union is developing the military capacity to support its design for world domination. The Soviet Union actually possesses armed forces far in excess of those necessary to defend its national territory. These armed forces are probably not yet considered by the Soviet Union to be sufficient to initiate a war which would involve the United States. This excessive strength, coupled now with an atomic capability, provides the Soviet Union with great coercive power for use in time of peace in furtherance of its objectives and serves as a deterrent to the victims of its aggression from taking any action in opposition to its tactics which would risk war.

Should a major war occur in 1950 the Soviet Union and its satellites are considered by the Joint Chiefs of Staff to be in a sufficiently advanced state of preparation immediately to undertake and carry out the following campaigns.

a. To overrun Western Europe, with the possible exception of the Iberian and Scandinavian Peninsulas, to drive toward the oil-bearing areas of the Near and Middle East; and to consolidate Communist gains in the Far East;

b. To launch air attacks against the British Isles and air and sea attacks against the lines of communications of the Western Powers in the Atlantic and the Pacific;

c. To attack selected targets with atomic weapons, now including the likelihood of such attacks against targets in Alaska, Canada, and the United States. Alternatively, this capability, coupled with other actions open to the Soviet Union, might deny the United Kingdom as an effective base of operations for allied forces. It also should be possible for the Soviet Union to prevent any allied "Normandy" type amphibious operations intended to force a reentry into the continent of Europe.

After the Soviet Union completed its initial campaigns and consolidated its positions in the Western European area, it could simultaneously conduct:

a. Full-scale air and limited sea operations against the British Isles;

b. Invasions of the Iberian and Scandinavian Peninsulas;

c. Further operations in the Near and Middle East, continued air operations against the North American continent, and air and sea operations against Atlantic and Pacific lines of communication; and

d. Diversionary attacks in other areas.

e. During the course of the offensive operations listed in the second and third paragraphs above, the Soviet Union will have an air defense capability with respect to the vital areas of its own and its satellites' territories which can oppose but cannot prevent allied air operations against these areas.

It is not known whether the Soviet Union possesses war reserves and arsenal capabilities sufficient to supply its satellite armies or even its own forces throughout a long war. It might not be in the interest of the Soviet Union to equip fully its satellite armies, since the possibility of defections would exist.

It is not possible at this time to assess accurately the finite disadvantages to the Soviet Union which may accrue through the implementation of the Economic Cooperation Act of 1948, as amended, and the Mutual Defense Assistance Act of 1949. It should be expected that, as this implementation progresses, the internal security situation of the recipient nations should improve concurrently. In addition, a strong United States military position, plus increases in the armaments of the nations of Western Europe, should strengthen the determination of the recipient nations to counter Soviet moves and in event of war could be considered as likely to delay operations and increase the time required for the Soviet Union to overrun Western Europe. In all probability, although United States backing will stiffen their determination, the armaments increase under the present aid programs will not be of any major consequence prior to 1952. Unless the military strength of the Western European nations is increased on a much larger scale than under current programs and at an accelerated rate, it is more than likely that those nations will not be able to oppose even by 1960 the Soviet armed forces in war with any degree of effectiveness. Considering the Soviet Union military capability, the long-range allied military objective in Western Europe must envisage an increased military strength in that area sufficient possibly to deter the Soviet Union from a major war or, in any event, to delay materially the overrunning of Western Europe and, if feasible, to hold a bridgehead on the continent against Soviet Union offensives.

We do not know accurately what the Soviet atomic capability is but the Central Intelligence Agency intelligence estimates, concurred in by State, Army, Navy, Air Force, and Atomic Energy Commission, assign to the Soviet Union a production capability giving it a fission bomb stockpile within the following ranges:

By mid-1950 10-20
By mid-1951 25-45
By mid-1952 45-90
By mid-1953 70-135
By mid-1954 200

This estimate is admittedly based on incomplete coverage of Soviet activities and represents the production capabilities of known or deducible Soviet plants. If others exist, as is possible, this estimate could lead us into a feeling of superiority in our atomic stockpile that might be dangerously misleading, particularly with regard to the timing of a possible Soviet offensive. On the other hand, if the Soviet Union experiences operating difficulties, this estimate would be reduced. There is some evidence that the Soviet Union is acquiring certain materials essential to research on and development of thermonuclear weapons.

The Soviet Union now has aircraft able to deliver the atomic bomb. Our Intelligence estimates assign to the Soviet Union an atomic bomber capability already in excess of that needed to deliver available bombs. We have at present no evaluated estimate regarding the Soviet accuracy of delivery on target. It is believed that the Soviets cannot deliver their bombs on target with a degree of accuracy comparable to ours, but a planning estimate might well place it at 40-60 percent of bombs sortied. For planning purposes, therefore, the date the Soviets possess an atomic stockpile of 200 bombs would be a critical date for the United States, for the delivery of 100 atomic bombs on targets in the United States would seriously damage this country.

At the time the Soviet Union has a substantial atomic stockpile and if it is assumed that it will strike a strong surprise blow and if it is assumed further that its atomic attacks will be met with no more effective defense opposition than the United States and its allies have programmed, results of those attacks could include

a. Laying waste to the British Isles and thus depriving the Western Powers of their use as a base;

b. Destruction of the vital centers and of the communications of Western Europe, thus precluding effective defense by the Western Powers; and

c. Delivering devastating attacks on certain vital centers of the United States and Canada.

The possession by the Soviet Union of a thermonuclear capability in addition to this substantial atomic stockpile would result in tremendously increased damage.

During this decade, the defensive capabilities of the Soviet Union will probably be strengthened, particularly by the development and use of modern aircraft, aircraft warning and communications devices, and defensive guided missiles.

### VI.  US Intentions and Capabilities—Actual and Potential

### A. POLITICAL AND PSYCHOLOGICAL

Our overall policy at the present time may be described as one designed to foster a world environment in which the American system can survive and flourish. It therefore rejects the concept of isolation and affirms the necessity of our positive participation in the world community.

This broad intention embraces two subsidiary policies. One is a policy which we would probably pursue even if there were no Soviet threat. It is a policy of attempting to develop a healthy international community. The other is the policy of "containing" the Soviet system. These two policies are closely interrelated and interact on one another. Nevertheless, the distinction between them is basically valid and contributes to a clearer understanding of what we are trying to do.

The policy of striving to develop a healthy international community is the long-term constructive effort which we are engaged in. It was this policy which gave rise to our vigorous sponsorship of the United Nations. It is of course the principal reason for our long continuing endeavors to create and now develop the Inter-American system. It, as much as containment, underlay our efforts to rehabilitate Western Europe. Most of our international economic activities can likewise be explained in terms of this policy.

In a world of polarized power, the policies designed to develop a healthy international community are more than ever necessary to our own strength.

As for the policy of "containment," it is one which seeks by all means short of war to (1) block further expansion of Soviet power, (2) expose the falsities of Soviet pretensions, (3) induce a retraction of the Kremlin's control and influence, and (4) in general, so foster the seeds of destruction within the Soviet system that the Kremlin is brought at least to the point of modifying its behavior to conform to generally accepted international standards.

It was and continues to be cardinal in this policy that we possess superior overall power in ourselves or in dependable combination with other like-minded nations. One of the most important ingredients of power is military strength. In the concept of "containment", the maintenance of a strong military posture is deemed to be essential for two reasons: (1) as an ultimate guarantee of our national security and (2) as an indispensable backdrop to the conduct of the policy of "containment". Without superior aggregate military strength, in being and readily mobilizable, a policy of "containment"—which is in effect a policy of calculated and gradual coercion—is no more than a policy of bluff.

At the same time, it is essential to the successful conduct of a policy of "containment" that we always leave open the possibility of negotiation with the USSR. A diplomatic freeze—and we are in one now—tends to defeat the very purposes of "containment" because it raises tensions at the same time that it makes Soviet retractions and adjustments in the direction of moderated behavior more difficult. It also tends to inhibit our initiative and deprives us of opportunities for maintaining a moral ascendancy in our struggle with the Soviet system.

In "containment" it is desirable to exert pressure in a fashion which will avoid so far as possible directly challenging Soviet prestige, to keep open the possibility for the USSR to retreat before pressure with a minimum loss of face and to secure political advantage from the failure of the Kremlin to yield or take advantage of the openings we leave it.

We have failed to implement adequately these two fundamental aspects of "containment." In the face of obviously mounting Soviet military strength ours has declined relatively. Partly as a byproduct of this, but also for other reasons, we now find ourselves at a diplomatic impasse with the Soviet Union, with the Kremlin growing bolder, with both of us holding on grimly to what we have, and with ourselves facing difficult decisions.

In examining our capabilities it is relevant to ask at the outset— capabilities for what? The answer cannot be stated solely in the negative terms of resisting the Kremlin design. It includes also our capabilities to attain the fundamental purpose of the United States, and to foster a world environment in which our free society can survive and flourish.

Potentially we have these capabilities. We know we have them in the economic and military fields. Potentially we also have them in the political and psychological fields. The vast majority of Americans are confident that the system of values which animates our society—the principles of freedom, tolerance, the importance of the individual, and the supremacy of reason over will—are valid and more vital than the ideology which is the fuel of Soviet dynamism. Translated into terms relevant to the lives of other peoples—our system of values can become perhaps a powerful appeal to millions who now seek or find in authoritarianism a refuge from anxieties, bafflement, and insecurity.

Essentially, our democracy also possesses a unique degree of unity. Our society is fundamentally more cohesive than the Soviet system, the solidarity of which is artificially created through force, fear, and favor. This means that expressions of national consensus in our society are soundly and solidly based. It means that the possibility of revolution in this country is fundamentally less than that in the Soviet system.

These capabilities within us constitute a great potential force in our international relations. The potential within us of bearing witness to the values by which we live holds promise for a dynamic manifestation to the rest of the world of the vitality of our system. The essential tolerance of our world outlook, our generous and constructive impulses, and the absence of covetousness in our international relations are assets of potentially enormous influence.

These then are our potential capabilities. Between them and our capabilities currently being utilized is a wide gap of unactualized power. In sharp contrast is the situation of the Soviet world. Its capabilities are inferior to those of our allies and to our own. But they are mobilized close to the maximum possible extent.

The full power which resides within the American people will be evoked only through the traditional democratic process: This process requires, firstly, that sufficient information regarding the basic political, economic, and military elements of the present situation be made publicly available so that an intelligent popular opinion may be formed. Having achieved a comprehension of the issues now confronting this Republic, it will then be possible for the American people and the American Government to arrive at a consensus. Out of this common view will develop a determination of the national will and a solid resolute expression of that will. The initiative in this process lies with the Government.

The democratic way is harder than the authoritarian way because, in seeking to protect and fulfill the individual, it demands of him understanding, judgment, and positive participation in the increasingly complex and exacting problems of the modern world. It demands that he exercise discrimination: that while pursuing through free inquiry the search for truth he knows when he should commit an act of faith; that he distinguish between the necessity for tolerance and the necessity for just suppression. A free society is vulnerable in that it is easy for people to lapse into excesses—the excesses of a permanently open mind wishfully waiting for evidence that evil design may become noble purpose, the excess of faith becoming prejudice, the excess of tolerance degenerating into indulgence of conspiracy and the excess of resorting to suppression when more moderate measures are not only more appropriate but more effective.

In coping with dictatorial governments acting in secrecy and with speed, we are also vulnerable in that the democratic process necessarily operates in the open and at a deliberate tempo. Weaknesses in our situation are readily apparent and subject to immediate exploitation. This Government therefore cannot afford in the face of the totalitarian challenge to operate on a narrow margin of strength. A democracy can compensate for its natural vulnerability only if it maintains clearly superior overall power in its most inclusive sense.

The very virtues of our system likewise handicap us in certain respects in our relations with our allies. While it is a general source of strength to us that our relations with our allies are conducted on a basis of persuasion and consent rather than compulsion and capitulation, it is also evident that dissent among us can become a vulnerability. Sometimes the dissent has its principal roots abroad in situations about which we can do nothing. Some times it arises largely out of certain weaknesses within ourselves, about which we can do something—our native impetuosity and a tendency to expect too much from people widely divergent from us.

The full capabilities of the rest of the free world are a potential increment to our own capabilities. It may even be said that the capabilities of the Soviet world, specifically the capabilities of the masses who have nothing to lose but their Soviet chains, are a potential which can be enlisted on our side.

Like our own capabilities, those of the rest of the free world exceed the capabilities of the Soviet system. Like our own they are far from being effectively mobilized and employed in the struggle against the Kremlin design. This is so because the rest of the free world lacks a sense of unity, confidence, and common purpose. This is true in even the most homogeneous and advanced segment of the free world—Western Europe.

As we ourselves demonstrate power, confidence, and a sense of moral and political direction, so those same qualities will be evoked in Western Europe. In such a situation, we may also anticipate a general improvement in the political tone in Latin America, Asia, and Africa and the real beginnings of awakening among the Soviet totalitariat.

In the absence of affirmative decision on our part, the rest of the free world is almost certain to become demoralized. Our friends will become more than a liability to us; they can eventually become a positive increment to Soviet power.

In sum, the capabilities of our allies are, in an important sense, a function of our own. An affirmative decision to summon up the potential within ourselves would evoke the potential strength within others and add it to our own.

## B. ECONOMIC

*1. Capabilities.* In contrast to the war economy of the Soviet world (cf. Ch V-B), the American economy (and the economy of the free world as a whole) is at present directed to the provision of rising standards of living. The military budget of the United States represents 6 to 7 percent of its gross national product (as against 13.8 percent for the Soviet Union). Our North Atlantic Treaty [NAT] allies devoted 4.8 percent of their national product to military purposes in 1949.

This difference in emphasis between the two economies means that the readiness of the free world to support a war effort is tending to decline relative to that of the Soviet Union. There is little direct investment in production facilities for military end-products and in dispersal. There are relatively few men receiving military training and a relatively low rate of production of weapons. However, given time to convert to a war effort, the capabilities of the United States economy and also of the Western European economy would be tremendous. In the light of Soviet military capabilities, a question which may be of decisive importance in the event of war is the question whether there will be time to mobilize our superior human and material resources for a war effort (cf. Chs. VIII and IX).

The capability of the American economy to support a build-up of economic and military strength at home and to assist a build-up abroad is limited not, as in the case of the Soviet Union, so much by the ability to produce as by the decision on the proper allocation of resources to this and other purposes. Even Western Europe could afford to assign a substantially larger proportion of its resources to defense, if the necessary foundation in public understanding and will could be laid, and if the assistance needed to meet its dollar deficit were provided.

A few statistics will help to clarify this point.

*Table 1. Percentage of Gross Available Resources Allocated to Investment, National Defense and Consumption in East and West, 1949 (in percent of total).*

| Country | Gross Investment | Defense | Consumption |
|---|---|---|---|
| USSR | 25.4 | 13.8 | 60.8 |
| Soviet Orbit | 22.0[a] | 4.0[b] | 74.0[a] |
| US | 13.6 | 6.5 | 79.9 |
| European NAT countries | 20.4 | 4.8 | 74.8 |

[a] Crude estimate. [Footnote in the source text.]

[b] Includes soviet zone of Germany; otherwise 5 percent [Footnote in the source text.]

The Soviet Union is now allocating nearly 40 percent of its gross available resources to military purposes and investment, much of which is in war-supporting industries. It is estimated that even in an emergency the Soviet Union could not increase this proportion to much more than 50 percent, or by one-fourth. The United States, on the other hand, is allocating only about 20 percent of its resources to defense and investment (or 22 percent including foreign assistance), and little of its investment outlays are directed to war-supporting industries. In an emergency the United States could allocate more than 50 percent of its resources to military purposes and foreign assistance, or five to six times as much as at present.

The same point can be brought out by statistics on the use of important products. The Soviet Union is using 14 percent of its ingot steel, 47 percent of its primary aluminum, and 18.5 percent of its crude oil for military purposes, while the corresponding percentages for the United States are 1.7, 8.6. and 5.6. Despite the tremendously larger production of these goods in the United States than the Soviet Union, the latter is actually using, for military purposes, nearly twice as much steel as the United States and 8 to 26 percent more aluminum.

Perhaps the most impressive indication of the economic superiority of the free world over the Soviet world which can be made on the basis of available data is provided in comparisons (based mainly on the *Economic Survey of Europe, 1948*) [Table 2].

It should be noted that these comparisons understate the relative position of the NAT countries for several reasons: (1) Canada is excluded because comparable data were not available; (2) the data for the USSR are the 1950 targets (as stated in the fourth five-year plan) rather than actual rates of production and are believed to exceed in many cases the production actually achieved; (3) the data for the European NAT countries are actual data for 1948, and production has generally increased since that time.

Furthermore, the United States could achieve a substantial absolute increase in output and could thereby increase the allocation of resources to a build-up of the economic and military strength of itself and its allies without suffering a decline in its real standard of living. Industrial production declined by 10 percent between the first quarter of 1948 and the last quarter of 1949, and by approximately one-fourth between 1944 and 1949. In March 1950 there were approximately 4,750,000 unemployed, as compared to 1,070,000 in 1943 and 670,000 in 1944. The gross national product declined slowly in 1949 from the peak reached in 1948 ($262 billion in 1948 to an annual rate of $256 billion in the last six months of 1949), and in terms of constant prices declined by about 20 percent between 1944 and 1948.

With a high level of economic activity, the United States could soon attain a gross national product of $300 billion per year, as was pointed out in the President's Economic Report (January 1950). Progress in this direction would permit, and might itself be aided by, a buildup of the economic and military strength of the United States and the free world; furthermore, if a dynamic expansion of the economy were achieved, the necessary build-up could be accomplished without a decrease in the national standard of living because the required resources could be obtained by siphoning off a part of the annual increment in the gross national product. These are facts of fundamental importance in considering the courses of action open to the United States (cf. Ch. IX).

2. *Intentions*. Foreign economic policy is a major instrument in the conduct of United States foreign relations. It is an instrument which can powerfully influence the world environment in ways favorable to the security and welfare of this country. It is also an instrument which, if unwisely formulated and employed, can do actual harm to our national interests. It is an instrument uniquely suited to our capabilities, provided we have the tenacity of purpose and the understanding requisite to a realization of its potentials. Finally, it is an instrument peculiarly appropriate to the cold war.

*Table 2. Comparative Statistics on Economic Capabilities of East and West*

| | US 1948-49 | European NAT Countries 1948-49 | Total | USSR (1950 Plan) | Satellites 1948-49 | Total |
|---|---|---|---|---|---|---|
| Population (millions) | 149 | 173 | 322 | 198[a] | 75 | 273 |
| Employment in non-agricultural establishments (millions | 45 | - | - | 31[a] | - | - |
| Gross national production (billion dollars) | 250 | 84 | 334 | 65[a] | 21 | 86 |
| National income per capita (current dollars) | 1700 | 480 | 1040 | 330 | 280 | 315 |
| Production data Coal (million tons) | 582 | 306 | 888 | 250 | 88 | 338 |
| Electric power (billion kwh) | 356 | 124 | 480 | 82 | 15 | 97 |
| Crude petroleum (million tons) | 277 | 1 | 278 | 35 | 5 | 40 |
| Pig iron (million tons) | 55 | 24 | 79 | 19.5 | 3.2 | 22.7 |
| Steel (million tons) | 80 | 32 | 112 | 25 | 6 | 31 |
| Cement (million tons) | 35 | 21 | 56 | 10.5 | 2.1 | 12.6 |
| Motor vehicles (thousands) | 5273 | 580 | 5853 | 500 | 25 | 525 |

[a] 1949 data. [Footnote in the source text.]

[b] For the European NAT countries and for the satellites, the data include output by major producers. [Footnote in the source text.]

The preceding analysis has indicated that an essential element in a program to frustrate the Kremlin design is the development of a successfully functioning system among the free nations. It is clear that economic conditions are among the fundamental determinants of the will and the strength to resist subversion and aggression.

United States foreign economic policy has been designed to assist in the building of such a system and such conditions in the free world. The principal features of this policy can be summarized as follows:

1. assistance to Western Europe in recovery and the creation of a viable economy (the European Recovery Program);

2. assistance to other countries because of their special needs arising out of the war or the cold war and our special interests in or responsibility for meeting them (grant assistance to Japan, the Philippines, and Korea, loans and credits by the Export-Import Bank, the International Monetary Fund, and the International Bank to Indonesia, Yugoslavia, Iran, etc.);

3. assistance in the development of underdeveloped areas (the Point IV program and loans and credits to various countries, overlapping to some extent with those mentioned under 2);

4. military assistance to the North Atlantic Treaty countries. Greece, Turkey, etc.;

5. restriction of East-West trade in items of military importance to the East;

6. purchase and stockpiling of strategic materials; and

7. efforts to reestablish an international economy based on multilateral trade, declining trade barriers, and convertible currencies (the GATT-ITO program, the Reciprocal Trade Agreements program, the IMF-ERD program, and the program now being developed to solve the problem of the United States balance of payments).

In both their short and long term aspects, these policies and programs are directed to the strengthening of the free world and therefore to the frustration of the Kremlin design. Despite certain inadequacies and inconsistencies, which are now being studied in connection with the problem of the United States balance of payments, the United States has generally pursued a foreign economic policy which has powerfully supported its overall objectives. The question must nevertheless be asked whether current and currently projected programs will adequately support this policy in the future, in terms both of need and urgency.

The last year has been indecisive in the economic field. The Soviet Union has made considerable progress in integrating the satellite economies of Eastern Europe into the Soviet economy, but still faces very large problems, especially with China. The free nations have important accomplishments to record, but also have tremendous problems still ahead. On balance, neither side can claim any great advantage in this field over its relative position a year ago. The important question therefore becomes: what are the trends?

Several conclusions seem to emerge. First, the Soviet Union is widening the gap between its preparedness for war and the unpreparedness of the free world for war. It is devoting a far greater proportion of its resources to military purposes than are the free nations and, in significant components of military power, a greater absolute quantity of resources. Second, the Communist success in China, taken with the politico-economic situation in the rest of South and South-East Asia, provides a springboard for a further incursion in this troubled area. Although Communist China faces serious economic problems which may impose some strains on the Soviet economy, it is probable that the social and economic problems faced by the free nations in this area present more than offsetting opportunities for Communist expansion. Third, the Soviet Union holds positions in Europe which, if it maneuvers skillfully, could be used to do great damage to the Western European economy and to the maintenance of the Western orientation of certain countries, particularly Germany and Austria. Fourth, despite (and in part because of) the Titoist' defection,[1] the Soviet Union has accelerated its efforts to integrate satellite economy with its own and to increase the degree of autarchy within the areas under its control.

Fifth, meanwhile, Western Europe, with American (and Canadian) assistance, has achieved a record level of production. However, it faces the prospect of a rapid tapering off of American assistance without the possibility of achieving, by its own efforts, a satisfactory equilibrium with the dollar area. It has also made very little progress toward "economic integration," which would in the long run tend to improve its productivity and to provide an economic environment conducive to political stability. In particular, the movement toward economic integration does not appear to be rapid enough to provide Western Germany with adequate economic opportunities in the West The United Kingdom still faces economic problems which may require a moderate but politically difficult decline in the British standard of living or more American assistance than is contemplated. At the same time, a strengthening of the British position is needed if the stability of the Commonwealth is not to be impaired and if it is to be a focus of resistance to Communist expansion in South and South-East Asia. Improvement of the British position is also vital in building up the defensive capabilities of Western Europe.

Sixth, throughout Asia the stability of the present moderate governments, which are more in sympathy with our purposes than any probable successor regimes would be, is doubtful. The problem is only in part an economic one. Assistance in economic development is important as a means of holding out to the peoples of Asia some prospect of improvement in standards of living under their present governments. But probably more important are a strengthening of central institutions, an improvement in administration, and generally a development of an economic and social structure within which the peoples of Asia can make more effective use of their great human and material resources.

Seventh, and perhaps most important, there are indications of a let-down of United States efforts under the pressure of the domestic budgetary situation, disillusion resulting from excessively optimistic expectations about the duration and results of our assistance programs, and doubts about the wisdom of continuing to strengthen the free nations as against preparedness measures in light of the intensity of the cold war.

Eighth, there are grounds for predicting that the United States and other free nations will within a period of a few years at most experience a decline in economic activity of serious proportions unless more positive governmental programs are developed than are now available.

In short, as we look into the future, the programs now planned will not meet the requirements of the free nations. The difficulty does not lie so much in the inadequacy or misdirection of policy as in the inadequacy of planned programs, in terms of timing or impact, to achieve our objectives. The risks inherent in this situation are set forth in the following chapter and a course of action designed to reinvigorate our efforts in order to reverse the present trends and to achieve our fundamental purpose is outlined in Chapter IX.

## C. MILITARY

The United States now possesses the greatest military potential of any single nation in the world. The military weaknesses of the United States vis-à-vis the Soviet Union, however, include its numerical inferiority in forces in being and in total manpower. Coupled with the inferiority of forces in being, the United States also lacks tenable positions from which to employ its forces in event of war and munitions power in being and readily available.

It is true that the United States armed forces are now stronger than ever before in other times of apparent peace; it is also true that there exists a sharp disparity between our actual military strength and our commitments. The relationship of our strength to our present commitments, however, is not alone the governing factor. The world situation, as well as commitments, should govern; hence, our military strength more properly should be related to the world situation confronting us. When our military strength is related to the world situation and balanced against the likely exigencies of such a situation, it is clear that our military strength is becoming dangerously inadequate.

If war should begin in 1950, the United States and its allies will have the military capability of conducting defensive operations to provide a reasonable measure of protection to the Western Hemisphere, bases in the Western Pacific, and essential military lines of communication; and an inadequate measure of protection to vital military bases in the United Kingdom and in the Near and Middle East. We will have the capability of conducting powerful offensive air operations against vital elements of the Soviet war-making capacity.

The scale of the operations listed in the preceding paragraph is limited by the effective forces and material in being of the United

States and its allies vis-à-vis the Soviet Union. Consistent with the aggressive threat facing us and in consonance with overall strategic plans, the United States must provide to its allies on a continuing basis as large amounts of military assistance as possible without serious detriment to the United States operational requirements.

If the potential military capabilities of the United States and its allies were rapidly and effectively developed, sufficient forces could be produced probably to deter war, or if the Soviet Union chooses war, to withstand the initial Soviet attacks, to stabilize supporting attacks, and to retaliate in turn with even greater impact on the Soviet capabilities. From the military point of view alone, however, this would require not only the generation of the necessary military forces but also the development and stockpiling of improved weapons of all types.

Under existing peacetime conditions, a period of from two to three years is required to produce a material increase in military power. Such increased power could be provided in a somewhat shorter period in a declared period of emergency or in wartime through a full-out national effort. Any increase in military power in peacetime, however, should be related both to its probable military role in war, to the implementation of immediate and long-term United States foreign policy vis-à-vis the Soviet Union, and to the realities of the existing situation. If such a course of increasing our military power is adopted now, the United States would have the capability of eliminating the disparity between its military strength and the exigencies of the situation we face; eventually of gaining the initiative in the "cold" war and of materially delaying if not stopping the Soviet offensives in war itself.

## VII. Present Risks

### A. GENERAL

It is apparent from the preceding sections that the integrity and vitality of our system is in greater jeopardy than ever before in our history. Even if there were no Soviet Union we would face the great problem of the free society, accentuated many fold in this industrial age, of reconciling order, security, the need for participation, with the requirement of freedom. We would face the fact that in a shrinking world the absence of order among nations is becoming less and less tolerable. The Kremlin design seeks to impose order among nations by means which would destroy our free and democratic system. The Kremlin's possession of atomic weapons puts new power behind its design, and increases the jeopardy to our system. It adds new strains to the uneasy equilibrium-without-order which exists in the world and raises new doubts in men's minds whether the world will long tolerate this tension without moving toward some kind of order, on somebody's terms.

The risks we face are of a new order of magnitude, commensurate with the total struggle in which we are engaged. For a free society there is never total victory, since freedom and democracy are never wholly attained, are always in the process of being attained. But defeat at the hands of the totalitarian is total defeat. These risks crowd in on us, in a shrinking world of polarized power, so as to give us no choice, ultimately, between meeting them effectively or being overcome by them.

## B. SPECIFIC

It is quite clear from Soviet theory and practice that the Kremlin seeks to bring the free world under its dominion by the methods of the cold war. The preferred technique is to subvert by infiltration and intimidation. Every institution of our society is an instrument which it is sought to stultify and turn against our purposes. Those that touch most closely our material and moral strength are obviously the prime targets, labor unions, civic enterprises, schools, churches, and all media for influencing opinion. The effort is not so much to make them serve obvious Soviet ends as to prevent them from serving our ends, and thus to make them sources of confusion in our economy, our culture, and our body politic. The doubts and diversities that in terms of our values are part of the merit of a free system, the weaknesses and the problems that are peculiar to it, the rights and privileges that free men enjoy, and the disorganization and destruction left in the wake of the last attack on our freedoms, all are but opportunities for the Kremlin to do its evil work. Every advantage is taken of the fact that our means of prevention and retaliation are limited by those principles and scruples which are precisely the ones that give our freedom and democracy its meaning for us. None of our scruples deter those whose only code is "morality is that which serves the revolution."

Since everything that gives us or others respect for our institutions is a suitable object for attack, it also fits the Kremlin's design that where, with impunity, we can be insulted and made to suffer indignity the opportunity shall not be missed, particularly in any context which can be used to cast dishonor on our country, our system, our motives, or our methods. Thus the means by which we sought to restore our own economic health in the '30's, and now seek to restore that of the free world, come equally under attack. The military aid by which we sought to help the free world was frantically denounced by the Communists in the early days of the last war, and of course our present efforts to develop adequate military strength for ourselves and our allies are equally denounced.

At the same time the Soviet Union is seeking to create overwhelming military force, in order to back up infiltration with intimidation. In the only terms in which it understands strength, it is seeking to demonstrate to the free world that force and the will to use it are on the side of the Kremlin, that those who lack it are decadent and doomed. In local incidents it threatens and encroaches both for the sake of local gains and to increase anxiety and defeatism in all the free world.

The possession of atomic weapons at each of the opposite poles of power, and the inability (for different reasons) of either side to place any trust in the other, puts a premium on a surprise attack against us. It equally puts a premium on a more violent and ruthless prosecution of its design by cold war, especially if the Kremlin is sufficiently objective to realize the improbability of our prosecuting a preventive war. It also puts a premium on piecemeal aggression against others, counting on our unwillingness to engage in atomic war unless we are directly attacked. We run all these risks and the added risk of being confused and immobilized by our inability to weigh and choose, and pursue a firm course based on a rational assessment of each.

The risk that we may thereby be prevented or too long delayed in taking all needful measures to maintain the integrity and vitality of our system is great The risk that our allies will lose their determination is greater. And the risk that in this manner a descending spiral of too little and too late, of doubt and recrimination, may present us with ever narrower and more desperate alternatives, is the greatest risk of all. For example, it is clear that our present weakness would prevent us from offering effective resistance at any of several vital pressure points. The only deterrent we can present to the Kremlin is the evidence we give that we may make any of the critical points which we cannot hold the occasion for a global war of annihilation.

The risk of having no better choice than to capitulate or precipitate a global war at any of a number of pressure points is bad enough in itself, but it is multiplied by the weakness it imparts to our position in the cold war. Instead of appearing strong and resolute we are continually at the verge of appearing and being alternately irresolute and desperate; yet it is the cold war which we must win, because both the Kremlin design, and our fundamental purpose give it the first priority.

The frustration of the Kremlin design, however, cannot be accomplished by us alone, as will appear from the analysis in Chapter IX, B. Strength at the center, in the United States, is only the first of two essential elements. The second is that our allies and potential allies do not as a result of a sense of frustration or of Soviet intimidation drift into a course of neutrality eventually leading to Soviet domination. If this were to happen in Germany the effect upon Western Europe and eventually upon us might be catastrophic.

But there are risks in making ourselves strong. A large measure of sacrifice and discipline will be demanded of the American people. They will be asked to give up some of the benefits which they have come to associate with their freedoms. Nothing could be more important than that they fully understand the reasons for this. The risks of a superficial understanding or of an inadequate appreciation of the issues are obvious and might lead to the adoption of measures which in themselves would jeopardize the integrity of our system. At any point in the process of demonstrating our will to make good our fundamental purpose, the Kremlin may decide to precipitate a general war, or in testing us, may go too far. These are risks we will invite by making ourselves strong, but they are lesser risks than those we seek to avoid. Our fundamental purpose is more likely to be defeated from lack of the will to maintain it, than from any mistakes we may make or assault we may undergo because of asserting that will. No people in history have preserved their freedom who thought that by not being strong enough to protect themselves they might prove inoffensive to their enemies.

## VIII. Atomic Armaments

### A. MILITARY EVALUATION OF US AND USSR ATOMIC CAPABILITIES

1. The United States now has an atomic capability, including both numbers and deliverability, estimated to be adequate, if effectively utilized, to deliver a serious blow against the war-making capacity of the USSR. It is doubted whether such a blow, even if it resulted in the complete destruction of the contemplated target systems, would cause the USSR to sue for terms or prevent Soviet forces from occupying Western Europe against such ground resistance as could presently be mobilized. A very serious initial blow could, however, so reduce the capabilities of the USSR to supply and equip its military organization and its civilian population as to give the United States the prospect of developing a general military superiority in a war of long duration.

2. As the atomic capability of the USSR increases, it will have an increased ability to hit at our atomic bases and installations and thus seriously hamper the ability of the United States to carry out an attack such as that outlined above. It is quite possible that in the near future the USSR will have a sufficient number of atomic bombs and a sufficient deliverability to raise a question whether Britain with its present inadequate air defense could be relied upon as an advance base from which a major portion of the US attack could be launched.

It is estimated that, within the next four years, the USSR will attain the capability of seriously damaging vital centers of the United States, provided it strikes a surprise blow and provided further that the blow is opposed by no more effective opposition than we now have programmed. Such a blow could so seriously damage the United States as to greatly reduce its superiority in economic potential.

Effective opposition to this Soviet capability will require among other measures greatly increased air warning systems, air defenses, and vigorous development and implementation of a civilian defense program which has been thoroughly integrated with the military defense systems.

In time the atomic capability of the USSR can be expected to grow to a point where, given surprise and no more effective opposition than we now have programmed, the possibility of a decisive initial attack cannot be excluded.

3. In the initial phases of an atomic war, the advantages of initiative and surprise would be very great. A police state living behind

an iron curtain has an enormous advantage in maintaining the necessary security and centralization of decision required to capitalize on this advantage.

4. For the moment our atomic retaliatory capability is probably adequate to deter the Kremlin from a deliberate direct military attack against ourselves or other free peoples. However, when it calculates that it has a sufficient atomic capability to make a surprise attack on us, nullifying our atomic superiority and creating a military situation decisively in its favor, the Kremlin might be tempted to strike swiftly and with stealth. The existence of two large atomic capabilities in such a relationship might well act, therefore, not as a deterrent, but as an incitement to war.

5. A further increase in the number and power of our atomic weapons is necessary in order to assure the effectiveness of any US retaliatory blow, but would not of itself seem to change the basic logic of the above points. Greatly increased general air, ground, and sea strength, and increased air defense and civilian defense programs would also be necessary to provide reasonable assurance that the free world could survive an initial surprise atomic attack of the weight which it is estimated the USSR will be capable of delivering by 1954 and still permit the free world to go on to the eventual attainment of its objectives. Furthermore, such a build-up of strength could safeguard and increase our retaliatory power, and thus might put off for some time the date when the Soviet Union could calculate that a surprise blow would be advantageous. This would provide additional time for the effects of our policies to produce a modification of the Soviet system.

6. If the USSR develops a thermonuclear weapon ahead of the US, the risks of greatly increased Soviet pressure against all the free world, or an attack against the US, will be greatly increased.

7. If the US develops a thermonuclear weapon ahead of the USSR, the US should for the time being be able to bring increased pressure on the USSR.

## B. STOCKPILING AND USE OF ATOMIC WEAPONS

1. From the foregoing analysis it appears that it would be to the longterm advantage of the United States if atomic weapons were to be effectively eliminated from national peacetime armaments; the additional objectives which must be secured if there is to be a reasonable prospect of such effective elimination of atomic weapons are discussed in Chapter IX. In the absence of such elimination and the securing of these objectives, it would appear that we have no alternative but to increase our atomic capability as rapidly as other considerations make appropriate. In either case, it appears to be imperative to increase as rapidly as possible our general air, ground, and sea strength and that of our allies to a point where we are militarily not so heavily dependent on atomic weapons.

2. As is indicated in Chapter IV, it is important that the United States employ military force only if the necessity for its use is clear

and compelling and commends itself to the overwhelming majority of our people. The United States cannot therefore engage in war except as a reaction to aggression of so clear and compelling a nature as to bring the overwhelming majority of our people to accept the use of military force. In the event war comes, our use of force must be to compel the acceptance of our objectives and must be congruent to the range of tasks which we may encounter.

In the event of a general war with the USSR, it must be anticipated that atomic weapons will be used by each side in the manner it deems best suited to accomplish its objectives. In view of our vulnerability to Soviet atomic attack, it has been argued that we might wish to hold our atomic weapons only for retaliation against prior use by the USSR. To be able to do so and shall have hope of achieving our objectives, the non-atomic military capabilities of ourselves and our allies would have to be fully developed and the political weaknesses of the Soviet Union fully exploited. In the event of war, however, we could not be sure that we could move toward the attainment of these objectives without the USSR's resorting sooner or later to the use of its atomic weapons. Only if we had overwhelming atomic superiority and obtained command of the air might the USSR be deterred from employing its atomic weapons as we progressed toward the attainment of our objectives.

In the event the USSR develops by 1954 the atomic capability which we now anticipate, it is hardly conceivable that, if war comes, the Soviet leaders would refrain from the use of atomic weapons unless they felt fully confident of attaining their objectives by other means.

In the event we use atomic weapons either in retaliation for their prior use by the USSR or because there is no alternative method by which we can attain our objectives, it is imperative that the strategic and tactical targets against which they are used be appropriate and the manner in which they are used be consistent with those objectives.

It appears to follow from the above that we should produce and stockpile thermonuclear weapons in the event they prove feasible and would add significantly to our net capability. Not enough is yet known of their potentialities to warrant a judgment at this time regarding their use in war to attain our objectives.

3. It has been suggested that we announce that we will not use atomic weapons except in retaliation against the prior use of such weapons by an aggressor. It has been argued that such a declaration would decrease the danger of an atomic attack against the United States and its allies.

In our present situation of relative unpreparedness in conventional weapons, such a declaration would be interpreted by the USSR as an admission of great weakness and by our allies as a clear indication that we intended to abandon them. Furthermore, it is doubtful whether such a declaration would be taken sufficiently seriously by the Kremlin to constitute an important factor in determining whether or not to attack the United States. It is to be anticipated that the Kremlin would weigh the facts of our capability far more heavily than a declaration of what we proposed to do with that capability.

Unless we are prepared to abandon our objectives, we cannot make such a declaration in good faith until we are confident that we will be in a position to attain our objectives without war, or, in the event of war, without recourse to the use of atomic weapons for strategic or tactical purposes.

## C. INTERNATIONAL CONTROL OF ATOMIC ENERGY

1. A discussion of certain of the basic considerations involved in securing effective international control is necessary to make clear why the additional objectives discussed in Chapter IX must be secured.

2. No system of international control could prevent the production and use of atomic weapons in the event of a prolonged war. Even the most effective system of international control could, of itself, only provide (a) assurance that atomic weapons had been eliminated from national peacetime armaments and (b) immediate notice of a violation. In essence, an effective international control system would be expected to assure a certain amount of time after notice of violation before atomic weapons could be used in war.

3. The time period between notice of violation and possible use of atomic weapons in war which a control system could be expected to assure depends upon a number of factors.

The dismantling of existing stockpiles of bombs and the destruction of casings and firing mechanisms could by themselves give little assurance of securing time. Casings and firing mechanisms are presumably easy to produce, even surreptitiously, and the assembly of weapons does not take much time.

If existing stocks of fissionable materials were in some way eliminated and the future production of fissionable materials effectively controlled, war could not start with a surprise atomic attack.

In order to assure an appreciable time lag between notice of violation and the time when atomic weapons might be available in quantity, it would be necessary to destroy all plants capable of making large amounts of fissionable material. Such action would, however, require a moratorium on those possible peacetime uses which call for large quantities of fissionable materials.

Effective control over the production and stockpiling of raw materials might further extend the time period which effective international control would assure. Now that the Russians have learned the technique of producing atomic weapons, the time between violation of an international control agreement and production of atomic weapons will be shorter than was estimated in 1946, except possibly in the field of thermonuclear or other new types of weapons.

4. The certainty of notice of violation also depends upon a number of factors. In the absence of good faith, it is to be doubted whether any system can be designed which will give certainty of notice of violation. International ownership of raw materials and fissionable

materials and international ownership and operation of dangerous facilities, coupled with inspection based on continuous unlimited freedom of access to all parts of the Soviet Union (as well as to all parts of the territory of other signatories to the control agreement) appear to be necessary to give the requisite degree of assurance against secret violations. As the Soviet stockpile of fissionable materials grows, the amount which the USSR might secretly withhold and not declare to the inspection agency grows. In this sense, the earlier an agreement is consummated the greater the security it would offer. The possibility of successful secret production operations also increases with developments which may reduce the size and power consumption of individual reactors. The development of a thermonuclear bomb would increase many fold the damage a given amount of fissionable material could do and would, therefore, vastly increase the danger that a decisive advantage could be gained through secret operations.

5. The relative sacrifices which would be involved in international control need also to be considered. If it were possible to negotiate an effective system of international control the United States would presumably sacrifice a much larger stockpile of atomic weapons and a much larger production capacity than would the USSR. The opening up of national territory to international inspection involved in an adequate control and inspection system would have a far greater impact on the USSR than on the United States. If the control system involves the destruction of all large reactors and thus a moratorium on certain possible peacetime uses, the USSR can be expected to argue that it, because of greater need for new sources of energy, would be making a greater sacrifice in this regard than the United States.

6. The United States and the peoples of the world as a whole desire a respite from the dangers of atomic warfare. The chief difficulty lies in the danger that the respite would be short and that we might not have adequate notice of its pending termination. For such an arrangement to be in the interest of the United States, it is essential that the agreement be entered into in good faith by both sides and the probability against its violation high.

7. The most substantial contribution to security of an effective international control system would, of course, be the opening up of the Soviet Union, as required under the UN plan. Such opening up is not, however, compatible with the maintenance of the Soviet system in its present rigor. This is a major reason for the Soviet refusal to accept the UN plan.

The studies which began with the Acheson-Lilienthal committee and culminated in the present UN plan made it clear that inspection of atomic facilities would not alone give the assurance of control; but that ownership and operation by an international authority of the world's atomic energy activities from the mine to the last use of fissionable materials was also essential. The delegation of sovereignty which this implies is necessary for effective control and, therefore, is as necessary for the United States and the rest of the free world as it is presently unacceptable to the Soviet Union.

It is also clear that a control authority not susceptible directly or indirectly to Soviet domination is equally essential. As the Soviet Union would regard any country not under its domination as under the potential if not the actual domination of the United States, it is clear that what the United States and the non-Soviet world must insist on, the Soviet Union at present rejects.

The principal immediate benefit of international control would be to make a surprise atomic attack impossible, assuming the elimination of large reactors and the effective disposal of stockpiles of fissionable materials. But it is almost certain that the Soviet Union would not agree to the elimination of large reactors, unless the impracticability of producing atomic power for peaceful purposes had been demonstrated beyond a doubt. By the same token, it would not now agree to elimination of its stockpile of fissionable materials.

Finally, the absence of good faith on the part of the USSR must be assumed until there is concrete evidence that there has been a decisive change in Soviet policies. It is to be doubted whether such a change can take place without a change in the nature of the Soviet system itself.

The above considerations make it clear that at least a major change in the relative power positions of the United States and the Soviet Union would have to take place before an effective system of international control could be negotiated. The Soviet Union would have had to have moved a substantial distance down the path of accommodation and compromise before such an arrangement would be conceivable. This conclusion is supported by the Third Report of the United Nations Atomic Energy Commission to the Security Council, May 17, 1948, in which it is stated that "...the majority of the Commission has been unable to secure...their acceptance of the nature and extent of participation in the world community required of all nations in this field.... As a result, the Commission has been forced to recognize that agreement on effective measures for the control of atomic energy is itself dependent on cooperation in broader fields of policy".

In short, it is impossible to hope than an effective plan for international control can be negotiated unless and until the Kremlin design has been frustrated to a point at which a genuine and drastic change in Soviet policies has taken place.

### IX. Possible Courses of Action

*Introduction.* Four possible courses of action by the United States in the present situation can be distinguished. They are:

    a. Continuation of current policies, with current and currently projected programs for carrying out these policies;

    b. Isolation;

    c. War; and

d. A more rapid building up of the political, economic, and military strength of the free world than provided under a, with the purpose of reaching, if possible, a tolerable state of order among nations without war and of preparing to defend ourselves in the event that the free world is attacked.

*The role of negotiation.* Negotiation must be considered in relation to these courses of action. A negotiator always attempts to achieve an agreement which is somewhat better than the realities of his fundamental position would justify and which is, in any case, not worse than his fundamental position requires. This is as true in relations among sovereign states as in relations between individuals. The Soviet Union possesses several advantages over the free world in negotiations on any issue:

a. It can and does enforce secrecy on all significant facts about conditions within the Soviet Union, so that it can be expected to know more about the realities of the free world's position than the free world knows about its position;

b. It does not have to be responsive in any important sense to public opinion;

c. It does not have to consult and agree with any other countries on the terms it will offer and accept; and

d. It can influence public opinion in other countries while insulating the peoples under its control.

These are important advantages. Together with the unfavorable trend of our power position, they militate, as is shown in Section A below, against successful negotiation of a general settlement at this time. For although the United States probably now possesses, principally in atomic weapons, a force adequate to deliver a powerful blow upon the Soviet Union and to open the road to victory in a long war, it is not sufficient by itself to advance the position of the United States in the cold war.

The problem is to create such political and economic conditions in the free world, backed by force sufficient to inhibit Soviet attack, that the Kremlin will accommodate itself to these conditions, gradually withdraw, and eventually change its policies drastically. It has been shown in Chapter VIII that truly effective control of atomic energy would require such an opening up of the Soviet Union and such evidence in other ways of its good faith and its intent to co-exist in peace as to reflect or at least initiate a change in the Soviet system.

Clearly under present circumstances we will not be able to negotiate a settlement which calls for a change in the Soviet system. What, then, is the role of negotiation?

In the first place, the public in the United States and in other free countries will require, as a condition to firm policies and adequate programs directed to the frustration of the Kremlin design, that the free world be continuously prepared to negotiate agreements with the Soviet Union on equitable terms. It is still argued by many people here and abroad that equitable agreements with the Soviet Union are possible, and this view will gain force if the Soviet Union begins to show signs of accommodation, even on unimportant issues.

The free countries must always, therefore, be prepared to negotiate and must be ready to take the initiative at times in seeking negotiation. They must develop a negotiating position which defines the issues and the terms on which they would be prepared—and at what stages—to accept agreements with the Soviet Union. The terms must be fair in the view of popular opinion in the free world. This means that they must be consistent with a positive program for peace—in harmony with the United Nations' Charter and providing, at a minimum, for the effective control of all armaments by the United Nations or a successor organization. The terms must not require more of the Soviet Union than such behavior and such participation in a world organization. The fact that such conduct by the Soviet Union is impossible without such a radical change in Soviet policies as to constitute a change in the Soviet system would then emerge as a result of the Kremlin's unwillingness to accept such terms or of its bad faith in observing them.

A sound negotiating position is, therefore, an essential element in the ideological conflict. For some time after a decision to build up strength, any offer of, or attempt at, negotiation of a general settlement along the lines of the Berkeley speech by the Secretary of State could be only a tactic.[2] Nevertheless, concurrently with a decision and a start on building up the strength of the free world, it may be desirable to pursue this tactic both to gain public support for the program and to minimize the immediate risks of war. It is urgently necessary for the United States to determine its negotiating position and to obtain agreement with its major allies on the purposes and terms of negotiation.

In the second place, assuming that the United States in cooperation with other free countries decides and acts to increase the strength of the free world and assuming that the Kremlin chooses the path of accommodation, it will from time to time be necessary and desirable to negotiate on various specific issues with the Kremlin as the area of possible agreement widens.

The Kremlin will have three major objectives in negotiations with the United States. The first is to eliminate the atomic capabilities of the United States; the second is to prevent the effective mobilization of the superior potential of the free world in human and material resources; and the third is to secure a withdrawal of United States forces from, and commitments to, Europe and Japan. Depending on its evaluation of its own strengths and weaknesses as against the West's (particularly the ability and will of the West to sustain its efforts), it will or will not be prepared to make important concessions to achieve these major objectives. It is unlikely that the Kremlin's evaluation is such that it would now be prepared to make significant concessions.

The objectives of the United States and other free countries in negotiations with the Soviet Union (apart from the ideological objectives discussed above) are to record, in a formal fashion which will facilitate the consolidation and further advance of our position, the process of Soviet accommodation to the new political, psychological, and economic conditions in the world which will result from adoption of the fourth course of action and which will be supported by the increasing military strength developed as an integral part of that course of action. In short, our objectives are to record, where desirable, the gradual withdrawal of the Soviet Union and to facilitate that process by making negotiation, if possible, always more expedient than resort to force.

It must be presumed that for some time the Kremlin will accept agreements only if it is convinced that by acting in bad faith whenever and wherever there is an opportunity to do so with impunity, it can derive greater advantage from the agreements than the free world. For this reason, we must take care that any agreements are enforceable or that they are not susceptible of violation without detection and the possibility of effective counter-measures.

This further suggests that we will have to consider carefully the order in which agreements can be concluded. Agreement on the control of atomic energy would result in a relatively greater disarmament of the United States than of the Soviet Union, even assuming considerable progress in building up the strength of the free world in conventional forces and weapons. It might be accepted by the Soviet Union as part of a deliberate design to move against Western Europe and other areas of strategic importance with conventional forces and weapons. In this event, the United States would find itself at war, having previously disarmed itself in its most important weapon, and would be engaged in a race to redevelop atomic weapons.

This seems to indicate that for the time being the United States and other free countries would have to insist on concurrent agreement on the control of nonatomic forces and weapons and perhaps on the other elements of a general settlement, notably peace treaties with Germany, Austria, and Japan and the withdrawal of Soviet influence from the satellites. If, contrary to our expectations, the Soviet Union should accept agreements promising effective control of atomic energy and conventional armaments, without any other changes in Soviet policies, we would have to consider very carefully whether we could accept such agreements. It is unlikely that this problem will arise.

To the extent that the United States and the rest of the free world succeed in so building up their strength in conventional forces and weapons that a Soviet attack with similar forces could be thwarted or held, we will gain increased flexibility and can seek agreements on the various issues in any order, as they become negotiable.

In the third place, negotiation will play a part in the building up of the strength of the free world, apart from the ideological strength discussed above. This is most evident in the problems of Germany, Austria, and Japan. In the process of building up strength, it may be desirable for the free nations, without the Soviet Union, to conclude separate arrangements with Japan, Western Germany, and Austria which would enlist the energies and resources of these countries in support of the free world. This will be difficult unless it has been demonstrated by attempted negotiation with the Soviet Union that the Soviet Union is not prepared to accept treaties of peace which would leave these countries free, under adequate safeguards, to participate in the United Nations and in regional or broader associations of states consistent with the United Nations' Charter and providing security and adequate opportunities for the peaceful development of their political and economic life.

This demonstrates the importance, from the point of view of negotiation as well as for its relationship to the building up of the strength of the free world (see Section D below), of the problem of closer association—on a regional or a broader basis—among the free countries.

In conclusion, negotiation is not a possible separate course of action but rather a means of gaining support for a program of building strength, of recording, where necessary and desirable, progress in the cold war, and of facilitating further progress while helping to minimize the risks of war. Ultimately, it is our objective to negotiate a settlement with the Soviet Union (or a successor state or states) on which the world can place reliance as an enforceable instrument of peace. But it is important to emphasize that such a settlement can only record the progress which the free world will have made in creating a political and economic system in the world so successful that the frustration of the Kremlin's design for world domination will be complete. The analysis in the following sections indicates that the building of such a system requires expanded and accelerated programs for the carrying out of current policies.

## A. THE FIRST COURSE—CONTINUATION OF CURRENT POLICIES, WITH CURRENT AND CURRENTLY PROJECTED PROGRAMS FOR CARRYING OUT THESE POLICIES

*1. Military aspects.* On the basis of current programs, the United States has a large potential military capability but an actual capability which, though improving, is declining relative to the USSR, particularly in light of its probable fission bomb capability and possible thermonuclear bomb capability. The same holds true for the free world as a whole relative to the Soviet world as a whole. If war breaks out in 1950 or in the next few years, the United States and its allies, apart from a powerful atomic blow, will be compelled to conduct delaying actions, while building up their strength for a general offensive. A frank evaluation of the requirements, to defend the United States and its vital interests and to support a vigorous initiative in the cold war, on the one hand, and of present capabilities, on the other, indicates that there is a sharp and growing disparity between them.

A review of Soviet policy shows that the military capabilities, actual and potential, of the United States and the rest of the free world, together with the apparent determination of the free world to resist further Soviet expansion, have not induced the Kremlin to relax its pressures generally or to give up the initiative in the cold war. On the contrary, the Soviet Union has consistently pursued a bold foreign policy, modified only when its probing revealed a determination and an ability of the free world to resist encroachment upon it. The relative military capabilities of the free world are declining, with the result that its determination to resist may also decline and that the security of the United States and the free world as a whole will be jeopardized.

From the military point of view, the actual and potential capabilities of the United States, given a continuation of current and projected programs, will become less and less effective as a war deterrent. Improvement of the state of readiness will become more and more important not only to inhibit the launching of war by the Soviet Union but also to support a national policy designed to reverse the present ominous trends in international relations. A building up of the military capabilities of the United States and the free world is a precondition to the achievement of the objectives outlined in this report and to the protection of the United States against disaster.

Fortunately, the United States military establishment has been developed into a unified and effective force as a result of the policies laid down by the Congress and the vigorous carrying out of these policies by the Administration in the fields of both organization and economy. It is, therefore, a base upon which increased strength can be rapidly built with maximum efficiency and economy.

2. *Political aspects.* The Soviet Union is pursuing the initiative in the conflict with the free world. Its atomic capabilities, together with its successes in the Far East, have led to an increasing confidence on its part and to an increasing nervousness in Western Europe and the rest of the free world. We cannot be sure, of course, how vigorously the Soviet Union will pursue its initiative, nor can we be sure of the strength or weakness of the other free countries in reacting to it. There are, however, ominous signs of further deterioration in the Far East. There are also some indications that a decline in morale and confidence in Western Europe may be expected. In particular, the situation in Germany is unsettled. Should the belief or suspicion spread that the free nations are not now able to prevent the Soviet Union from taking, if it chooses, the military actions outlined in Chapter V, the determination of the free countries to resist probably would lessen and there would be an increasing temptation for them to seek a position of neutrality.

Politically, recognition of the military implications of a continuation of present trends will mean that the United States and especially other free countries will tend to shift to the defensive, or to follow a dangerous policy of bluff, because the maintenance of a firm initiative in the cold war is closely related to aggregate strength in being and readily available.

This is largely a problem of the incongruity of the current actual capabilities of the free world and the threat to it, for the free world has an economic and military potential far superior to the potential of the Soviet Union and its satellites. The shadow of Soviet force falls darkly on Western Europe and Asia and supports a policy of encroachment. The free world lacks adequate means—in the form of forces in being—to thwart such expansion locally. The United States will therefore be confronted more frequently with the dilemma of reacting totally to a limited extension of Soviet control or of not reacting at all (except with ineffectual protests and half measures). Continuation of present trends is likely to lead, therefore, to a gradual withdrawal under the direct or indirect pressure of the Soviet Union, until we discover one day that we have sacrificed positions of vital interest. In other words, the United States would have chosen, by lack of the necessary decisions and actions, to fall back to isolation in the Western Hemisphere. This course would at best result in only a relatively brief truce and would be ended either by our capitulation or by a defensive war—on unfavorable terms from unfavorable positions—against a Soviet Empire compromising all or most of Eurasia (See Section B).

*3. Economic and social aspects.* As was pointed out in Chapter VI, the present foreign economic policies and programs of the United States will not produce a solution to the problem of international economic equilibrium, notably the problem of the dollar gap, and will not create an economic base conducive to political stability in many important free countries.

The European Recovery Program has been successful in assisting the restoration and expansion of production in Western Europe and has been a major factor in checking the dry rot of Communism in Western Europe. However, little progress has been made toward the resumption by Western Europe of a position of influence in world affairs commensurate with its potential strength. Progress in this direction will require integrated political, economic, and military policies and programs, which are supported by the United States and the Western European countries and which will probably require a deeper participation by the United States than has been contemplated.

The Point IV Program and other assistance programs will not adequately supplement, as now projected, the efforts of other important countries to develop effective institutions, to improve the administration of their affairs, and to achieve a sufficient measure of economic development. The moderate regimes now in power in many countries, like India, Indonesia, Pakistan, and the Philippines, will probably be unable to restore or retain their popular support and authority unless they are assisted in bringing about a more rapid improvement of the economic and social structure than present programs will make possible.

The Executive Branch is now undertaking a study of the problem of the United States balance of payments and of the measures which might be taken by the United States to assist in establishing international economic equilibrium. This is a very important project and work on it should have a high priority. However, unless such an economic program is matched and supplemented by an equally far-sighted and vigorous political and military program, we will not be successful in checking and rolling back the Kremlin's drive.

*4. Negotiation.* In short, by continuing along its present course the free world will not succeed in making effective use of its vastly superior political, economic and military potential to build a tolerable state of order among military situation of the free world is already unsatisfactory and will become less favorable unless we act to reverse present trends.

This situation is one which militates against successful negotiations with the Kremlin—for the terms of agreements on important pending issues would reflect present realities and would therefore be unacceptable, if not disastrous, to the United States and the rest of the free world. Unless a decision had been made and action undertaken to build up the strength, in the broadest sense, of the United States and the free world, an attempt to negotiate a general settlement on terms acceptable to us would be ineffective and probably long drawn out, and might thereby seriously delay the necessary measures to build up our strength.

This is true despite the fact that the United States now has the capability of delivering a powerful blow against the Soviet Union in the event of war for one of the present realities is that the United States is not prepared to threaten the use of our present atomic superiority to coerce the Soviet Union into acceptable agreements. In light of present trends, the Soviet Union will not withdraw and the only conceivable basis for a general settlement would be spheres of influence and of no influence—a "settlement" which the Kremlin could readily exploit to its great advantage. The idea that Germany or Japan or other important areas can exist as islands of neutrality in a divided world is unreal, given the Kremlin design for world domination.

## B. THE SECOND COURSE—ISOLATION

Continuation of present trends, it has been shown above, will lead progressively to the withdrawal of the United States from most of its present commitments in Europe and Asia and to our isolation in the Western Hemisphere and its approaches. This would result not from a conscious decision but from a failure to take the actions necessary to bring our capabilities into line with our commitments and thus to a withdrawal under pressure. This pressure might come from our present Allies, who will tend to seek other "solutions" unless they have confidence in our determination to accelerate our efforts to build a successfully functioning political and economic system in the free world.

There are some who advocate a deliberate decision to isolate ourselves. Superficially, this has some attractiveness as a course of action, for it appears to bring our commitments and capabilities into harmony by reducing the former and by concentrating our present, or perhaps even reduced, military expenditures on the defense of the United States.

This argument overlooks the relativity of capabilities. With the United States in an isolated position, we would have to face the probability that the Soviet Union would quickly dominate most of Eurasia, probably without meeting armed resistance. It would thus acquire a potential far superior to our own, and would promptly proceed to develop this potential with the purpose of eliminating our power, which would, even in isolation, remain as a challenge to it and as an obstacle to the imposition of its kind of order in the world. There is no way to make ourselves inoffensive to the Kremlin except by complete submission to its will. Therefore isolation would in the end condemn us to capitulate or to fight alone and on the defensive, with drastically limited offensive and retaliatory capabilities in comparison with the Soviet Union. (These are the only possibilities, unless we are prepared to risk the future on the hazard that the Soviet Empire, because of over-extension or other reasons, will spontaneously destroy itself from within.)

The argument also overlooks the imponderable, but nevertheless drastic, effects on our belief in ourselves and in our way of life of a deliberate decision to isolate ourselves. As the Soviet Union came to dominate free countries, it is clear that many Americans would feel a deep sense of responsibility and guilt for having abandoned their former friends and allies. As the Soviet Union mobilized the resources of Eurasia, increased its relative military capabilities, and heightened its threat to our security, some would be tempted to accept "peace" on its terms, while many would seek to defend the United States by creating a regimented system which would permit the assignment of a tremendous part of our resources to defense. Under such a state of affairs our national morale would be corrupted and the integrity and vitality of our system subverted.

Under this course of action, there would be no negotiation, unless on the Kremlin's terms, for we would have given up everything of importance.

It is possible that at some point in the course of isolation, many Americans would come to favor a surprise attack on the Soviet Union and the area under its control, in a desperate attempt to alter decisively the balance of power by an overwhelming blow with modern weapons of mass destruction. It appears unlikely that the Soviet Union would wait for such an attack before launching one of its own. But even if it did and even if our attack were successful, it is clear that the United States would face appalling tasks in establishing a tolerable state of order among nations after such a war and after Soviet occupation of all or most of Eurasia for some years. These tasks appear so enormous and success so unlikely that reason dictates an attempt to achieve our objectives by other means.

## C. THE THIRD COURSE—WAR

Some Americans favor a deliberate decision to go to war against the Soviet Union in the near future. It goes without saving that the idea of "preventive"—in the sense of a military attack not provoked by a military attack upon us or our allies—is generally unacceptable to Americans. Its supporters argue that since the Soviet Union is in fact at war with the free world now and that since the failure of the Soviet Union to use all-out military force is explainable on grounds of expediency, we are at war and should conduct ourselves accordingly. Some further argue that the free world is probably unable, except under the crisis of war, to mobilize and direct its resources to the checking and rolling back of the Kremlin's drive for world dominion. This is a powerful argument in the light of history, but the considerations against war are so compelling that the free world must demonstrate that this argument is wrong. The case for war is premised on the assumption that the United States could launch and sustain an attack of sufficient impact to gain a decisive advantage for the free world in a long war and perhaps to win an early decision.

The ability of the United States to launch effective offensive operations is now limited to attack with atomic weapons. A powerful blow could be delivered upon the Soviet Union, but it is estimated that these operations alone would not force or induce the Kremlin to capitulate and that the Kremlin would still be able to use the forces under its control to dominate most or all of Eurasia. This would probably mean a long and difficult struggle during which the free institutions of Western Europe and many freedom-loving people would be destroyed and the regenerative capacity of Western Europe dealt a crippling blow.

Apart from this, however, a surprise attack upon the Soviet Union, despite the provocativeness of recent Soviet behavior, would be repugnant to many Americans. Although the American people would probably rally in support of the war effort, the shock of responsibility for a surprise attack would be morally corrosive. Many would doubt that it was a "just war" and that all reasonable possibilities for a peaceful settlement had been explored in good faith. Many more, proportionately, would hold such views in other countries, particularly in Western Europe and particularly after Soviet occupation, if only because the Soviet Union would liquidate articulate opponents. It would, therefore, be difficult after such a war to create a satisfactory international order among nations. Victory in such a war would have brought us little if at all closer to victory in the fundamental ideological conflict.

These considerations are no less weighty because they are imponderable, and they rule out an attack unless it is demonstrably in the nature of a counter-attack to a blow which is on its way or about to be delivered. (The military advantages of landing the first blow become increasingly important with modern weapons, and this is a fact which requires us to be on the alert in order to strike with our full weight as soon as we are attacked, and, if possible, before the Soviet blow is actually delivered.) If the argument of Chapter IV is accepted, it follows that there is no "easy" solution and that the only sure victory lies in the frustration of the Kremlin design by the steady development of the moral and material strength of the free world and its projection into the Soviet world in such a way as to bring about an internal change in the Soviet system.

## D. THE REMAINING COURSE OF ACTION—A RAPID BUILD-UP OF POLITICAL, ECONOMIC, AND MILITARY STRENGTH IN THE FREE WORLD

A more rapid build-up of political, economic, and military strength and thereby of confidence in the free world than is now contemplated is the only course which is consistent with progress toward achieving our fundamental purpose. The frustration of the Kremlin design requires the free world to develop a successfully functioning political and economic system and a vigorous political offensive against the Soviet Union. These, in turn, require an adequate military shield under which they can develop. It is necessary, to have the military power to deter, if possible, Soviet expansion, and to defeat, if necessary, aggressive Soviet or Soviet-directed actions of a limited or total character. The potential strength of the free world is great; its ability to develop these military capabilities and its will to resist Soviet expansion will be determined by the wisdom and will with which it undertakes to meet its political and economic problems.

*1. Military aspects.* It has been indicated in Chapter VI that US military capabilities are strategically more defensive in nature than offensive and are more potential than actual. It is evident, from an analysis of the past and of the trend of weapon development, that there is now and will be in the future no absolute defense. The history of war also indicates that a favorable decision can only be achieved through offensive action. Even a defensive strategy if it is to be successful, calls not only for defensive forces to hold vital positions while mobilizing and preparing for the offensive, but also for offensive forces to attack the enemy and keep him off balance.

The two fundamental requirements which must be met by forces in being or readily available are support of foreign policy and protection against disaster. To meet the second requirement, the forces in being or readily available must be able, at a minimum, to perform certain basic tasks:

a. To defend the Western Hemisphere and essential allied areas in order that their war-making capabilities can be developed;

b. To provide and protect a mobilization base while the offensive forces required for victory are being built up;

c. To conduct offensive operations to destroy vital elements of the Soviet war-making capacity, and to keep the enemy off balance until the full offensive strength of the United States and its allies can be brought to bear;

d. To defend and maintain the lines of communication and base areas necessary to the execution of the above tasks; and

e. To provide such aid to allies as is essential to the execution of their role in the above tasks.

In the broadest terms, the ability to perform these tasks requires a build-up of military strength by the United States and its allies to a point at which the combined strength will be superior for at least these tasks, both initially and throughout a war, to the forces that can be brought to bear by the Soviet Union and its satellites. In specific terms, it is not essential to match item for item with the Soviet Union, but to provide an adequate defense against air attack on the United States and Canada and an adequate defense against air and surface attack on the United Kingdom and Western Europe, Alaska, the Western Pacific, Africa, and the Near and Middle East, and on the long lines of communication to these areas. Furthermore, it is mandatory that in building up our strength, we enlarge upon our technical superiority by an accelerated exploitation of the scientific potential of the United States and our allies.

Forces of this size and character are necessary not only for protection against disaster but also to support our foreign policy. In fact, it can be argued that larger forces in being and readily available are necessary to inhibit a would-be aggressor than to provide the nucleus of strength and the mobilization base on which the tremendous forces required for victory can be built. For example, in both World Wars I and II the ultimate victors had the strength, in the end, to win though they had not had the strength in being or readily available to prevent the outbreak of war. In part, at least, this was because they had not had the military strength on which to base a strong foreign policy. At any rate, it is clear that a substantial and rapid building up of strength in the free world is necessary to support a firm policy intended to check and to roll back the Kremlin's drive for world domination.

Moreover, the United States and the other free countries do not now have the forces in being and readily available to defeat local Soviet moves with local action, but must accept reverses or make these local moves the occasion for war—for which we are not prepared. This situation makes for great uneasiness among our allies, particularly in Western Europe, for whom total war means, initially, Soviet occupation. Thus, unless our combined strength is rapidly increased, our allies will tend to become increasingly reluctant to support a firm foreign policy on our part and increasingly anxious to seek other solutions, even though they are aware that appeasement means defeat. An important advantage in adopting the fourth course of action lies in its psychological impact—the revival of confidence and hope in the future. It is recognized, of course, that any announcement of the recommended course of action could be exploited by the Soviet Union in its peace campaign and would have adverse psychological effects in certain parts of the free world until the necessary increase in strength has been achieved. Therefore, in any announcement of policy and in the character of the measures adopted, emphasis should be given to the essentially defensive character and care should be taken to minimize, so far as possible, unfavorable domestic and foreign reactions.

2. *Political and economic aspects.* The immediate objectives—to the achievement of which such a build-up of strength is a necessary though not a sufficient condition—are a renewed initiative in the cold war and a situation to which the Kremlin would find it expedient to accommodate itself, first by relaxing tensions and pressures and then by gradual withdrawal. The United States cannot alone provide the resources required for such a build up of strength. The other free countries must carry their part of the burden, but their ability and determination to do it will depend on the action the United States takes to develop its own strength and on the adequacy of its foreign political and economic policies. Improvement in political and economic conditions in the free world, as has been emphasized above, is necessary as a basis for building up the will and the means to resist and for dynamically affirming the integrity and vitality of our free and democratic way of life on which our ultimate victory depends.

At the same time, we should take dynamic steps to reduce the power and influence of the Kremlin inside the Soviet Union and other areas under its control. The objective would be the establishment of friendly regimes not under Kremlin domination. Such action is essential to engage the Kremlin's attention, keep it off balance, and force an increased expenditure of Soviet resources in counteraction. In other words, it would be the current Soviet cold war technique used against the Soviet Union.

A program for rapidly building up strength and improving political and economic conditions will place heavy demands on our courage and intelligence; it will be costly; it will be dangerous. But half-measures will be more costly and more dangerous, for they will be inadequate to prevent and may actually invite war. Budgetary considerations will need to be subordinated to the stark fact that our very independence as a nation may be at stake.

A comprehensive and decisive program to win the peace and frustrate the Kremlin design should be so designed that it can be sustained for as long as necessary to achieve our national objectives. It would probably involve:

1. The development of an adequate political and economic framework for the achievement of our long-range objectives.

2. A substantial increase in expenditures for military purposes adequate to meet the requirements for the tasks listed in Section D-1.

3. A substantial increase in military assistance programs, designed to foster cooperative efforts, which will adequately and efficiently meet the requirements of our allies for the tasks referred to in Section D-1-e.

4. Some increase in economic assistance programs and recognition of the need to continue these programs until their purposes have been accomplished.

5. A concerted attack on the problem of the United States balance of payments, along the lines already approved by the President.

6. Development of programs designed to build and maintain confidence among other peoples in our strength and resolution, and to wage overt psychological warfare calculated to encourage mass defections from Soviet allegiance and to frustrate the Kremlin design in other ways.

7. Intensification of affirmative and timely measures and operations by covert means in the fields of economic warfare and political and psychological warfare with a view to fomenting and supporting unrest and revolt in selected strategic satellite countries.

8. Development of internal security and civilian defense programs.

9. Improvement and intensification of intelligence activities.

10. Reduction of Federal expenditures for purposes other than defense and foreign assistance, if necessary by the deferment of certain desirable programs.

11. Increased taxes.

Essential as prerequisites to the success of this program would be (a) consultations with Congressional leaders designed to make the program the object of non-partisan legislative support, and (b) a presentation to the public of a full explanation of the facts and implications of present international trends.

The program will be costly, but it is relevant to recall the disproportion between the potential capabilities of the Soviet and non-Soviet worlds (cf. Chapters V and VI). The Soviet Union is currently devoting about 40 percent of available resources (gross national product plus reparations, equal in 1949 to about $65 billion) to military expenditures (14 percent) and to investment (26 percent), much of which is in war-supporting industries. In an emergency the Soviet Union could increase the allocation of resources to these purposes to about 50 percent, or by one-fourth.

The United States is currently devoting about 22 percent of its gross national product ($255 billion in 1949) to military expenditures (6 percent), foreign assistance (2 percent), and investment (14 percent), little of which is in war-supporting industries. (As was pointed out in Chapter V, the "fighting value" obtained per dollar of expenditure by the Soviet Union considerably exceeds that obtained by the United States, primarily because of the extremely low military and civilian living standards in the Soviet Union.) In an emergency the United States could devote upward of 50 percent of its gross national product to these purposes (as it did during the last war), an increase of several times present expenditures for direct and indirect military purposes and foreign assistance.

From the point of view of the economy as a whole, the program might not result in a real decrease in the standard of living, for the economic effects of the program might be to increase the gross national product by more than the amount being absorbed for additional military and foreign assistance purposes. One of the most significant lessons of our World War II experience was that the American economy, when it operates at a level approaching full efficiency, can provide enormous resources for purposes other than civilian consumption while simultaneously providing a high standard of living. After allowing for price changes, personal consumption expenditures rose by about one-fifth between 1939 and 1944, even though the economy had in the meantime increased the amount of resources going into Government use by $60-$65 billion (in 1939 prices).

This comparison between the potentials of the Soviet Union and the United States also holds true for the Soviet world and the free world and is of fundamental importance in considering the courses of action open to the United States.

The comparison gives renewed emphasis to the fact that the problems faced by the free countries in their efforts to build a successfully functioning system lie not so much in the field of economics as in the field of politics. The building of such a system may require more rapid progress toward the closer association of the free countries in harmony with the concept of the United Nations. It is clear that our long-range objectives require a strengthened United Nations, or a successor organization, to which the world can look for the maintenance of peace and order in a system based on freedom and justice. It also seems clear that a unifying ideal of this kind might awaken and arouse the latent spiritual energies of free men everywhere and obtain their enthusiastic support for a positive program for peace going far beyond the frustration of the Kremlin design and opening vistas to the future that would outweigh short-run sacrifices.

The threat to the free world involved in the development of the Soviet Union's atomic and other capabilities will rise steadily and rather rapidly. For the time being, the United States possesses a marked atomic superiority over the Soviet Union which, together with the potential capabilities of the United States and other free countries in other forces and weapons, inhibits aggressive Soviet action. This provides an opportunity for the United States, in cooperation with other free countries, to launch a build-up of strength which will support a firm policy directed to the frustration of the Kremlin design. The immediate goal of our efforts to build a successfully functioning political and economic system in the free world backed by adequate military strength is to postpone and avert the disastrous situation which, in light of the Soviet Union's probable fission bomb capability and possible thermonuclear bomb capability, might arise in 1954 on a continuation of our present programs. By acting promptly and vigorously in such a way that this date is, so to speak, pushed into the future, we would permit time for the process of accommodation, withdrawal and frustration to produce the necessary changes in the Soviet system. Time is short, however, and the risks of war attendant upon a decision to build up strength will steadily increase the longer we defer it.

## CONCLUSIONS AND RECOMMENDATIONS

### Conclusions

The foregoing analysis indicates that the probable fission bomb capability and possible thermonuclear bomb capability of the Soviet Union have greatly intensified the Soviet threat to the security of the United States. This threat is of the same character as that described in NSC 20/4 (approved by the President on November 24, 1948) but is more immediate than had previously been estimated. In particular, the United States now faces the contingency that within the next four or five years the Soviet Union will possess the military capability of delivering a surprise atomic attack of such weight that the United States must have substantially increased general air, ground, and sea strength, atomic capabilities, and air and civilian defenses to deter war and to provide reasonable assurance, in the event of war, that it could survive the initial blow and so on to the eventual attainment of its objectives. In return, this contingency requires the intensification of our efforts in the fields of intelligence and research and development.

Allowing for the immediacy of the danger, the following statement of Soviet threats, contained in NSC 20/4, remains valid:

14. The gravest threat to the security of the United States within the foreseeable future stems from the hostile designs and formidable power of the USSR, and from the nature of the Soviet system.

15. The political, economic, and psychological warfare which the USSR is now waging has dangerous potentialities for weakening the relative world position of the United States and disrupting its traditional institutions by means short of war, unless sufficient resistance is encountered in the policies of this and other non-communist countries.

16. The risk of war with the USSR is sufficient to warrant, in common prudence, timely and adequate preparation by the United States.

a. Even though present estimates indicate that the Soviet leaders probably do not intend deliberate armed action involving the United States at this time, the possibility of such deliberate resort to war cannot be ruled out.

b. Now and for the foreseeable future there is a continuing danger that war will arise either through Soviet miscalculation of the determination of the United States to use all the means at its command to safe-guard its security, through Soviet misinterpretation of our intentions, or through US miscalculation of Soviet reactions to measures which we might take.

17. Soviet domination of the potential power of Eurasia, whether achieved by armed aggression or by political and subversive means, would be strategically and politically unacceptable to the United States.

18. The capability of the United States either in peace or in the event of war to cope with threats to its security or to gain its objectives would be severely weakened by internal development, important among which are:

a. Serious espionage, subversion and sabotage, particularly by concerted and well-directed communist activity.

b. Prolonged or exaggerated economic instability.

c. Internal political and social disunity.

d. Inadequate or excessive armament or foreign aid expenditures.

e. An excessive or wasteful usage of our resources in time of peace.

f. Lessening of US prestige and influence through vacillation or appeasement or lack of skill and imagination in the conduct of its foreign policy or by shirking world responsibilities.

g. Development of a false sense of security through a deceptive change in Soviet tactics.

Although such developments as those indicated in paragraph 18 above would severely weaken the capability of the United States and its allies to cope with the Soviet threat to their security, considerable progress has been made since 1948 in laying the foundation upon which adequate strength can now be rapidly built.

19. a. To reduce the power and influence of the USSR to limits which no longer constitute a threat to the peace, national independence, and stability of the world family of nations.

b. To bring about a basic change in the conduct of international relations by the government in power in Russia, to conform with the purposes and principles set forth in the UN Charter.

In pursuing these objectives, due care must be taken to avoid permanently impairing our economy and the fundamental values and institutions inherent in our way of life.

20. We should endeavor to achieve our general objectives by methods short of war through the pursuit of the following aims:

a. To encourage and promote the gradual retraction of undue Russian power and influence from the present perimeter areas around traditional Russian boundaries and the emergence of the satellite countries as entities independent of the USSR.

b. To encourage the development among the Russian peoples of attitudes which may help to modify current Soviet behavior and permit a revival of the national life of groups evidencing the ability and determination to achieve and maintain national independence.

c. To eradicate the myth by which people remote from Soviet military influence are held in a position of subservience to Moscow and to cause the world at large to see and understand the true nature of the USSR and the Soviet-directed world communist party, and to adopt a logical and realistic attitude toward them.

d. To create situations which will compel the Soviet Government to recognize the practical undesirability of acting on the basis of its present concepts and the necessity of behaving in accordance with precepts of international conduct, as set forth in the purposes and principles of the UN Charter.

21. Attainment of these aims requires that the United States:

a. Develop a level of military readiness which can be maintained as long as necessary as a deterrent to Soviet aggression, as indispensable support to our political attitude toward the USSR, as a source of encouragement to nations resisting Soviet political aggression, and as an adequate basis for immediate military commitments and for rapid mobilization should war prove unavoidable.

b. Assure the internal security of the United States against dangers of sabotage, subversion, and espionage.

c. Maximize our economic potential, including the strengthening of our peacetime economy and the establishment of essential reserves readily available in the event of war.

d. Strengthen the orientation toward the United States of the non-Soviet nations; and help such of those nations as are able and willing to make an important contribution to US security, to increase their economic and political stability and their military capability.

e. Place the maximum strain on the Soviet structure of power and particularly on the relationships between Moscow and the satellite countries.

f. Keep the US public fully informed and cognizant of the threats to our national security so that it will be prepared to support the measures which we must accordingly adopt.

In the light of present and prospective Soviet atomic capabilities, the action which can be taken under present programs and plans, however, becomes dangerously inadequate, in both timing and scope, to accomplish the rapid progress toward the attainment of the United States political, economic, and military objectives which is now imperative.

A continuation of present trends would result in a serious decline in the strength of the free world relative to the Soviet Union and its satellites. This unfavorable trend arises from the inadequacy of current programs and plans rather than from any error in our objectives and aims. These trends lead in the direction of isolation, not by deliberate decision but by lack of the necessary basis for a vigorous initiative in the conflict with the Soviet Union.

Our position as the center of power in the free world places a heavy responsibility upon the United States for leadership. We must organize and enlist the energies and resources of the free world in a positive program for peace which will frustrate the Kremlin design for world domination by creating a situation in the free world to which the Kremlin will be compelled to adjust. Without such a cooperative effort, led by the United States, we will have to make gradual withdrawals under pressure until we discover one day that we have sacrificed positions of vital interest.

It is imperative that this trend be reversed by a much more rapid and concerted build-up of the actual strength of both the United States and the other nations of the free world. The analysis shows that this will be costly and will involve significant domestic financial and economic adjustments.

The execution of such a build-up, however, requires that the United States have an affirmative program beyond the solely defensive one of countering the threat posed by the Soviet Union. This program must light the path to peace and order among nations in a system based on freedom and justice, as contemplated in the Charter of the United Nations. Further, it must envisage the political and economic measures with which and the military shield behind which the free world can work to frustrate the Kremlin design by the strategy of the cold war; for every consideration of devotion to our fundamental values and to our national security demands that we achieve our objectives by the strategy of the cold war, building up our military strength in order that it may not have to be used. The only sure victory lies in the frustration of the Kremlin design by the steady development of the moral and material strength of the free world and its projection into the Soviet world in such a way as to bring about an internal change in the Soviet system. Such a positive program—harmonious with our fundamental national purpose and our objectives—is necessary if we are to regain and retain the initiative and to win and hold the necessary popular support and cooperation in the United States and the rest of the free world.

This program should include a plan for negotiation with the Soviet Union, developed and agreed with our allies and which is consonant with our objectives. The United States and its allies, particularly the United Kingdom and France, should always be ready to negotiate with the Soviet Union on terms consistent with our objectives. The present world situation, however, is one which militates against successful negotiations with the Kremlin—for the terms of agreements on important pending issues would reflect present realities and would therefore be unacceptable, if not disastrous, to the United States and the rest of the free world. After a decision and a start on building up the strength of the free world has been made, it might then be desirable for the United States to take an initiative in seeking negotiations in the hope that it might facilitate the process of accommodation by the Kremlin to the new situation. Failing that, the unwillingness of the Kremlin to accept equitable terms or its bad faith in observing them would assist in consolidating popular opinion in the free world in support of the measures necessary to sustain the build-up.

In summary, we must, by means of a rapid and sustained build-up of the political, economic, and military strength of the free world, and by means of an affirmative program intended to wrest the initiative from the Soviet Union, confront it with convincing evidence of the determination and ability of the free world to frustrate the Kremlin design of a world dominated by its will. Such evidence is the only means short of war which eventually may force the Kremlin to abandon its present course of action and to negotiate acceptable agreements on issues of major importance.

The whole success of the proposed program hangs ultimately on recognition by this Government, the American people, and all free peoples, that the cold war is in fact a real war in which the survival of the free world is at stake. Essential prerequisites to success are consultations with Congressional leaders designed to make the program the object of non-partisan legislative support and a presentation to the public of a full explanation of the facts and implications of the present international situation. The prosecution of the program will require of us all the ingenuity, sacrifice, and unity demanded by the vital importance of the issue and the tenacity to persevere until our national objectives have been attained.

### Recommendations

That the President:

a. Approve the foregoing Conclusions.

b. Direct the National Security Council, under the continuing direction of the President, and with the participation of other Departments and Agencies as appropriate, to coordinate and insure the implementation of the Conclusions herein on an urgent and continuing basis for as long as necessary to achieve our objectives. For this purpose, representatives of the member Departments and Agencies, the Joint Chiefs of Staff or their deputies, and other Departments and Agencies as required should be constituted as a revised and strengthened staff organization under the National Security Council to develop coordinated programs for consideration by the National Security Council.

## NOTES

1.  Marshal Tito, the Communist leader of Yugoslavia, broke away from the Soviet bloc in 1948. [Ed. note]

2.  The Secretary of State listed seven areas in which the Soviet Union could modify its behaviour in such a way as to permit co-existence in reasonable security. These were: 1. Treaties of peace with Austria, Germany. Japan and relaxation of pressures in the Far East; 2. Withdrawal of Soviet forces and influence from satellite areas; 3. Cooperation in the United Nations; 4. Control of atomic energy and/or conventional armaments; 5. Abandonment of indirect aggression; 6. Proper treatment of official representatives of the United States; 7. Increased access to the Soviet Union of persons and ideas from other contries. [Note in source text]

# BIBLIOGRAPHIC ESSAY

For the most thorough recent analysis of the Truman Administration's diplomacy, see Melvyn P. Leffler, *A Preponderance of Power: National Security, the Truman Administration, and the Cold War* (Stanford, 1992). The run-up to the Cold War (Soviet actions, 1944-45) is found in John Lewis Gaddis, *We Now Know: Rethinking Cold War History* (New York, 1997) and, earlier, in *The United States and the Origins of the Cold War, 1941-1947* (New York, 1972); as well as Robert L. Messer, *The End of the Alliance: James F. Byrnes, Roosevelt, Truman, and the Origins of the Cold War* (Chapel Hill, NC, 1982). Also consult Joseph M. Siracusa, ed., *The American Diplomatic Revolution: A Documentary History of the Cold War, 1941-1947* (Sydney, 1976).

Traditionalist works that emphasize the protracted nature of Soviet aggressiveness include: John W. Spanier, *American Foreign Policy since World War II* (New York, 1960); Herbert Druks, *Harry S. Truman and the Russians 1945-1953* (New York, 1966); Dexter Perkins, *The Diplomacy of a New Age: Major Issues in U.S. Policy Since 1945* (Bloomington, IN, 1967); David Rees, *The Age of Containment: The Cold War, 1945-1965* (London, 1967); and Charles Burton Marshall, *The Cold War: A Concise History* (New York, 1965). For the so-called 'realist' interpretation of the Cold War, which underscores the role of power politics and tends to find fault with the execution of US foreign policy, one should begin with W.H. McNeil, *America, Britain and Russia: Their Co-operation and Conflict, 1941-1946* (London, 1953); the incomparable studies by Herbert Feis, *Churchill, Roosevelt, Stalin: The War They Waged and the Peace They Sought* (Princeton, NJ, 1957); *Between War and Peace: The Potsdam Conference* (Princeton, NJ, 1960); and *From Trust to Terror: The Onset of the Cold War, 1945-1950* (New York, 1970); the dated but still useful Norman A. Graebner, *Cold War Diplomacy, 1945-1960* (Princeton, NJ, 1962); Martin F. Hertz, *Beginnings of the Cold War* (Bloomington, IN, 1966); and Louis B. Halle, *The Cold War as History* (New York, 1967).

Other more critical works include Walter Lippmann, *The Cold War: A Study in U.S. Foreign Policy* (New York, 1947); K. Zilliacus, *I Choose Peace* (New York, 1949); Kenneth Ingram, *History and the*

*Cold War* (London, 1955); J.P. Morray, *From Yalta to Disarmament: Cold War Debate* (New York, 1961); Hans J. Morgenthau, *In Defense of National Interest* (New York, 1961); John Lukacs, *A New History of the Cold War* (3rd ed., expanded of *A History of the Cold War* (Garden City, NY, 1966); Marshall D. Shulman, *Beyond the Cold War* (New Haven, CN, 1966); Charles O. Lerche Jr., *The Cold War and After* (Englewood, NJ, 1965); Wilfrid Knapp, *A History of War and Peace, 1939-1965* (London, 1967); and Paul Seabury, *Rise and Decline of the Cold War* (New York, 1967).

For the antecedents of the New Left revisionism of the 1960s and 1970s, see D.F. Fleming, *The Cold War and Its Origins, 1917-1960* (2 vols., Garden City, NY, 1961); Frederick L. Schuman, *The Cold War: Retrospect and Prospect* (Baton Rouge, LA, 1962); and the seminal works of William A. Williams, *American-Russian Relations, 1781-1947* (New York, 1952); and *The Tragedy of American Diplomacy* (rev. and enlarged, New York, 1962). The classic New Left study of the Cold War with its emphasis on the foreign policy necessities of an "Open-Door empire" is still Walter LaFeber's *America, Russia, and the Cold War* (New York, 1967). For other revisionist works of merit consult Lloyd C. Gardner's *Economic Aspects of New Deal Diplomacy* (Madison, WI, 1965); *Architects of Illusion: Men and Ideas in American Foreign Policy, 1941-1949* (Chicago, 1970); and Diane Shaver Clemens's *Yalta* (New York, 1970). For New Left diplomatic history at its most tendentious, one need look no further than Gabriel Kolko, *The Politics of War: The World and United States Foreign Policy, 1945-1954* (New York, 1972); Joyce and Gabriel Kolko, *The Limits of Power: The World and United States Foreign Policy, 1945-1954* (New York, 1972); and David Horowitz, *The Free World Colossus: A Critique of American Foreign Policy in the Cold War* (New York, 1965).

An examination of the impact and significance of New Left scholarship in terms of its contribution to political science, American diplomatic historiography, and historical methodology is found, respectively, in Robert W. Tucker, The *Radical Left and American Foreign Policy* (Baltimore, 1971); Joseph M. Siracusa, *New Left Diplomatic Histories and Historians: The American Revisionists* (2nd ed., Claremont CA, 1993); and Robert James Maddox, *The New Left and the Origins of the Cold War* (Princeton, NJ, 1972).

Background of American perceptions of Soviet Russia is contained in Christopher Lasch, *The American Liberals and the Russian Revolution* (New York, 1972); Peter G. Filene, *Americans and the Soviet Experiment, 1917-1933* (Cambridge, MA, 1967); Robert P. Browder, *The Origins of Soviet-American Diplomacy* (Princeton, NJ, 1953); and William Welch, *American Images of Soviet Foreign Policy:*

*An Inquiry into Recent Appraisals from the Academic Community* (New Haven, CN, 1970). For a discussion of the American 'discovery' of totalitarianism in the 1930s with suggestive implications for the 1940s refer to Robert Allen Skotheim's seminal *Totalitarianism and American Social Thought* (New York, 1971). Also see Hugh De Santis, *The Diplomacy of Silence: The American Foreign Service, the Soviet Union and the Cold War, 1933-1947* (Chicago, 1980); and David Mayers, *The Ambassadors and America's Soviet Policy* (New York, 1995).

Of the other works dealing with the intellectual history of the period under consideration the most relevant are Cushing Strout, *The American Image of the Old World* (New York, 1963); chapters 11 and 12; Charles Alexander, *Nationalism in American Thought, 1930-1945* (New York, 1969); *The Irony of American History* (New York, 1952); and Arthur Schlesinger Jr., *The Vital Center* (Boston 1949). A model of its kind and one of the essential works for understanding the transformation of American foreign policy attitudes towards collective security is Robert A. Divine's *Second Chance: The Triumph of Internationalism in America during World War II* (New York, 1967). These should be read with Alonzo Hamby, *Beyond the New Deal: Harry S. Truman and American Liberalism* (New York, 1973) and *Man of the People: A Life of Harry S. Truman* (New York, 1995), as well as Robert J. Maddox, *From War to Cold War: The Education of Harry S. Truman* (Boulder, CO, 1988); Stephen J. Whitfield, *The Culture of the Cold War* (Baltimore, 1991), Paul Boyer, *By the Bomb's Early Light: American Thought and Culture at the Dawn of the Nuclear Age*, (2nd ed., Chapel Hill, NC, 1994); and Michael Wala, *The Council on Foreign Affairs and American Foreign Policy in the Early Cold War* (New York, 1994).

The origins of the Truman Doctrine and the Marshall Plan are examined at length in most of the Cold War histories cited. In addition to those works one will find much of interest in John L. Gaddis's "Was the Truman Doctrine a Real Turning Point," *Foreign Affairs* 52 (Jan. 1974): 386-402; Geoffrey Warner's "The Truman Doctrine and the Marshall Plan," *International Affairs* 50 (Jan. 1974): 82-92; and Henry Butterfield Ryan's "The American Intellectual Tradition Reflected in the Truman Doctrine," *American Scholar* 42 (Spring 1973): 294-307. Other important books and articles include Harry B. Price, *The Marshall Plan and its Meaning* (Ithaca, NY, 1955); Hadly Arkes, *Bureaucracy, The Marshall Plan, and the National Interest* (Princeton, NJ, 1972); Joseph M. Jones, *The Fifteen Weeks* (New York, 1955); and Michael J. Hogan, *The Marshall Plan: America, Britain and the Reconstruction of Western Europe, 1947-1952* (New York, 1987).

For the Cold War in Europe one should begin with Howard Jones and Randall B. Woods, "The Origins of the Cold War in Europe and the Near East: Recent Historiography and the National Security Imperative," *Diplomatic History* 17 (Spring 1993): 251-76; David Reynolds, ed., *The Origins of the Cold War in Europe* (New Haven, 1994); Robin Edmonds, *Setting the Mould: The United States and Britain, 1945-1950* (New York, 1986); and Thomas A. Schwartz, *America's Germany: John J. McCloy and the Federal Republic of Germany* (Cambridge, Mass., 1991). Also see Geir Lundestad, *The American Non-Policy towards Eastern Europe, 1943-1947* (New York, 1975); *America, Scandinavia, and the Cold War, 1945-1949* (New York, 1980); and *The American "Empire" and Other Studies of US Foreign Policy in Comparative Perspective* (New York, 1990).

The best analysis of Soviet war aims in World War II is still Vojtech Mastny, *Russia's Road to the Cold War: Diplomacy, Warfare and the Politics of Communism, 1941-1945* (New York, 1979). Important insights into Stalin's thinking are found in Jonathan Haslam, *The Soviet Union and the Struggle for Collective Security in Europe, 1933-39* (New York, 1984); *The Soviet Union and the Threat form the East, 1933-41: Moscow, Tokyo, and the Prelude to the Pacific War* (Pittsburgh, 1992); Jiri Hochman, *The Soviet Union and the Failure of Collective Security, 1934-1938* (Ithaca, NY, 1984); and R.C. Raack, *Stalin's Drive to the West, 1938-1945: The Origins of the Cold War* (Stanford, 1995). Soviet documents published in the Cold War International History Project *Bulletin* since 1992 show that Stalin had plenty of help in the foreign policy area. The following about, and from, this source suggest the strength and weaknesses of documents from Soviet archives: Jonathan Haslam, "Russian Archival Revelations and Our Understanding of the Cold War," Diplomatic *History* 21 (Spring 1997): 217-42; Melvyn P. Leffler, "Inside Enemy Archives: The Cold War Reopened," *Foreign Affairs* 75 (July/Aug. 1996): 122-34; and Kathryn Weatherby, "New Russian Documents on the Korean War," Cold War International History Project," *Bulletin* 6/7 (1996): 30-84. Finally, for a look at spheres of influence in Soviet wartime diplomacy, see *Molotov Remembers: Inside Kremlin Politics*, ed. Albert Resis (Chicago, 1993). Also see Henry Kissinger, *Diplomacy* (New York, 1994).

Earlier works on Soviet foreign policy and Soviet perceptions of the United States include: Frederick C. Barghoorn, *The Soviet Image of the United States: A Study in Distortion* (New York, 1950); Louis Fischer, *The Road to Yalta: Soviet Foreign Relations, 1941-1945* (New York, 1972); Alexander Dallin, ed., *Soviet Conduct in World Affairs* (New York, 1960); Marshall D. Schulman, *Stalins' Foreign Policy Reappraised* (Cambridge, MA, 1973); and Adam B. Ulam's two superb studies, *Expansion and Coexistence: The History of Soviet Foreign Policy, 1971-67* (New York, 1968); and *The Rivals: America and Russia since World War II* (New York, 1972). Also see Isaac Deutscher, *Ironies of History: Essays on Contemporary Communism* (London, 1966).

For an analysis of Stalin's leadership, consult the older but still useful Leon Trotsky, *Stalin: An Appraisal of the Man and His Influence* (New York, 1946) and Isaac Deutscher's classic *Stalin: A Political Biography* (New York, 1967). Other efforts to come to grips with Stalin include among others Adam B. Ulam, *Stalin: The Man and his Era* (New York, 1973); Robert C. Tucker, *Stalin and the Uses of Psychology* (Santa Monica, Cal., 1955); *The Soviet Political Mind: Studies in Stalinism and Post-Stalin Change* (New York, 1963); and *Stalin as Revolutionary, 1879-1929* (New York, 1973). (Also see works cited in footnotes.)

For background on American defense policy and nuclear issues, see Samuel P. Huntington, *The Common Defense: Strategic Programs in National Politics* (New York, 1961), and Warner R. Schilling, Paul Y. Hammond, and Glenn H. Snyder, *Strategy, Politics, and Defense Budgets* (New York, 1962). On nuclear issues in particular, the best studies are Herbert York, *The Advisors: Oppenheimer, Teller, and the Super-bomb* (San Francisco, 1976), and McGeorge Bundy, *Danger and Survival: Choices about the Bomb in the First Fifty Years* (New York, 1988).

Paul Nitze's autobiography is *From Hiroshima to Glasnost: At the Center of Decision, a Memoir* (New York, 1989). Works about him are Steven L. Rearden, *The Evolution of American Strategic Doctrine: Paul H. Nitze and the Soviet Challenge* (Boulder, CO, 1984); Strobe Talbott, *The Master of the Game: Paul Nitze and the Nuclear Peace* (New York, 1988); and David Callahan, *Dangerous Possibilities: Paul Nitze and the Cold War* (New York, 1990). For George F. Kennan see his *Memoirs*, 2 vols. (Boston, 1967-1972); Walter L. Hixson, *George F. Kennan: Cold War Iconoclast* (New York, 1989); David Allan Mayers, *George Kennan and the Dilemmas of U.S. Foreign Policy* (New York, 1989); Anders Stephanson, *Kennan and the Art of Foreign Policy* (Cambridge, MA, 1989), and Wilson D. Miscamble, *George F. Kennan and the Making of American Foreign Policy, 1947-1950* (Princeton, NJ, 1992).

For early American involvement in Vietnam, see David C. Marr, *Vietnam 1945: The Quest for Power* (Berkeley, 1995); Edward R. Drachman, *United States Policy toward Vietnam, 1940-1945* (Cranbury, NJ, 1970); and William J. Duiker, *The Communist Road to Power in Vietnam* (Boulder, CO, 1981). Also useful are George Kahin, *Intervention: How America Became Involved in Vietnam* (New York,

1986); Leslie Gelb and Richard K. Betts, *The Irony of Vietnam: The System Worked* (Washington, DC, 1978); Stanley Karnow, *Vietnam: A History* (New York, 1983); George C. Herring, "America's Path to Vietnam: A Historiographical Analysis," in *Vietnam: War, Myth and Memory*, ed. Jeffrey Grey and Jeff Doyle (Sydney, 1992), pp. 31-57; and his *America's Longest War: The United States and Vietnam, 1950-1975* (2nd ed., Philadelphia, 1986).

For the making of the ANZUS alliance see Joseph G. Starke, *The ANZUS Treaty Alliance* (Melbourne, 1965); H.C. Gelber, *The Australian-American Alliance: Costs and Benefits* (Baltimore, 1968); Trevor R. Reese, *Australia, New Zealand and the United States: A Survey of International Relations, 1941-1968* (London, 1969); Coral Bell, *Dependent Ally: A Study in Australian Foreign Policy* (Canberra, 1984); Henry S. Albinski, *ANZUS, the Untied States and Pacific Security* (Lanham, MD, 1987); Geoffrey Bolton, ed., *The Oxford History of Australia* (Melbourne, 1990); V: *1942-1988: The Middle Way*, by G. Bolton; Alan Burnett, *The ANZUS Triangle* and *The ANZUS Documents*, ed., by Alan Burnett (Canberra, 1988, 1991); and Joseph M. Siracusa and Yeong-Han Cheong, *America's Australia: Australia's America* (Claremont, CA, 1997). Finally for a different angle on the periphery of the Cold War, see the two important studies by Robert J. McMahon, *Colonialism and the Cold War: The United States and the Struggle for Indonesian Independence, 1945-49* (Ithaca, NY, 1981) and *The Cold War on the Periphery: The United States, India, and Pakistan* (New York, 1994).

# INDEX